I CARE ABOUT YOUR MARRIAGE

I CARE ABOUT YOUR MARRIAGE

EVERETT WORTHINGTON, Ph.D.

MOODY PRESS
CHICAGO

ISBN: 0-8024-1575-X

1 3 5 7 9 10 8 6 4 2

Printed in the United States of America

To Frank & Lucy, Steve & Danielle,
Scott & Amy, Rob & Carol,
Gene & Molly, John & Christie,
Leo & Kathy, Scotty & Lynnmarie,
Andy & Caroline, Yugi & Kyomi
Friends helping friends

CONTENTS

PREFACE

This book has been one of my dreams for years.

In our first year of marriage, Kirby and I were close friends with a couple who had been married for (what seemed then) a long time. During that time, we talked, grew together in the Lord, and discussed our marriages. Those interactions formed the dream that showed me beyond doubt that friends could help each other make a more lasting and Christ-centered marriage. Since that first year of marriage twenty-three years ago, I have wanted to pass that dream to others.

This book is built on five convictions. First, whether you are single or married, you can help a friend improve his or her marriage. Second, you can help more effectively if you know more about both helping and marriage. Third, the most important parts of helping are listening, supporting, knowing your limitations and strengths, and recognizing your dependence on the Lord for your helping. Fourth, the most important truth about marriage is that it is God's metaphor for a relationship with Him—one that is built on Christian discipleship, which requires faith, work, and love—and practicing faith working through love (Galatians 5:6) is God's pattern for Christian discipleship and marriage. Fifth, you, as a Christian helper, are an agent of hope to a world that often finds hope in short supply.

I pray that you will catch the dream and use the knowledge and skills that you develop through reading this book to further God's kingdom.

ACKNOWLEDGMENTS

A hot Richmond sun blazed. A group of children sat around a backyard swimming pool and splashed their hands in the water, each trying to cool off a friend who sat in the middle of the pool. Despite their churning, the children hardly perturbed the surface of the water. One splish here canceled a splush there.

Then one child began to scrape his hand alongside the pool. Another followed suit. Then another. When the group worked together, the water rushed about the periphery, and waves sloshed over the friend who was the center of their attention.

A book isn't produced by an author alone, which is one reason I think of myself as a writer, not an author. A book is a team effort. One member of the team merely lends a hand to write down the words.

I Care About Your Marriage is the product of many hands in the water. My lifelong mate, Kirby, has taught me most of what I know about marriage by her continuous loving example. She has been a constant lighthouse of God's love. Doug McMurry, my pastor, worked with me on an earlier book and taught me much about marriage counseling. The graduate students and colleagues with whom I've worked on research and shared professional (and personal) experiences have influenced my thinking, as have the students in classes I've taught at Virginia Commonwealth University (VCU), Liberty University, and Denver Seminary. People I've supervised at counseling have changed my ideas. Even more importantly, the people who have sought counseling from me or from people I have supervised have influenced my ideas, because those people have permitted me to see how they have dealt with their marriage problems courageously. They have followed advice and counsel and have showed what works (and sometimes what doesn't work). The undergraduate students in my Effective Behavior and Contemporary Psychology classes at VCU through the years have challenged me with new understandings about marriage, helping, and helping friends with marriage difficulties.

Other people have helped me write the book. Kirby and our children gave up time in the summer while I punished a computer terminal. Bill Watkins encouraged me to publish the book. Jim Bell, editorial director at Moody Press, also encouraged me in its publication. Cheryl Dunlop, an editor at Moody Press, stuck with me through the labor of revision and shaping the writing into something readable.

Most of all, I believe Jesus Christ had a hand in the book from its conception to its completion. I believe that marriage is a special case of discipleship, and helping needy friends is similarly discipleship. That Jesus Christ wants people to help friends and family members with marital difficulties is clear. I have prayed and desire so much to be faithful to that calling in writing this book. I hope that the book will be an honor to Him. I believe He wants Christians showing love to friends and family in their times of need and doing so with as much compassion and skill as we can.

All these hands and others I haven't named have contributed in unison to swirling the waters. I pray that the waters that flow from this book will bless you, your family, and your friends, and help you to be a closer disciple of Jesus.

PART ONE

UNDERSTANDING THE NEED FOR MARITAL HELPING

CHAPTER ONE

"HELP, I HAVE MARRIAGE PROBLEMS"

"He had an affair?" Nan said, looking at the phone as if it were from outer space.

Nan could hear Lindsay crying, gasping in herky-jerky breaths. Lindsay still didn't speak.

"This happened last night?" Nan said. She willed Lindsay to talk. Still silence.

"I'm sorry, Lindsay. What happened?"

Lindsay sniffed. "Patrick came home after midnight. Drunk again. He had a hickey, a passion mark, on his neck. I saw it, and—well, I hit the ceiling. I yelled at him, and he yelled at me. He was drunk. It was the booze, I guess. He said the most dreadful things. He told me about having sex with *her*. With Thelma." Lindsay laughed, too high-pitched.

"I shouted at him to stop talking about it. I put my fingers in my ears, but he kept describing their sex. It was disgusting. Finally, I threw a trivet at him, and it hit him in the chest. He got so mad that he grabbed our globe and threw it at me. It missed, but it smashed the chandelier. I ran into the bedroom and locked the door. For a while I thought he was going to break in. He kicked the door and screamed, but after a while he went away. This morning, he wasn't at home, so I called you. Should I get a divorce?"

Nan's mind was spinning. *What can I tell her? I'm scared I might make a mistake. Patrick can be such a jerk sometimes. Maybe Lindsay is better off without him. On the other hand, I don't believe in divorce.*

"Help me, Nan. I don't know what I should do."

Nan ran her fingers through her frazzled hair. Fresh from bed at 7:00 on a Saturday morning, she felt like crying herself. Lindsay was a dear friend, and Nan and Alan had spent a lot of time with Patrick and Lindsay since Patrick and Lindsay had married two years ago. *I've put a lot of effort into their relationship. I don't want to see it end.*

"Nan, are you there?"

"I'm here, Linds. I was thinking. Have you told anyone else?"

Lindsay's voice went up into the upper register. "Who am I supposed to tell? My mother's, uh, gone, and—" Nan could not remember Lindsay ever being able to say that her mother was dead. "And my stepdad—" She paused. "I had a dream after Patrick got violent last night. I dreamed my stepdad was beating me again. It woke me. I can't even call Dr. Lucas. He and the elders are on retreat this weekend."

Nan felt cornered. What could she say? She and Alan had talked with Lindsay and Patrick about their different needs for closeness, inability (sometimes it seemed to be unwillingness) to talk about serious topics, arguing, and tendency to say hurtful things to each other. *But a drunken fight,* thought Nan, *isn't something I have any experience with.*

"I'm so depressed. I want it over. I want to end it."

Oh, no. Lindsay had been depressed for about a month. *She's thinking of suicide,* thought Nan.

"I'm out of my depth," said Nan. "I don't know how to help."

"You're all I have," yelled Lindsay. She swore and broke the connection. Nan quickly dialed Lindsay's number and listened to the burr of twenty rings before she hung up.

Will I Ever Need to Counsel a Friend with Marital Problems?

Since 1860, every decade has seen an increased expectancy of divorce. Family sociologist Andrew Cherlin estimates that divorce rate is now in the mid-50 percent for first marriages and mid-60 percent for remarriages.[1] About 4 percent of the adults in the United States have married three or more times.[2]

Distressed couples usually try to solve their problems themselves, but if they can't, they seek help. In numerous studies, marital problems are the problems most frequently presented to pastors, who do most of the professional counseling in the United States.[3] In one study of help-seeking from friends, marital problems were the most frequently mentioned problems for which people sought help.[4]

Practically speaking, this means that almost every family in the country has a member who is seeking help from someone for marital problems. To get personal, *you* will probably be asked for advice or help with a marital problem, if not this year, certainly in the next few years.

Most of us are like Nan. When a marital crisis comes, we feel out of our depth, confused, uncertain of whether we will help or hurt, afraid of saying the wrong thing. We love the friends who desperately seek our advice and support, but we simply don't know what to do. Perhaps you have never been married. *What do I know about marriage?* you think. Or perhaps you have been divorced, or you are not happy in your own marriage. You may have little confidence that you can help your friend. Or maybe you're simply unsure that you have anything of value to say. You are hesitant to help, yet you are pulled to help, and you long to give wise counsel.

Training in Lay Counseling

That's why many people have sought training in lay counseling. They know that they will likely be called to help a friend, so they have entered formal programs in lay counseling through organizations like Ken Haugk's Stephen Ministries,[5] Larry Crabb's biblical counseling,[6] Gary Collins's people helping,[7] Jay Adams's nouthetic counseling,[8] Gary Sweeten's discipleship counseling,[9] Horace Lukens's body life training,[10] William Backus's misbelief counseling,[11] and Innovations in Learning's videotapes.[12] Addresses and phone numbers are listed on pages 16–17.

Training is often available in large churches. For example, in 1991 Elmbrook Church in Waukesha, Wisconsin, hosted a national conference on lay counseling that was attended by more than 200 representatives from large churches.

Not everyone has the resources or desire to seek formal training in lay counseling, though, and hundreds of thousands of people have learned basics of helping through reading books about lay or friendship counseling. Some of these books are listed at the end of this chapter. Yet, despite the many resources for learning to be a better helper in general, no resource has helped people learn directly how to help their friends and family members *with marital problems.* That's the purpose of this book.

**Some Examples of Formal
Lay Counseling Training Programs**

Dr. Kenneth Haugk
Stephen Ministries
1325 Boland
St. Louis, MO 63117
(314) 645–5511

Dr. Lawrence J. Crabb, Jr.
Institute of Biblical Counseling
16075 West Belleview Avenue
Morrison, CO 80465
(303) 697–5425

Gary R. Collins, Ph.D.
People Helpers International
20720 North Meadow Court
Kildeer, IL 60047
(708) 438–9673

Dr. Timothy Clinton, Associate Dean
Liberty University School of LifeLong Learning
Box 20000
Lynchburg, VA 24506
(804) 582–2183

Dr. Gary Sweeten
Equipping Ministries International
4015 Executive Park Drive
Suite 309
Cincinnati, OH 45241
(513) 769–5353

John C. Broger
Biblical Counseling Foundation
P.O. Box 925
Rancho Mirage, CA 92270
(619) 773–2667

Jay Adams's Competent to Counsel Training Kit
c/o National Association of Evangelicals
450 Gunderson Drive
Wheaton, IL 60187
(708) 665–0500

Dr. Horace Lukens
7320 South Yale
Tulsa, OK 74136
(918) 496–9588

Dr. William Backus
2701 North Rice Street
Roseville, MN 55113
(612) 484–2049

William H. "Skip" Hunt
P.O. Box 10855
Tampa, FL 33679
(813) 874–5509

Innovations in Learning
7018 El Paso Street
Long Beach, CA 90815
(310) 594–4823

Marital Problems Are Different from Individual Problems

Helping a friend with marital problems is different from helping a friend with an individual problem like depression, anxiety, self-concept, or career choice. The marriage partner is covenantally bound to another individual, and the partners' behaviors are intertwined in a complex marital dance. Although family and marriage conflicts both have the interlocking nature, marriages are different from families because marriages are voluntary adult unions while parents and children are bound by blood and dependency.

Helping a troubled marriage partner improve his or her marriage is like trying to move a person anchored by a truck. The patterned behavior within the marriage is especially difficult to change, even if one person is willing to change. The spouse is an anchor holding the marriage in place. A helper can feel like an ineffectual breeze, attempting to blow the Queen Elizabeth II onto course. To help people with marital problems, you must develop knowledge and skills concerning both helping and marriage.

You Can Learn to Help More Effectively

Substantial research has shown that people can gain knowledge and skills to help more effectively (for a good review, see Tan, 1991).[13]

You can prove this to yourself with this book. Think about how you would have reacted to Lindsay's call for help. Would you have been more helpful than Nan was? If you want to test yourself, write the answers to the following ten questions about Lindsay.

1. *What common mistakes in helping should you avoid?*

   ____

   ____

2. *What is the main root cause of problems in Lindsay's and Patrick's marriage?*

   ____

3. *What are the main areas in which the problem is surfacing?*

   ____

   ____

4. *How would you help Lindsay deal with her current crisis?*

   ____

5. *How would you answer her question, "Should I get a divorce?"*

   ____

   ____

6. *Is Lindsay depressed? Is she suicidal?*

   ____

   ____

7. *How concerned are you about each of the complicating factors?*
   a. Infidelity ______________________________
   b. Drinking ______________________________
   c. Physical abuse __________________________
8. *In the longer term, how would you help with:*
   a. Intimacy ______________________________
   b. Communication __________________________
   c. Conflict management ______________________
   d. Negative thinking ________________________

9. *How would you help strengthen their commitment?*

____

____

10. *Do you think Lindsay and Patrick will remain married?*

____

Save your written answers. Throughout this book, we will learn to deal with problems like Lindsay's through

- the information I provide,
- the conversations I describe,
- the additional resources you consult,
- the cases we follow.

A word about the cases: We will return several times in various chapters to four cases.

Fromma and Leo, newly wedded, struggle with several adjustments and crises and are helped by their friends.

Dorothy and Dan have developed some negative views of their marriage and their future. Marie tries to help them develop a more hopeful vision.

Jane and Edward divorce after many years of marriage. Faithful Roberta sticks with Jane through her efforts to cope with this tragedy.

Raphael and Donna's marriage is split by Donna's affair. Carlos tries to help Raphael forgive and reestablish intimacy with the repentant Donna.

Each of these cases is fictitious and is not simply a disguised version of a real couple. I have created these characters to illustrate how helping can take place within friendships. That each case is fictional does not mean that it isn't true to life. Each is based on composites of experiences I have had with my friends, clients, research participants, and supervisees' clients. However, using fictional composites not only protects the confidentiality of those who have trusted me with their stories, but it also allows me to illustrate points directly and use dialogue to teach efficiently rather than be bound by actual events. I hope you will find the cases engaging and instructive.

In the final chapter, we will revisit Lindsay's case. You can then assess what you have learned.

You are on the threshold to improving yourself as an effective helper. Let's get started.

Some Books about Lay Counseling

Jay E. Adams, *How to Help People Change: The Four-Step Biblical Process* (Grand Rapids: Zondervan, 1986).

W. V. Arnold and M. A. Fohl, *Christians and the Art of Caring* (Philadelphia: Westminster, 1988).

William Backus, *Telling the Truth to Troubled People* (Minneapolis: Bethany House, 1985).

C. L. Baldwin, *Friendship Counseling: Biblical Foundations for Helping Others* (Grand Rapids: Zondervan, 1988).

Colleen Birchett, ed., *How to Help Hurting People* (Chicago: Urban Ministries, 1990).

M. Bobgan and D. Bobgan, *How to Counsel from Scripture* (Chicago: Moody, 1985).

Duncan Buchanan, *The Counselling of Jesus* (Downers Grove, Ill.: InterVarsity, 1985).

Harold Ewing Burchett, *People Helping People: How Every Christian Can Counsel* (Chicago: Moody, 1979).

Robert R. Carkhuff, *Helping and Human Relations: A Primer for Lay and Professional Helpers,* vols. 1, 2 (New York: Holt, Rinehart and Winston, 1969).

Shelley Chapin, *Counselors, Comforters, & Friends: Establishing a Caregiving Ministry in Your Church* (Wheaton, Ill.: Victor, 1992), 93–148.

Gary R. Collins, *The Biblical Basis of Christian Counseling for People Helpers* (Colorado Springs: NavPress, 1993).

__________. *How to Be a People Helper: You Can Help the Others in Your Life* (Santa Ana, Calif.: Vision House, 1976).

__________. *Innovative Approaches to Counseling* (Waco, Tex.: Word, 1986).

__________. *People Helper Growth Book* (Santa Ana, Calif.: Vision House, 1976).

John W. Drakeford, *People to People Therapy* (New York: Harper & Row, 1978).

John W. Drakeford and Claude V. King, *WiseCounsel: Skills for Lay Counseling* (Nashville: The Sunday School Board of the Southern Baptist Convention, 1988).

Gerard Egan, *The Skilled Helper* 5th ed. (Monterey, Calif.: Brooks/Cole, 1994).

T. Foster, *Called To Counsel* (Nashville: Oliver Nelson, 1986).

Michael Gershon and Henry B. Biller, *The Other Helpers* (Lexington, Mass.: Lexington Books, 1977).

S. Gruland and D. Lambrides, *Healing Relationships* (Camp Hill, Pa.: Christian Publications, 1984).

Kenneth C. Haugk, *Christian Caregiving* (Minneapolis: Augsburg, 1984).

S. Hughes, *A Friend in Need* (Eastbourne, England: Kingsway, 1982).

E. Kennedy, *On Becoming a Counselor: A Basic Guide for Non-Professional Counselors* (New York: Seabury, 1977).

I. Lim and S. Lim, *Comfort My People: Christian Counseling—A Lay Challenge* (Singapore: Methodist Book Room, 1988).

S. E. Lindquist, *Action Helping Skills* (Fresno, Calif.: LinkCare Foundation Press, 1976).

P. M. Miller, *Peer Counseling in the Church* (Scottdale, Pa.: Herald, 1978).

P. D. Morris, *Love Therapy* (Wheaton, Ill.: Tyndale House, 1974).

E. Peterson, *Who Cares? A Handbook of Christian Counseling* (Wilton, Conn.: Morehouse-Barlow, 1980).

H. Sala, *Coffee Cup Counseling: How to Be Ready When Friends Ask for Help* (Nashville: Nelson, 1989).

Abraham Schmitt, *The Art of Listening with Love* (Waco, Tex.: Word, 1977).

Abraham Schmitt and D. Schmitt, *When a Congregation Cares* (Scottdale, Pa.: Herald, 1984).

C. R. Solomon, *Counseling with the Mind of Christ* (Old Tappan, N.J.: Revell, 1977).

R. B. Sommerville, *Help for Hotliners: A Manual for Christian Telephone Crisis Counselors* (Phillipsburg, N.J.: Presbyterian & Reformed, 1978).

M. J. Steinbron, *Can the Pastor Do It Alone? A Model for Preparing Lay People for Lay Pastoring* (Ventura, Calif.: Regal, 1987).

J. Sturkie and G. Bear, *Christian Peer Counseling: Love in Action* (Dallas: Word, 1989).

Siang-Yang Tan, *Lay Counseling: Equipping Christians for a Helping Ministry* (Grand Rapids: Zondervan, 1991).

B. B. Varenhorst, with L. Sparks, *Training Teenagers for Peer Ministry* (Loveland, Colo.: Group, 1988).

R. P. Walters, *The Amity Book: Exercises in Friendship Skills* (Grand Rapids: Christian Helpers, 1983).

Waylon O. Ward, *The Bible in Counseling* (Chicago: Moody, 1977).

Paul Welter, *Connecting with a Friend: Eighteen Proven Counseling Skills to Help You Help Others* (Wheaton, Ill.: Tyndale House, 1985).

__________. *How to Help a Friend* (Wheaton, Ill.: Tyndale House, 1978).

Everett L. Worthington, Jr., *How to Help the Hurting: When Friends Face Problems with Self-esteem, Self-control, Fear, Depression, Loneliness* (Downers Grove, Ill.: InterVarsity, 1985).

__________. *When Someone Asks for Help: A Practical Guide for Counseling* (Downers Grove, Ill.: InterVarsity, 1982).

H. Norman Wright, *Training Christians to Counsel* (Eugene, Oreg.: Harvest House, 1977).

PART TWO

UNDERSTANDING MARRIAGE

CHAPTER TWO

THE CAUSE OF MARITAL PROBLEMS

For years, John and Emily delighted in joking at each other's expense. They were hilarious wisecrackers. Entire Bible studies guffawed. They have now been in counseling for a year, and if it weren't for their strong Christian commitment, they would have divorced years ago. As it is now, they rarely speak to each other. John likes to work on cars, and when he isn't doing that, he watches television and grunts occasionally at Emily. Emily does crafts and reads books. Both feel devalued, worthless, and unloved.

Linda and Mel have been married a long time, but their marriage died slowly. They developed some minor disagreements and lost a sense of intimacy; eventually, Mel coasted into an affair. Linda didn't even get angry. She initiated an affair with a co-worker. Both affairs are still ongoing. The couple remains married, growing further apart each day.

Al and Cloe don't believe that anything can be done to improve their relationship. By mutual consent, they have had no sexual relations for about three years. They gave it up because they couldn't bring Cloe to orgasm. After many frustrating attempts, they quit trying. Their sexual relationship is a metaphor for their entire relationship.

The Most Basic Need of a Marriage Counselor

As a Christian, you are a member of Jesus Christ's body. As part of the priesthood of believers, you present God to struggling people in your priestly role. Both you and they need God's help. Besides priestly gifts, you also need basic helping skills and an understanding of the cause of marital problems. There are many ways to think about the cause of marital problems, but throughout this book, I'll work with one. Marriages are troubled because partners mutually fail to practice God's pattern of Christian discipleship.

God's Pattern

God has a pattern for marriage which, not surprisingly, is also a vision for Christian discipleship. In Galatians 5:6, Paul reveals the pattern: "For in Christ Jesus neither circumcision nor uncircumcision is of any avail, but faith working through love" (RSV). In 2 Timothy 1:13, he reiterates it: "Follow the pattern of the sound words which you have heard from me, in the faith and love which are in Christ Jesus" (RSV). God's pattern is easily said, easily understood, and easily put aside for our own plan.

God's pattern is *faith working through love*.[1]

When you help a person with marital problems, look for failures in this pattern. You'll see an abundance. Don't get sidetracked by other issues. Looking for failures in faith working through love doesn't mean that you don't listen to people's concerns. You *must* listen to and value people. Valuing people is God's plan. Let's look closer at the three parts of God's pattern.

Love

Love is defined as willfully valuing and not devaluing the other person.

Will to value. How does a partner willfully value the spouse? He or she says, "I will give something important to you because I value you." We have a model in Jesus. Jesus gave His life for us *while we were yet sinners.* He didn't wait until we deserved the price He paid. He thought we were valuable when we were in our nastiest mood, even if we cursed Him, even if we rejected Him repeatedly.

In Matthew 13:45–46, Jesus told His shortest parable. He said, "The kingdom of heaven is like a merchant looking for fine pearls.

When he found one of great value, he went away and sold everything he had and bought it." Jesus is the merchant. Each of us is a pearl of great value. Jesus, in search of valuable pearls, found each of us. He sold all He had, His life, to purchase us.

Because Jesus values people, people can value others—if they will to do so. Loving is willing to value.

What do spouses spend to show that they value each other?

- Time
- Effort to communicate
- Experiences, feelings, thoughts, secrets, goals, ambitions, fears—whatever people protect from others because they don't want to be vulnerable
- Willingness to help and care for the partner
- Effort to know him or her
- Money and material possessions

Will not to devalue. How can a man or woman avoid devaluing his or her partner? Some ways: Don't put down the partner. Don't use sarcasm. Be respectful. Don't presume on the partner (instead, ask). Don't look disgusted. Don't call names, even in the heat of conflict. Will to value. Never devalue. In so doing, you love.

Working

A good marriage requires effort to improve. Without effort, a marriage declines. If we don't add energy, disorder increases. It's a fundamental law of nature. Water runs downhill. Gardens grow weeds. Buildings run down and crumble.

Marriage requires work, or it degenerates too.

Without work, a couple cannot progress. Without work, it is as if they were steering a ship that is dead in the water. The ship floats with the current and eventually washes into the ocean. Any marriage, vibrant or recovering from troubled times, requires work.

Faith

What is faith? The writer of Hebrews tells us, "Faith is the assurance of things hoped for, the conviction of things not seen" (Hebrews 11:1 RSV). When partners *will to value,* when they *will not to devalue,* when they *work* to love more, they may not always see a direct return on their investment of love and work in a marriage. People need faith to realize their hopes.

When Christen, my oldest daughter, was six years old, I put a thousand dollars in the bank. I haven't seen that thousand dollars since then, but by faith I expect that when she starts college this fall, I'll get the thousand dollars plus another thousand dollars in interest.

Love is Jesus' currency. When we invest it, love pays enormous interest. Who is worthier of our faith—our bank or Jesus Christ, Lord of creation? Jesus, of course. He tells us that there are eternal dividends in following His pattern, and He challenges us to trust Him.

The faith that people need for a good marriage is multifaceted. Ultimately, it is faith in God—in His care for those He loves and His provision for that care through Jesus, His Son, and the Holy Spirit. But people's faith must extend to their own obedience. They need faith that if they try to conform their lives as living sacrifices (Romans 12:1), then the Lord will work His love through them into their marriage. They need faith that trials will end, that flaws can be corrected, that effort will be rewarded. They need faith that the marriage can improve. They need faith that helpers can help. Each of these objects of faith proceeds from faith in the loving and holy character of God. As we help friends with marital struggles, we can see few of these outcomes, so we must maintain faith that Jesus Christ can bring about positive outcomes in the lives of our friends.

Applications

Knowing that failures of faith working through love cause marital problems is not enough to help friends in pain over their marriage. You must recognize the specific failures in their story and gently help them see those failures without their feeling that you are condemning them. Recognizing failures requires practice. Let's recall those three couples with whom I began this chapter.

Couple 1: *Failure in Faith Working through* ***Love***

John and Emily, the jokesters, put each other down and poured their time into hobbies, leaving each other feeling worthless and devalued. What caused their problem?

A failure in faith working through love.

In particular, their put-down humor devalued each other publicly. In private, they ignored each other, which devalued each other. Thus, they failed to love each other. They also refused to work on their relationship, preferring to allow the marriage to deteriorate while they avoided each other. They had no confidence that their relationship was redeemable; no faith that anything could be changed through their own efforts, their counselor's help, or God's intervention. Their problem involved failures in faith, working, and love; but for John and Emily, their major problem was a failure in love.

How would you help them? After helping them see God's pattern, help them discuss their lives together and recognize the times when they were not valuing each other or were actively devaluing each other. It is important not to allow them to point out each other's failures of love. Each should only point out his or her own failures. To repair their marriage, they must work to stop devaluing each other, start showing love, and rekindle their faith.

Couple 2: *Failure in Faith **Working** Through Love*

Linda and Mel, who were having separate affairs, stopped putting effort into their relationship, and the relationship inevitably crashed.

Their problem is a failure in faith working through love. The problem majors in lack of working and minors in failures in faith and love.

If you were helping Linda and Mel, your main job would be to motivate them to work on their marriage again.

- Express your faith in God and in their willingness to work on their marriage.
- Give homework and expect the homework to be done.
- Characterize success as depending on their work.
- Help them make small changes to achieve some success.

Linda's and Mel's affairs decrease the prospects that their marriage will improve. Encourage each partner to stop the affair and to work seriously and single-mindedly on their marriage.

Couple 3: *Failure in **Faith** Working Through Love*

Al and Cloe, the couple whose relationship died in the marriage bed, also have a problem in faith working through love. They have given up their faith and they need to recapture it. The erosion of their faith has demotivated them from working on their marriage and has caused love to faint. They need faith in God's sovereign ability to change their marriage, in the helpfulness of their work on the marriage, and in the helpfulness of the help they receive.

They will challenge each aspect of faith in any help you provide. Assure them of things hoped for. Help develop the conviction of things not seen. Only if they regain their lost faith can their marriage survive as more than a hollow shell.

Test Yourself

In the following graphic, I have included five brief descriptions of couples. Identify how failures in faith working through love show up in their marriages.

Five Examples to Practice Finding Instances of Failure in Faith Working Through Love

In each of the five cases below, test yourself. See if you can find at least one way that there is a failure in faith, working, and love for each case. You'll get the most out of this exercise if you actually formulate your answers by saying them aloud or by writing them before you check your answers. Then turn the page and check your answers against some of the answers I've provided.

CASE 1:

Marie: I don't believe Lon cares about our marriage anymore. I get up in the morning and he's off at work. He doesn't come home until after the kids are in bed; and most of the time, I'm already in bed when he gets home.

CASE 2:

Richard: I don't feel connected to Caroline anymore. I feel like I've lost my reason for being married. It's like the marriage within has died and left a hollow outer shell. I think our marriage is over.

CASE 3:

Yonette: He yells at me. Every time I try to do anything, he screams, criticizes, and fusses. I can't stand it anymore.

CASE 4:

Will: How could God have done this to me? I love the Lord, and I've tried to live a dedicated Christian life. Then, my wife of fifteen years has an affair. She's no good. I'm angry at her and angry at God. I feel betrayed all around.

CASE 5:

Kitty: You're so kind to me. You're not like him at all. He runs me down. He never listens. He's just an unfeeling machine. But you —you're different. You are so kind and sensitive. I wish I had married you instead of Rick.

CASE 1: Marie has a failure in faith in Lon and she believes that he has lost his faith in the marriage too. Marie claims that Lon isn't interested in working on the marriage because he is pouring all his energy into other pursuits. Marie feels devalued because Lon is unwilling to treat her and the children as valuable.

CASE 2: Richard has decided that his marriage to Caroline is over, signifying that he is no longer committed to making the marriage live. He has lost faith in the marriage's ability to revive. As a consequence, he has given up any desire to work on the marriage. He doesn't value Caroline enough to work on the seemingly hopeless marriage.

CASE 3: Yonette is critical of her spouse for actively devaluing her. At the same time, though, she is actively devaluing him, so both are showing a lack of love. Yonette states that she can't stand it anymore, which might indicate that she is experiencing a failure in faith and a loss of willingness to work on the marriage.

CASE 4: Will is experiencing a loss of faith. He believes that God has suddenly changed character and seeks to do harm to him. Further, he doesn't believe that God can have anything positive come out of the affair. Rather than work on the marriage, Will believes that it's over. He shows a devaluing of God as well as a devaluing of his spouse, showing a deficit in love for both.

CASE 5: Kitty is hurt and is devaluing Rick at the same time that she is valuing the helper. Her effort is aimed at soothing her wounds, her feelings of having made a mistake in marrying Rick, and she is exerting effort in attracting the helper. Chances are that her attraction to the helper is motivated more out of a desire to hurt Rick than out of an attraction to the helper. By trying to attract the helper, she is losing her faith in God's covenantal binding of her to her husband. While the betrayal has apparently not become sexual at this point, it could if the helper is not alert and does not stand firmly against a violation of his faith.

Marriages have problems because they don't conform to God's pattern of discipleship. As one of the priesthood of believers, you have the awesome opportunity and the terrifying responsibility to try to make a difference when people ask your help.

CHAPTER THREE

WHERE PROBLEMS SURFACE

Failures in faith working through love occur in several areas simultaneously. Marital problems aren't *caused by* disagreements over sex, in-laws, child rearing, chores and responsibilities, finances, personal habits, work priorities, or even the toothpaste (rolled or squeezed) or toilet paper (flap over or under) problem. Those are topics of conflict. Don't be deluded into thinking that if you can resolve those differences through clever compromise, marital problems will disappear.

Some Hard Thinking About Causes of Marital Problems

There is no single, *real* cause for failed marriages. A medical model presumes that a "germ" or damaged tissue is the real cause of symptoms. Marriage problems are not like medical problems, and the task of the helper is not like the task of the physician, who first discovers the germ or tissue damage that is causing the problem, then prescribes the correct treatment. People's minds don't operate like their bodies. Germs are present whether we know they are there or not, and we can't make a broken arm or fever worse by worrying about it, but we can make psychological difficulties worse by dwelling on them. Sometimes psychological problems are even *created* by paying attention to something that never before was a problem.

A couple might be perfectly happy. Then one partner reads a book about marital communication. Convinced that a problem exists, the person worries about it until there is a real problem. Or, a couple may resolve a problem, and then one or both begin to dwell on the problem again, bringing it back into the marriage.

Sally and Mark

When marriages are stressed, they often suffer in many areas at the same time. The couple will usually only pay close attention to one or two problems and generally ignore the others. For example, Sally and Mark had a chronic problem since their marriage as teens. They couldn't agree on how to handle their money.

Sally was reared in a financially conservative home. Her father was a postman, and her mother stayed at home with the children. When her parents saw something they wanted, they weighed the options carefully. Saving money for the three children's college educations was usually the highest priority, so Sally's family lived in austere surroundings. Sally adopted that attitude.

Mark was reared in a free-spending family. His parents didn't make more money than Sally's, but to them, money was made in order to enjoy life. They thought little about saving for the future, believing that God would provide.

In their own marriage, Sally and Mark argued incessantly for twenty years about money. Sally thought that the problem was due to Mark's impulsiveness and rash decision making, which often resulted in his foolish spending. Mark thought that the problem was due to Sally's lack of spontaneity.

Looking at the marriage objectively, though, we can see that many problems exist. For example, the two aren't feeling emotionally close to each other, their communication isn't good, they can't resolve conflict, they blame each other for deliberately hurting each other, they lack forgiveness, and they don't have a common vision of marriage. Also, their long-term commitment to marriage is wavering.

As long as Sally thinks Mark's irresponsible personality is the problem and Mark thinks Sally's uptight, repressed personality is the problem, they won't resolve their differences and get their marriage back on track. You, their friend, probably couldn't help either. It is simply too hard to change a person's personality in less than several years of intense psychological counseling—short of a direct miracle by God, which, I am happy to say, He does at times.

For you to help a married couple, look for areas that the couple might change immediately—areas that might have a long-term effect on the couple. Larry Christenson, in *The Renewed Mind*,[1] once likened change to building a concrete structure. First, build a wooden form in the shape of the structure. Then, insert steel rods and secure them by wires. Finally, pour the concrete. Over time, the concrete hardens into a permanent structure. For marital change, help married partners erect temporary forms by changing their behavior, and insert steel rods and wires by encouraging them to sustain improved behavior. Then pray for God to pour the concrete of changed hearts, personalities, and attitudes of love.

A Brief Overview of Marriage

Whenever marriages are troubled, difficulties occur in nine areas that provide targets for helping marriages change.

Human Needs

With Adam and Eve, God created people who needed a sense of meaning. First, He saw that it was not good for man to be alone, so He created Eve to meet human relationship needs. Second, He created Adam to work in the Garden of Eden and Eve to help Adam. Adam and Eve had the same fundamental needs: to have meaningful relationships and to do meaningful work. People show their fidelity to God by living out His love and doing His work, with His help.

When Adam and Eve fell from grace, their needs remained, but because sin indwelt them, they sinned to meet those needs. That continues today. We needn't be ashamed of our needs for love, work, and meaning. But loving God and being grateful for His redemption, we must practice the discipleship pattern of faith working through love in every area of the most precious human relationship He provides for us to learn about Him—marriage.

A Preview of the Major Areas

At the most fundamental level of marriage is the Christian core, which consists of three areas. At the center is each individual's Christian foundation; those beliefs and values affect all other areas. Springing from that foundation is the couple's vision for marriage. Partners actualize that vision in every area of marriage. Because people are fallen, they inevitably hurt their partners. They sin against them and against God. Therefore, a fundamental aspect of marriage is confession of those hurts and repentance from further hurts. Seeking and granting forgiveness is needed in all areas of marriage. These three areas—Christianity, core beliefs, and confession-forgiveness—are the heart of the marriage (see graphic, page 35). They are the lifeblood, pumping vitality into the outer body.

Four areas are mostly responsible for a couple's marital satisfaction—closeness, communication, conflict resolution, and cognition (expectations and negative thinking). If Christianity, core vision, and confession-forgiveness is the heart of the marriage, then closeness, communication, conflict resolution, and cognition are the muscles, bones, ligaments, and tendons that keep the body in motion and empower it.

Complicating factors—psychological or physical problems, infidelity, alcohol abuse, physical abuse, and sexual abuse—can make solving problems extremely difficult. Like cancers that run out of control and gnaw at the body's tender parts, complicating factors often run rampant and threaten the existence of the marriage body.

Finally, covenantal commitment holds the relationship together. Like skin, which gives shape and stability to the body and is seen by the outer world, covenantal commitment holds the inner parts together.

Faith working through love is the spirit of the marriage. It is the motivation, the raison d'être, the ennobling part of the marriage. The marriage, like the miracle of the physical body, depends on proper functioning of its parts. The spirit must pervade the body. If an individual area of the marriage is stressed or untouched by the spirit, the effects are felt throughout the entire system.

Faith Working Through Love in Nine Areas of Marriage

Christian Foundation

Recently, I observed a conflict at church. The elders had proposed an action that one active couple in the church found to be an anathema to their concept of the church. The pastor and an elder met with the couple in their home to discuss the difficulty. The meeting was characterized by civility, and both sides presented logical arguments. By the end of the evening, both sides felt as if they had been heard and respected, but the feelings were not positive. Until they prayed. Through prayer together, a spirit of Christian unity was sensed that was far more important than any personal or philosophical issue about the business of the church. The meeting ended in love.

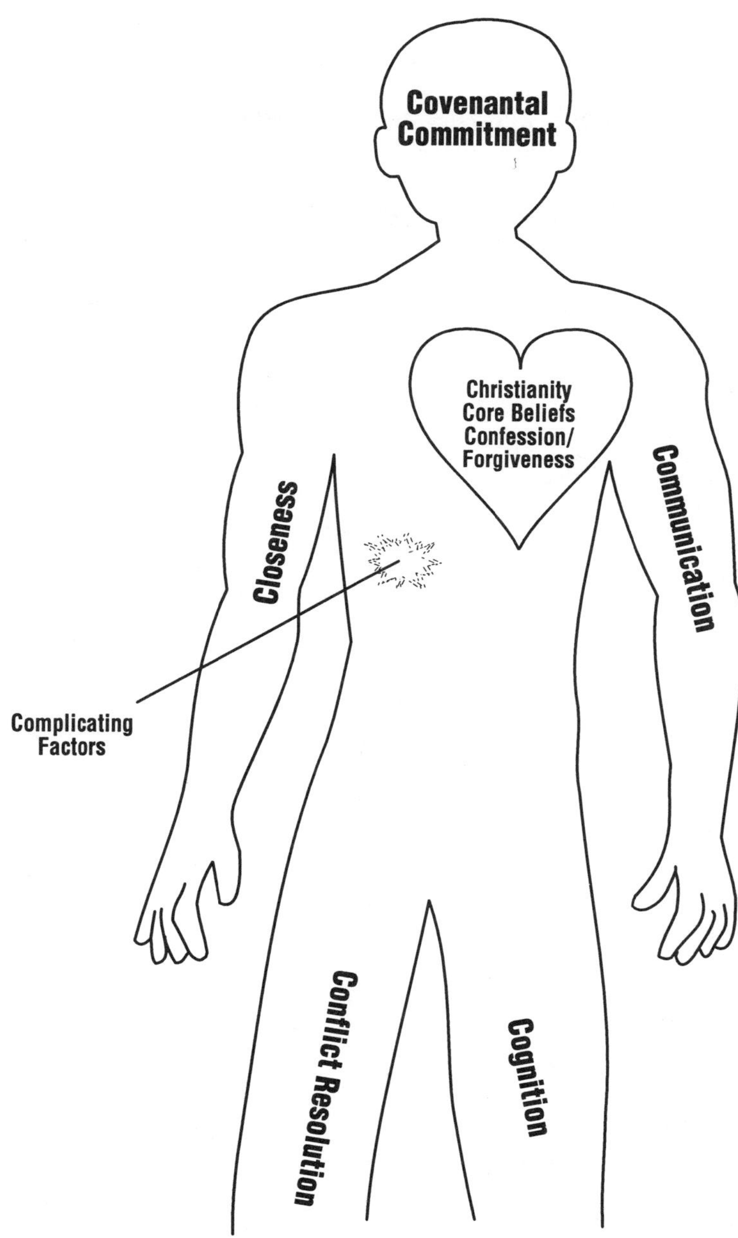
Covenantal
Commitment
Christianity
Core Beliefs
Confession/
Forgiveness
Closeness
Communication
Complicating
Factors
Conflict Resolution
Cognition

The adage that the couple who prays together stays together is true. Research has supported it,[2] and I have found only a few instances in my experience counseling couples in which intense marital problems continued if the couple prayed for and with each other.

God forges a spiritual tie between husband and wife. Marriage is a type of the relationship between God and Israel, Jesus and the church, and Jesus and the believer. God wants marriage to succeed.

When partners seek God for themselves and their marriage, they reinforce those spiritual ties, like exercise strengthens muscles. Spiritual lifeblood flows into the marriage, fighting against tensions, misunderstandings, dysfunctional family backgrounds, sinful pride, and the desire to retaliate for hurts that (because of our fallenness) inevitably occur. Sometimes the spiritual connection simply isn't strong enough to heal the strains on marriage, but the spiritual connection certainly helps.

When people practice faith working through love, they exercise spiritually, which will strengthen the muscles. When they fail to practice faith working through love, it is like lifting weights incorrectly. Vital muscles are damaged, and the body needs healing.

Core Beliefs

Everyone has both a positive and negative mental picture of marriage. The positive picture says, "This is the way my marriage should be." The negative picture says, "I'll never let this happen in my marriage." The pictures are formed in the family-of-origin; modified through watching others in life, reading, viewing movies and television; and fine-tuned in our own romantic relationships (with the spouse and previous romantic partners).

Core beliefs consist of things you say about your marriage and things you believe but have never said. Paradoxically, the things one hasn't put into words seem to have the most impact on marriage. A husband and wife both grew up observing how their parents treated each other as marriage partners. They observed the ways parents spoke to, touched, and disagreed with each other. They didn't consciously attend to those behaviors, but the observations made an indelible impact on them. Later, in their marriage, they copied parental behaviors or irrationally tried to avoid them. Those are unspoken core beliefs.

Core beliefs can be modified. A person isn't doomed to unhappy marriage because his family-of-origin was troubled. Knowing that one is to practice faith working through love as a fundamental part of

Christian life and pondering how to do that in marriage can irreversibly change one's mental pictures of marriage.

Confession

This morning I was fixing breakfast when I stepped backwards onto Katy Anna's toes. Waaugh—a wail. With athleticism rivaling Carl Lewis's, I leaped deftly from her foot. And placed my hand in the raw eggs I had prepared. I jerked my hand up and slimed my shirt as I apologized to Katy Anna. I found the egg-slime tracks after I arrived at work. It's Monday. It is going to be a long week.

Living with others means occasionally hurting them, like I did when I stepped on Katy Anna's toes. A proper response to hurting a loved one is confession. The loved one's proper response is forgiveness. Because of sin, though, people often justify themselves when they hurt others. They blame others, harbor resentment and bitterness, and seek revenge.

In a troubled marriage, hurts are more numerous and last longer than smashed toes, so helping troubled couples involves much confession and forgiveness. Each partner is responsible for both confessing and forgiving wrongs. Confession and forgiveness lubricate the marriage machinery.

Confession and forgiveness are at the core of faith working through love. People love their partners by confessing their hurtfulness because they show them that they value them enough to bow in confession. When people forgive, they express faith in their partners' desire to try not to hurt them again. They know that failures and hurts are inevitable, but they have faith in their partners' willingness to try not to hurt deliberately. Confession and forgiveness are not easy; they require work. Without the willingness to work, a relationship is doomed to swing back and forth, going nowhere like a door swinging on its hinges. Faith working through love: that principle is at the heart of the Christian gospel as it works into lives through confession and forgiveness.

Closeness

God created individuals with free will to choose responsible behavior. But He also created people to be in intimate relationship with Him and with others. There is always a tension, then, between individual freedom and relationship responsibility. That tension is often acute in marriages.

When people marry, they become one flesh, but they retain individuality. If partners are too independent, they lose touch, feel isolated and lonely, out of contact. But partners can be so close that they stifle each other. They can demand total union, joined like Siamese twins until they tire of the prison of each other's company.

Because God created individuals, husband and wife often have different needs for closeness and distance. If they try to satisfy all their intimacy needs with their spouse alone—without having intimacy with best friends or relatives—they might feel strained. Sid described Joni as a black hole of emotion, draining him of every ounce of emotional support, sucking the life from his spirit. Joni described Sid as being withdrawn and cold, incapable of showing emotion, a man with so many barriers that it was hard to touch him. They needed different amounts of emotional expression.

Sid and Joni had to practice faith working through love to escape the intimacy trap that had snared them. They communicated that they valued each other, regardless of their different styles of showing love. They had faith that each was trying to lay down his or her life for the other, trying to go against the natural patterns of self-protection and instead show love and value to the other. They concentrated their efforts on the "hard" loving of self-denial and seeking good for the other. In fact, it was only after Joni developed a close friendship with Susan that Joni was able to stop making so many demands for emotional support on Sid. For his part, Sid stopped complaining each time Joni tried to talk with him. Over time, they worked out a balance of closeness and distance that pleased both.

Communication

People communicate on several levels. They *exchange rituals,* such as "Hi. How are you today?" "Fine. How are you?" "Good." "See you." "See you."

They also *exchange information,* such as what happened at work or how the children behaved.

They *self-disclose* important information and feelings, which might involve saying things like, "I'm worried about whether I will get that promotion that my boss promised me last year." Or discussion might involve disclosures such as, "When you eat crackers in bed, it makes me angry. I also fear that you're telling me that we have a crumby relationship. You know, marriage to you isn't all it was cracked up to be either." Self-disclosure requires knowing how and when to level—discuss feelings directly—with the mate and when to edit—not tell feelings when the result might harm. Self-disclosure involves telling the mate about positive and negative feelings, and it involves telling others what you are thinking.

Finally, people may *meta-communicate,* which means they talk about how they are communicating. For instance, they might say, "I think we are in a power struggle. We have to break free if we are going to resolve our differences."

Communication can break down at any level, though usually most feelings that communication is not going well occur when people self-disclose or meta-communicate. Restoring faith working through love in broken communication is necessary in almost all marital problems.

Conflict Resolution

Differences are inevitable. Couples must resolve conflicts. For instance, Edward and Robin were married in 1983. They had no arguments for their first two years of marriage. Whenever they had a difference of opinion, one would simply give in. After six months, both were moody and angry most of the time. By the time they had been married one year, they criticized each other. Only after two years did they argue and fight openly. When the feelings were unleashed, the damage was enormous. Edward and Robin hurt each other with every sentence. They used counseling to argue more viciously. They soon separated and later divorced.

In contrast, Kirby and I began our marriage living in California while both our sets of parents were living in the southeastern United States. During the first year, we squabbled. In the style that I had perfected in my family-of-origin, I sulked, fumed, and tried to make Kirby feel guilty when she disagreed with me. Instead of meekly giving in or getting angry, Kirby insisted that we talk about our differences. I sulked, but she continued to ask that we discuss our disagreements. So we did, and we resolved our differences. Kirby taught me how to resolve conflicts productively. She valued me enough to insist lovingly that I talk with her instead of manipulating her. She had faith that if we talked, we could work out our differences.

Cognition: Negative Thinking

Troubled marriages are plagued by negative thinking. Partners violate expectations so often that negative expectations replace positive expectations of the new marriage. Each partner assumes the worst about the spouse and blames the other for anything that goes wrong (and for some things that didn't go wrong), making it unlikely that the spouse can redeem himself or herself. Negative self-talk also is common in a troubled marriage. *Why can't I make this work?* partners may think. *I should be able to deal with these frustrations without losing my perspective and blowing sky-high. But I can't.*

With negative expectations, assumptions, attributions of blame, and self-talk, the entire atmosphere of marriage feels negative. Faith in the future and faith in God's ability to redeem the marriage are at a low ebb. The partners are unmotivated to work on the relationship because they believe that working on the marriage is hopeless. Love has eroded and partners devalue each other. Failures of faith working through love show up repeatedly in each partner's thought-life.

Complicating Factors

Sometimes ongoing problems not directly associated with the relationship might exacerbate existing marital tensions. Some of the complicating problems can be serious in themselves, claiming priority of treatment over the marital difficulties. For example, physical problems such as chronic illness or handicapping conditions can place extra strains on the marriage. Life-threatening illnesses may mobilize a family around the ill person while marital concerns are put on hold. Dorothy and Dan endured twenty years of marital conflict, which came to a head only when she discovered she had breast cancer.

Psychological problems can also create difficulties in marriage. Depression is often related to marital problems. Many people become depressed because of marriage disruption. In other cases, depression disrupts good marriages. In both cases, depression focuses the depressed spouse on marriage weaknesses and burdens the other partner.

Infidelity almost always disrupts a marriage. Dealing with the betrayal of trust that occurs with infidelity, handling the guilt, and forgiving the unfaithful partner can challenge the vitality of any relationship.

Alcohol or drug abuse disrupts marriage as partners organize to deal with addiction. Failures to give up the addiction may be characterized as failures in love. Repeated failures exhaust both partners' will to simultaneously battle the addiction and work on the marriage.

Sexual or physical abuse can also complicate the marriage. Sexual abuse of a child strikes at the heart of the family. It is infidelity and incest rolled into one. Physical abuse of a partner can create life-threatening situations for both partners as anger, self-protection, shame, and a desire to cover up create a coercive and secretive marital environment that is not conducive to promoting faith working through love. Also insidious is past sexual or physical abuse within one person's family-of-origin. The betrayal of love may be experienced by one partner in a way that affects the current marriage, leaving the other partner feeling puzzled, angry, and helpless.

Commitment

God has always been faithful to humans, but we have continually rebelled against Him due to our indwelling sinful human nature. God covenanted with His chosen servant Abraham. Today, we use the word *covenant* loosely to mean "agreement," but in Abraham's day, covenant meant that the parties were pledged to place the other person's needs above the self's needs. Covenants were lifelong (and since God is eternal, *His* covenant is everlasting). Shed blood made a covenant official.

Generally, a Christian understanding of marriage presumes a *covenantal commitment.* Marriages fail when people weaken their commitment to each other under Christ.

A lifelong agreement to remain committed to another person who is virtually unknown at the time of marriage would not be a likely prospect were it to be made solely in the strength of human will power. God's grace and (at times) His supernatural intervention are necessary for a lasting marriage. Heavy doses of faith, work, and love are the prescription for covenantal commitment.

Faith working through love acts in each aspect of the marriage. Let's apply these concepts in the next two chapters.

CHAPTER FOUR

HELPING AFTER MARRIAGE

After marriage, people seek help during two especially vulnerable times: shortly after marriage and during long-term or crisis problems.

Marriage? No Problema, Amigo

"Sure lots of marriages end in divorce today. It seems like everyone I know has been divorced or is considering divorce. But it will never happen to Suzy and me because . . ."

". . . we have an unusually strong love."

". . . we *really* know each other."

". . . we're compatible."

". . . we've discussed the potentially troublesome areas and agree on everything."

". . . we've had premarital counseling."

". . . we've had counseling and have our acts together."

". . . neither of us has ever had counseling. We've got our acts together."

". . . everyone is behind us—our parents, our friends, the church, everyone."

". . . we're both Christians."

". . . we have peace about getting married, so we know it's God's will."

". . . we've decided never to let the D-word [divorce] cross our lips."

". . . we've both been married before. We now realize the mistakes we made before, and we won't make those again."

Why Do Newlyweds Seek Help?

Before a couple marries, they feel invulnerable. Love sweeps them along on a cloud from which they can't see the ground, much less the pit—even if they wished to look, which they don't.

Then they come back from the honeymoon.

Making Their Own Rules for Marriage

Fromma and Leo were reared in Christian homes. Throughout their engagement, they talked constantly. They knew each other's position on Bosnia, reduction of the national debt, number of children they wanted (three), type of car (cheap at first, later a Volvo), debt (don't go into debt except for a house), pets (a dog), vacations (camping in the national parks), and many other controversial topics. They were unusually compatible. They had never thought to talk about who should take the trash out. That was obvious—beyond question.

Fromma's father always took out the trash. Leo's mother always took it out.

For three weeks after they returned from their honeymoon, trash collected in the kitchen. They stepped over it. They each neatened the piles when the mate wasn't around. Both were too polite, too much in love to mention how the other was shirking a minor responsibility.

"Honey," said Fromma in their fourth week. "Would you mind emptying the trash?"

Leo smiled. "Sure, darling. I'd be glad to." *But it's a woman's work,* he thought.

Three weeks later, Fromma tripped over an empty milk carton. "Honey, please take the trash out."

Leo's lips smiled but his teeth were clenched. "Sure, lamb chop, darling."

Two and a half weeks later, summer's heat was making the kitchen an aromatic place. "Leo, can you take out the trash? It stinks in here."

Leo slammed the wastebasket around and threw scraps of potato into an empty vegetable can. "We're going to have to talk about this trash thing," he snapped.

The honeymoon was *really* over this time.

Fromma and Leo had come from different families and the "trash thing" was merely one of many differences they would uncover in their marriage. Early in the marriage, small differences are ignored, but a necessary part of forming a marriage is discussing the differences that partners bring to marriage and working out how the partners are going to resolve the differences (as well as working out a solution to the specific differences). In some research I did several years ago,[1] I found that happily married couples who had been married less than three years had *more disagreements* than did unhappy couples who had been married less than three years. However, the happily married couples who discussed their differences grumbled about their relationships less than did unhappy couples who did not discuss their differences. For couples married from three to fifty-six years, fewer disagreements were associated with marital happiness. Not so for newly wedded couples.

Working out inevitable differences is often emotional and painful. Yet some conflict is necessary, as long as the couple works on the differences in love and with a primary objective of valuing the partner rather than winning a war.

Young couples seek help with their early conflicts. They need to know that such conflicts are normal—which doesn't make conflict any less traumatic but should encourage them to work on resolving the issues rather than burying the conflict and grumbling about each other.

Dealing with the (Almost) Inevitable Disillusionment

Usually, within the first six months of marriage, partners become disillusioned with each other. Regardless of how careful people are, they marry their ideal of the spouse rather than an accurate picture of the spouse. Once reality bursts through the ideal, the partner feels betrayed. "You're not the person I married," she might wail. She's right. She married a figment of her imagination. Everyone does. Disillusionments are almost inevitable. The question is, What is the newly married partner to do about the disillusionment?

It can be helpful for a newly married spouse in the midst of disillusionment, feeling a wrenching catch in the chest each time a deep breath is drawn, to talk with someone who has survived disillusionment. Merely the encouragement to keep faith in the partner might be enough to spur the person to continue to work to build love with the "new" person he or she is discovering.

Adjusting to New Roles and Behaviors

People who haven't previously been married soon find marriage a bit like bushwhacking through a jungle. Marriage has hidden beauties and unsuspected dangers. Despite conscientious efforts to prepare for marriage, people simply can't know how they're going to adjust until they try it out.

Problems pop up. "Our sexual relationship isn't like the movies. We don't enjoy sex very often, and my wife almost never has an orgasm when we make love."

"We don't have devotions together."

"We can't decide how to divide the household work fairly."

Eventually, couples establish routines and become more comfortable in their roles, but information from someone who has been married for a while might smooth the tracks to adjustment and reduce the bumps. So newly married couples often seek information to aid their adjustment to new roles.

Seeking Help

Having to negotiate the patterns and rules of a new marriage, handling the almost inevitable disillusionment, and getting used to new roles guarantee that newly married couples will need adjustment to marriage. Some couples try to solve the difficulties on their own, but most seek help and support. They may call home and ask parents for advice, seek the counsel of a married brother or sister, talk with a friend or colleague at work about their adjustments, seek help from their pastor, or join a support group for newly wedded couples. Most people seek some help,[2] though they may ask only indirectly.

Leo was having problems dealing with his adjustment to marriage. He and Fromma had argued three times during the last week, only once over the trash problem. The most recent disagreement had occurred as they left for work that morning. He told Fromma he would be home late because he was playing basketball with the guys, and she blew up. Leo was exasperated with his inability to solve his marriage problems with the same facility that he dealt with his problems at work.

He was part of a group of design engineers, all men, who had worked closely for five years. Before the marriage, the group took Leo out for dinner and a surprise party afterward. Leo had been the target of teasing and the butt of many jokes about being newly married.

Recently the group had conducted a field test, which required Leo to work extra. Fromma couldn't understand why he had to stay late every night. Then, on the one night he got off early, he wanted to relax with basketball. Over the group's lunch of sandwiches and coffee, Leo started a conversation with Russell, Mac, and Gabe by saying, "My dad said he had the hardest time with the first year of marriage. He said that he and Mom almost divorced by their first anniversary. But Mom got pregnant with me and when Dad came home from work, he went into the bedroom to change clothes and Mom had laid some baby booties on his pillow. He said that having a child was what held their marriage together. Did you guys have any difficulty during your first year of marriage?"

Each launched into his war stories. Leo listened intently, hoping for some tidbits of wisdom that he could apply to his marriage. Occasionally, he asked questions casually, such as, "Did you have any fights? How'd you handle those?"

Two days later, Mac caught Leo alone at the water fountain. "Hey, Leo. I don't mean to pry, but when we were talking, it seemed as if you were concerned about your marriage."

"Nah," said Leo. "Oh, we've had a few little disagreements. Naturally I'm concerned. Nobody likes disagreements, do they?"

Mac slapped Leo on the back. "Sure, everybody sometimes disagrees. I wasn't saying that anything was *wrong*. Just, well, Cara and I had some disagreements when we married, and I thought you and I might talk about it sometime if you wanted."

Leo ran his fingers through his hair. "Yeah, it'd be interesting to know how you handled those. Fromma and I are having more disagreements than I can handle on my own, and I could use some ideas about how to get things right."

Mac, a good helper, was sensitive to what Leo was really asking, and he sensed that Leo might want to talk. When he approached Leo head-on, though, Mac correctly heard Leo's defensiveness. So Mac helped Leo feel comfortable talking about his marriage by revealing some of his own difficulties. Leo opened up so the two could talk. After that, Mac and Leo talked frequently—over an occasional lunch or after work in either Mac's or Leo's office. Mac was Leo's lifeline during the turbulent first-year storms.

Helping Enrich Marriage

Some Friendly Advice

"If it ain't broke, don't fix it," said my seventy-year-old neighbor, Mr. Barrington. (He never told me his first name in the three years we were neighbors.) The 100-plus degree heat was oppressive. I could see the heat waves shimmering from the ground. Mr. Barrington leaned on the fence and talked about his life in mid-Missouri. "It's my philosophy. I always let well enough alone. When my job was going well—back before they made me retire—I didn't take to wondering how I might twittle some knob and make it a bit better. I let it be. My marriage has been the same way. The good Lord has blessed us with more than fifty years of good life. We got married after she finished high school. I didn't finish no more than the eighth grade 'cause my daddy needed me to work on the farm. Course we've fought. Lord knows, we've fought like cats and dogs sometimes. But we always make up. Anyway, ain't nothing wrong with our marriage, so we don't bother with it. You psychology people think you can always make life better. It just ain't so."

Mr. Barrington was holding forth about psychologists—one of his favorite pastimes—after I had described a marriage enrichment program that several interns were developing at the University of Missouri-Columbia's Counseling Services. He voiced the sentiments of many people toward marriage enrichment. Most people do not seek help enriching their marriages when they are content.

Does Marriage Enrichment Work?

Should satisfied couples seek help? Can psychology make good marriages better? Some research has investigated the effectiveness of marriage enrichment. For instance, Doherty and Walker (1982) and Doherty et al. (1986)[3] investigated Marriage Encounter, usually an intensive weekend in which couples hear short talks, discuss them briefly in a group, and communicate alone as a couple. Partners communicate in writing first, each person writing for ten minutes (or more) about his or her feelings. As the weekend progresses, partners share more intimately. Doherty and Walker found a moderately positive effect of Marriage Encounter. In a second study on the same program, Doherty et al. found that not all couples improved their marriages as a result of the weekend encounter. Rather, couples who already had the strongest marriages improved the most. Troubled couples got worse by the end of the weekend. The authors speculated that requiring troubled couples to communicate without supervision increased marital tensions. Most couples did not benefit, nor were they harmed by the marriage encounter weekend. To them, the weekend made no difference after their initial enthusiasm had worn off.

When Can You Help Enrich Good Marriages?

Marriage enrichment usually occurs in groups rather than one-on-one or couple-to-couple. Whereas marriage counseling usually involves a single couple so special attention can be paid to particular troubles, marriage enrichment is more information-centered. Well-functioning couples are usually able to apply the information to their lives. In groups, opportunities arise continually for sharing about marriage. Each opportunity is a chance to help others improve their marriage if people are alert to describing helpful marital interactions. Discussing experiences and providing social support as a couple can have a lasting impact on other couples—even when the contact is brief.[4]

Helping with Ongoing Problems

Don't Get Frustrated

We all know someone, or perhaps several someones, who have marital difficulties. Whenever we talk to them, the talk often turns to their marriages. At times we may feel that we are caught in a game in which we make suggestions that are never followed or that always prove ineffective. We offer suggestion after suggestion, only to come up frustrated.

In ongoing problems, your friend is usually dissatisfied with his or her present life—dissatisfied enough to complain about the marriage, though often not dissatisfied enough to want to change. The misery of the uncertainty of change is greater than the certainty of the misery of remaining unchanged.

Sometimes, however, we feel that we've said something that might help. Perhaps just being with them and supporting them may have encouraged them in their trials.

Speaking Faith Working Through Love into an Ongoing Problem

Into this usually stable unhappy situation, you are called to speak words of faith working through love. Emphasize love. Encourage the person not to devalue his or her spouse. Speak words of love to the person, calling him or her into the activity that Jesus said would set Christians apart from others. He said, "My command is this: Love each other as I have loved you. Greater love has no one than this, that one lay down his life for his friends. You are my friends if you do what I command" (John 15:12–14). He also said, "A new commandment I give you: Love one another. As I have loved you, so you must love one another. All men will know that you are my disciples if you love one another" (John 13:34–35).

Such disciplined love takes work, effort, labor. So, become an encourager who gently prods the person into loving, who works to guide the person in how to love, who gently spurs the person to give up hurtful ways, who notices when the person is working hard on his or her relationship, who praises his or her effort, who supports attempts to change, who follows up on efforts to change to see whether they succeeded, and who suggests other changes.

Faith is required too. The person may feel that God isn't willing or able to change his or her marriage. Speak words of faith that extol God's goodness and His willingness to help. Speak words of faith after the person has risked loving and has been rejected by the spouse. Speak words of faith anytime change is discernible. You are an agent of faith.

The Instability of Motivation

Motivation to work on ongoing problems ebbs and flows. It changes like the weather, with times of low pressure which bring clouds and instability and times of high pressure which usher in clear skies. Through emotional drought and tearful monsoons, you are the weather forecaster who faithfully predicts God's working in the couple's life, and you live your own life in faith working through love so that the person can know what a life of Christian discipleship looks like.

Helping in a Crisis

Mariners in a Hurricane

When a crisis blows up like a hurricane, inexperienced helpers hold onto their hats and crawl for shelter. They fear the crisis because chaos reigns. Tears and anger flow like an angry, storm-driven river loosed from its banks. Shouting, recriminations, and cursing rip apart the quiet misery of unsatisfactory lives. Helpers don't want to get caught and battered in the onslaught.

I recall seeing a picture of a storm, ripping the tops off waves that soared twenty feet in the air only to crash into a trough below. Old men, mariners with gray beards and wrinkled faces, strained to launch a rescue craft into the holocaust. The determination on their faces made the storm's fury as insignificant as a summer breeze. "People are caught in a storm," their faces seemed to say, "and we're going after them."

The mariners have ridden the boat through waves to rescue panicked people caught in countless storms prior to this one. In wisdom, they know what they can and can't do. Experienced helpers look at crisis not as a disaster but as an opportunity. Crises upset sailing, tearing the tattered sails from the main mast. Crises make the troubled couples long for change, and crises destabilize the boat so that change is easier.

Can you imagine tourists trying to save the shipwrecked sailors? It could be disaster. For a friend, a crisis can be an unsettling turmoil in which it is easy to be pulled into the vortex of the maelstrom while attempting a heroic rescue. Treat a crisis cautiously.

Faith Working Through Love

Faith working through love is needed. Faith is demanded. The faith needed during crises is not the glib name-it-claim-it faith that affirms that everything will come out right and God will redeem any mistakes. Rather, it is a confidence that God is in charge, tempered with humility to accept that you don't always know how He intends to work.

In crisis, work. Consult experts. Who are the counseling mariners? Are they the elders, the pastor, an experienced counselor within the lay counseling program at church? Can you consult a professional?

Love is essential. In crisis, people feel that their moorings have been cut. They are adrift in a hostile sea. A person who has experienced rejection and pain wonders about his value as a mate and even as a human. Provide love that helps him sense that an anchor stabilizes him. Help him not devalue the spouse who has hurt him in retaliation for being hurt.

You can help the couple after their marriage, in crisis and over the long haul. Sometimes, though, despite your efforts, tragedy will occur.

CHAPTER FIVE

HELPING PREVENT DIVORCE OR DEAL WITH DIVORCE AND REMARRIAGE

When we counsel people in a troubled marriage, we usually do not want to encourage them to think about divorce as even a possibility. Unfortunately, though, many people divorce. As much as we wish we never had to deal with divorce, chances are that divorce will touch each of us.

In this chapter, we will examine the pain of divorce and the experiences of those divorcing, so that you know what can occur. We will also briefly examine remarriage, because more than two-thirds of those who divorce or are widowed remarry within three years of the divorce or death.

One theme of the present chapter is that the more you know about divorce and remarriage, the more you are prepared to help a couple avoid divorce. Or, if the divorce has already occurred or if the person has been widowed, your knowledge can help a person prepare realistically for remarriage.

As always, faith working through love is a guiding principle of helping. Faith working through love emphasizes faith in the future through Christ. The divorced person often sees marriage as a time of blackness, and he or she needs the light of faith. Work is needed to cope with the pain and loss of divorce. Love is the big challenge after divorce because the partners have usually been repeatedly devalued. Even after widowhood, love can be a challenge because it is easy to idealize a dead spouse, which prevents others from measuring up to the spouse's memory.

Throughout the chapter, we'll touch on the theology and psychology of divorce and remarriage, but we will concentrate on how to help someone experiencing those trials.

What Does the Bible Say About Divorce?

Almost everyone believes that divorce is not in God's *perfect* will and that God hates divorce (Malachi 2:16). Theologians differ about the extent to which divorce is in God's *permissive* will. There are three major positions.[1]

No Divorce

One position argues that marriage is permanent, no exceptions. Separation is permitted but not divorce. Annulment might be recognized by church tribunal or civil authority when the marriage was fraudulent or never consummated.

Divorce Permissible in Cases of Adultery

A second position argues that marriage is permanent except when adultery occurs (see Matthew 5:32 and 19:9). If adultery occurs, divorce is not mandatory but is permissible. Prior to Jesus' time, adultery was punishable by death. However, the Roman government prohibited death by stoning, so (the argument goes) Jesus permitted divorce as a merciful alternative to stoning. Homosexual adultery is considered adultery.

Divorce Permitted in Exceptional Circumstances

The third position is that marriage is permanent except for certain circumstances. Besides adultery, which was specifically mentioned by Jesus, Paul argues that when a non-Christian spouse deserts his or her partner and wishes a divorce, the divorce is permissible (1 Corinthians 7:15). When Jesus discussed divorce, He referred to Moses' law in which "hardness of heart" was cited as a reason divorce was permitted. The interpretation of "hardness of heart" has been considered to include such things as repeated spouse or child abuse, unrepentant alcoholism or drug abuse, failure to care for one's family (1 Timothy 5:8), and refusal to allow one's spouse or children to worship God.

The Psychology of Divorce

Stages of Divorce

People experience divorce differently. For some, divorce threatens their mental health. For others, it is a relief. For some, divorce is an emotional roller coaster; for others, an emotional merry-go-round. Despite the differences, I have identified some frequent steps along the pathway to divorce.[2]

Watch out. Early warning signs of divorce include the feeling that closeness has declined—either slowly or precipitously. While intimacy is declining, the couple may maintain public behavior suggesting that their marriage is fine. Privately, they become increasingly disillusioned with each other. Although intimacy rises and falls with any couple, troubled couples take the downs as proof that their love is dying. They may try to recreate intimacy between them, or they may simply accept the dying love with resignation.

With the decline in closeness, communication suffers. Communication about values and ideas may cease or may become increasingly conflictual. Sometimes, the couple may "snipe" at each other, usually at home in the beginning but moving to more public gatherings as communication deteriorates.

Noticing more differences. As normal communication falters, differences that were previously glossed over as unimportant cry for resolution. Divorce is often the gruel made from marital scraps. Partners score points, trying to win arguments. They rehearse arguments with their spouse, and they often feel as if the spouse has violated their basic rights. Conflict resolution grinds to a standstill.

Whose fault is it? Someone once said, "Love is the quest, the proposal the request, the marriage the conquest, and divorce the inquest [investigating the cause of death]." As marriage dies, spouses try to explain why the relationship is troubled. They blame the partner, telling their tale to family members, friends, and counselors. The involvement of lawyers will often hasten the death of the marriage because the legal system is adversarial. But even friends and family can hasten divorce by polarizing spouses.

Commitment is kaput. Commitment wanes. Spouses consider the alternatives to marriage. Thoughts of single life or remarriage become frequent. Spouses may flirt with eligible partners and try to further relationships with other-sex co-workers or friends. Contact with the spouse is limited to intense conflict or emotional deadness. Sometimes, one spouse may try to reestablish the relationship, even when the other spouse has completely withdrawn from it. This can become a power struggle that has almost no chance of success.

Still legally married but emotionally divorced, people are often uncertain about their future. To end the uncertainty, some people rush into divorce. Usually, such people do not handle the divorce as well as those who allow the relationship more time either to decline or to get better.

Separation. Separation is often a giant step toward divorce. Although many separated couples ultimately reunite, most people who separate eventually divorce. Usually, the decision to separate and the actual period of separation are the most stressful parts of divorce, although a few people report relief after separation.

The Aftermath of Divorce

Just trying to survive. Most people rate divorce as extremely stressful. In one long-term study by Judith Wallerstein and Sandra Blakeslee,[3] divorce was described as an explosion that usually sent recurring shock waves throughout the marriage and family for up to fifteen years after it. In a real sense, divorce is a life-changing event that one never gets over. One merely encounters changes and makes adjustments to those changes.

Anne's story. Anne divorced Blaine at age thirty-six and received legal custody of their two children. Whereas Blaine remarried within a year, Anne was reluctant to remarry. "Once burned, twice shy," she was forever quoting to her friends who tried to interest her in romantic relationships. For the first year after the divorce, she felt psychologically devastated. She had poor self-esteem, feelings of hopelessness, helplessness, rejection, incompetence, and vulnerability. She complained, "I don't know who I am anymore. I was always Blaine's wife and the mother of my children. Now I don't know how to be anything else."

One of the biggest problems besides managing her depression and anger at Blaine was in parenting. The younger child, Seth, who was eight years old, appeared to take the divorce the hardest. He got into trouble at school frequently (he had never been in trouble before), and he was often moody. Anne didn't know what she could do differently. She had to work to earn money to support the children, which cut into the time she had previously spent with them.

The children complained because they had less freedom to participate in outside activities than before the divorce. They had especially enjoyed sailing prior to the divorce, but Blaine had been the enthusiast, and he had taken the sailboat. Although the children said they didn't blame their mother for their "restriction," Anne continually felt that they resented her.

Her resentment of Blaine was always near the surface too. Preoccupied with his recent marriage, he offered only minimal help in rearing the children. Blaine's new wife did not get along with the children well, and she pressured Blaine not to spend much time with them. He complied.

Anne's social life was in shambles. She believed that some people at her church were being judgmental about her divorce. Her years of being half of a couple with Blaine had restricted her to interactions with other couples. Since she was no longer part of a couple, her social engagements had dried up. Being in her thirties, she felt that she had little in common with the other singles in the congregation, most of whom were in college or early in their careers.

Anne, in a reflective moment, described herself, "I'm a ship without a rudder. All of the stable things in my life—the things I could count on—have been stripped away, and I don't know where I am drifting. I'm being taken by hostile currents and winds, without power to navigate and without even a compass."

Anne's experience was similar to many people's after divorce. They enter a new world and don't know the ground rules. Besides the emotion of their failed marriage and the trauma of separation, they must forge a new life from new circumstances.

Helping Someone Who Is Considering Divorce

In helping, don't get mired in theological debates. You may disagree with your friend's theology, but you can still help if you adhere to four principles.

- Understand Scripture, its guidance, and what it *doesn't* speak to.
- Remain humble about your ability to interpret Scripture perfectly.

- Encourage the person considering divorce to try to discern the will of God for him or her through prayer, reasoning, listening and looking for God's guidance, and being willing to follow that guidance.
- Act within your conscience while respecting others' rights to have different opinions.

When you counsel a friend or family member who is considering divorce, remember that your task is not to ensure that he or she makes the thoroughly correct scriptural decision, because such a goal arrogantly assumes that you know God's truth perfectly. Although you must act in accord with your beliefs, you must also demonstrate Christian love and forgiveness for the person, regardless of his or her decision about divorce or remarriage. The person dealing with divorce or remarriage is usually vulnerable and needy. Valuing him or her should not be conditioned on the decision made about divorce. Rather, empathically help the person; help at times might be tough and at other times tender, but it always should be understanding and compassionate.

Helping Someone Who Is Going Through Divorce

What Is the "Stage" of Divorce?

How you deal with a friend who is divorcing depends on the "stage" of the divorce. The person making initial explorations about divorce is obviously different from the person trying to adjust to divorce, rear a family, and reorient his or her life. To bring out some of the important issues, we will follow Jane as she divorced. Roberta, one of Jane's friends from church, began to help her at their pastor's request.

Jane and Edward's Marital History and Issues

Jane and Edward had been married for thirteen years. Both were thirty-eight. They had three children: Sarah, twelve; Eddie, nine; and Jill, six. They had sensed that their marriage was dying for years, but they had been too busy with PTA, Scouts, youth sports, church, and career to do anything about it.

They argued about fundamental issues more frequently as time went on. For example, Edward was reared Roman Catholic, and Jane was reared Baptist. They had attended a Presbyterian church throughout their marriage because it represented a compromise. However, both had become dissatisfied with the direction the church was taking and both wanted to move—in different directions.

They also differed in career aspirations. Both were college educated. Jane had not worked since the children were born, but with Jill in kindergarten, Jane had decided to return to work over Edward's objections.

They sought counseling from a local pastoral counselor because they did not think much of their pastor; but their counseling had not gone well, and their differences loomed even more troublesome over time. They discontinued counseling, feeling that their marriage was hopeless. Edward stopped attending church, and Jane attended only on Sunday.

Roberta, a Friend in Need

Roberta was a fifty-one-year-old mother of four. Her youngest child had entered college two years earlier, and she had volunteered for the lay counseling training program at her church. When Jane and Edward developed marital tensions, their pastor asked Roberta if she would help Jane. As often happens, Jane and Roberta became friends. Most of their contact was over the phone, but they got together for lunch or Roberta just "popped by" occasionally.

Roberta helped Jane several ways. Having read about divorce, counseled a cousin who had divorced, and worked with several people in the church during their divorces, Roberta provided information about what to expect and about what Jane was experiencing. This helped Jane feel that her experiences were "normal" and also helped her search for solutions rather than focus only on her emotions during crisis.

Second, Roberta helped Jane deal with her roller-coaster emotions during the years surrounding her divorce—anger, depression, anxiety, frustration, and bitterness. When Jane felt worthless, out of control, and incompetent, Roberta listened, affirmed Jane as a person, and helped her move beyond her feelings to coping with her problems.

Third, Roberta provided practical help in times of need. When Jane needed child care, Roberta baby-sat. When Jane needed money, Roberta provided. When Jane didn't know where to turn, Roberta helped find the resources. When Jane felt overwhelmed with housework, Roberta organized a house-cleaning party. Roberta showed practical love in action.

Trying to Prevent Divorce

Awaiting Divorce

Until the legal divorce was granted, Jane felt ambivalent. Some days she simply wanted the marriage to end. Other days, she wanted reconciliation so badly that she wept. The pre-divorce period is usually a time of mixed emotions. There are lingering feelings of attachment and investment in the marriage and periods of intimacy, tenderness, and warmth. But other days are filled with frustration, anger, and bitterness.

Advocating for Reconciliation

Roberta strongly supported marriage. She believed that marriage could be fulfilling; despite problems, she hoped that Jane and Edward would reconcile. She knew the dangers of counseling Jane alone, that she might come to see things from Jane's point of view and subtly advocate divorce. So, determinedly, Roberta tried to help Jane maintain her hope for a reconciliation.

At first, Roberta counseled Jane not to think about the possibility of divorce. Edward clearly thought of divorce. He refused to do activities with the family and withdrew physically as well as emotionally from Jane. Their interactions were almost literally confined to fighting.

Most of Roberta's help centered on dealing with Jane's emotional ups and downs. Jane felt that the entire pre-divorce period was one of intense stress, one in which her defenses needed almost daily mobilization.

The Decision to Separate

Helping deal with separation. When Edward moved out, Jane's feeling of stress intensified. She developed a respiratory infection. Her work suffered. She had difficulty falling asleep, and she worried about what she would do if Edward continued to press for a divorce. Over the six-month separation, she lost fifteen pounds and looked unhealthy.

Although some people experience separation as a time of relief from conflict, Jane felt it to be even more stressful than the pre-separation period. True, her contacts with Edward were less frequent, but she described herself as "having continual conversations with him in my mind."

Telephone mania. During the separation, Jane phoned Roberta almost daily. Thus, Roberta listened to the saga of events and helped Jane control her feelings and figure out how to respond. It became clear that Edward wanted most of the family resources. Both Edward and Jane engaged attorneys and had several emotional meetings to decide on an equitable distribution of property. Roberta largely served as emotional support after those periods of conflict.

The Decision to Divorce

Edward unilaterally decided to divorce. Although Jane objected, the state laws permitted divorce after a one-year separation. Jane was uncertain about the biblical correctness of divorce in her circumstances. No adultery had been committed, and Edward appeared to be a believer. So was divorce biblically acceptable?

She and Jane discussed the issue at length. While the marriage existed, Jane maintained that she did not want a divorce, though she clearly had mixed feelings. She was troubled, though, about the status of the marriage in God's eyes if Edward divorced her. Roberta did not state her position about this.

Dating While Still Married

After being separated about four months, Jane accepted an invitation to dinner with a man she had met at a Christian conference the previous year. She enjoyed the date and the company of an attractive man. Nothing sexual occurred—not even a good-night kiss—but the possibilities were definitely there.

Roberta and Jane discussed the date over coffee. Jane asked for Roberta's opinion. Roberta coughed nervously, apprehensive about what she wanted to say. "Jane, I know you feel hurt and unsure of yourself because Edward rejected you. The attraction of someone who offers intimacy and caring is great. If I were in your position, I would probably want an emotional Band-aid. I might have some darker desires, too—ones I might not be proud of. I'd like to hurt Edward by starting another relationship."

Roberta looked intently at Jane to see if there was a reaction. Seeing none, she continued. "Added to all that is the awareness that I'm not getting any younger, and I don't know many eligible men. I suppose, if I were in your shoes, the desire to date would be pretty overwhelming."

Jane looked down. "You're right," she said. "I do feel those things. It's not pretty, but I feel so *vulnerable.*"

Roberta said, "That's a good reason to allow more time before you start dating. Your feelings are stirred up, and it's easy to misinterpret stirred up feelings for attraction."

"That's right," said Jane. "I don't want to jump into another relationship. Maybe it is better if I don't date for a while. Besides, after being married for thirteen years and making love regularly, I feel some sexual attractions. I know I wouldn't do anything, but it's probably better not to tempt myself."

People who are separated may struggle with whether to date while still legally married. Technically, the marriage is still legal, and partners are committing adultery if sexual relations occur. They often are firmly convinced that the marriage is, in fact, dead and thus dating (without sexual contact) is OK. (Some people even feel free to have sex.)

What about dating that does not involve sexual contact—even kissing? Is that wrong if a marriage is still legally intact?

I believe that contact with a person of the other gender isn't wrong per se, but it is rarely, if ever, helpful. I believe it isn't wrong because in all marriages, spouses have interaction with other-sex individuals—business meetings, committee meetings, sitting together as they watch their children play a sport, as well as other interactions. Marriage does not mean that one will never speak to or be alone with a person to whom he or she isn't married.

On the other hand, though, I try to discourage dates by people who are separated but not divorced. There are several reasons for that. One, people aren't always aware of their motives. Many motives, especially some of the sexual motives, are hard to admit to ourselves. People may feel ambivalent about having sexual contact with a date —they want to but don't want to at the same time. Sometimes, when alone with a potential partner, they can do things they later regret. It is better not to put themselves in the position of being tempted. Two, people may date because they are angry at the spouse and want to punish the spouse, rather than because they are attracted to the date. Exercising a vindictive motive isn't good for people's spiritual lives, nor is it fair to the other person involved in the date. Three, people can't know the future. They cannot tell whether an anticipated divorce will occur or whether reconciliation will occur. By avoiding dating, they don't take chances with a marriage that might eventually reconcile. Four, there is rarely such a pressing reason to date that it can't wait until the divorce is complete. For people who feel pressured to date *immediately,* it might be good for them to consider *why* they are so driven to date immediately, why dating can't wait until the divorce is final.

Roberta offered other suggestions for Jane to consider, too. Generally, I don't think it's a good idea for people who are still married to date, but I realize it is the married people, not I, who will decide.

As a helper, try, therefore, not to moralize or exert psychological pressure on people not to date. (For avoiding sexual contact, though, the biblical position is clear—married or single, the Bible forbids sex outside marriage.) Pressuring friends can only backfire, weakening your relationship with them. But gently bringing up some of the reasons why it is best to avoid dating—as Roberta did with Jane— is usually a good idea.

The Divorce

Anger and Depression

At the time of the divorce, Jane was angry at Edward: for finally carrying out the divorce, for wresting more resources away from her than she felt was equitable, and for his "hiding" by immersing himself in work. Roberta supported Jane as she replayed her anger daily. After a month, anger subsided and depression spread.

Grief

In the divorce, Jane lost an important relationship. As when one loses a loved one through a lingering illness, the grief begins in force only after the death.

Numbed shock. Jane's grief followed a path similar to grief after the death of a loved one. Initially, she was stunned, unable to believe that the divorce was permanent. Jane's raging emotions alternated with stunned numbness. Sometimes she cried for no reason. At other times, she thought she should cry but felt nothing.

Broken record. Then she seemed to accept the divorce as permanent, but she replayed the details of the divorce repeatedly in her mind. She almost obsessively thought, *If only I had been more responsive, then things would have been different.*

She called Roberta even more often, and each conversation seemed the same to Roberta. The details of the failing marriage were recounted and rehashed, again and again, until Roberta felt at wit's end. Roberta listened because she knew that such repetition is a normal part of grieving. It helps the grieving person get a sense of meaning from the loss.

Jane also complained that her friends had abandoned her. Some had interacted with Jane and Edward as a couple and did not know how to relate to Jane alone. Others had been closer to Edward and were caught in loyalty conflicts, so they withdrew. For some, Jane's broken-record complaining drove them away.

Acceptance. About one year after the divorce, Jane reported that in the midst of her morning quiet time, she simply decided that life had to go on without the marriage and that moping about it served no useful purpose. So she resolved to get on with her life.

Conflict

Even then Jane did not find it easy to put the past behind her. The past kept straying into the future. She continued to argue with Edward over child care. Edward was adamant that when the children were with him on Sunday, they would not attend church, which was a continual barb in Jane's side.

Conflict is not uncommon among divorced couples. Constance Ahrons, a social worker, has studied relationships between former spouses five years after the divorce.[4] She found that about half of the couples still argued. Half of those she classified as "fiery foes." The remaining half she called "angry associates." About 40 percent had learned to get along and were called "cooperative colleagues." Most of their cooperation was over child care. They rarely discussed their own relationship. About 10 percent of the couples Ahrons called "perfect pals."

Roberta tried to help Jane deal with conflicts as they arose. Jane would come home, fresh from a disagreement with Edward and would call Roberta for support. Roberta would listen and help Jane cope with her feelings and with the situation.

During low-conflict times, Roberta helped Jane see that Jane still wanted to control Edward. Eventually, Jane saw that there would always be influences on her children that she did not approve of; rather than lose her own peace, she needed to strengthen her children's values to reduce the impact of those influences. As Jane accepted Roberta's advice, she could still be appropriately concerned and motivated to battle evil, but she jousted at windmills less and changed the things she could influence more. She pondered the positive values she wanted her children to develop, and she tried to build those values intentionally.

Child Rearing Trials

Even before the divorce, child rearing had challenged Jane. Edward withdrew, leaving Jane to rear the children. Almost immediately after the divorce, nine-year-old Eddie acted up in school. He got in trouble with his teacher almost weekly and was sent to the principal three times during the first year after the divorce. Roberta told Jane that boys often had difficulties after divorce, just as girls usually had more difficulties adjusting to remarriage; but that didn't make it easier to discipline Eddie.

Jane observed that Eddie seemed to need a good male role model, which made her consider remarriage for the first time. However, no eligible men were attractive to her.

She discussed the problem with her pastor, who recommended that she talk to the parents of several other boys who were Eddie's age. One parent coached a youth football team, and Eddie was invited to play. Another family went camping one weekend that summer and invited Eddie. Over time, Eddie got into trouble less, but even a year after the divorce he was still more sullen and prone to angry outbursts than before it.

Although Jane's handling of the children was somewhat chaotic before the divorce, she attributed it mostly to her being distracted by the conflict and trauma of the divorce. By six months after the divorce, she was exasperated. Not only had the handling not improved after the divorce was finalized, but it seemed to get worse. In discussing her difficulties with Roberta, Jane concluded that the divorce had irrevocably changed her. It had left her needing to redefine who she was and what the boundaries of her family were. New rules had to be made to fit her one-parent family. Each of the children had to assume new roles within the family. Further, Jane was trying out many new roles. Her standard of living had been drastically reduced, but she managed to hold a job, maintain a budget, and support her children emotionally. Although she felt more confident, she admitted to Roberta that she had liked her role as mother and homemaker better when she had the love and support of a man than when she was going it alone.

Practical Help

Jane adjusted to divorce largely because she knew Roberta, who helped on a practical level. Roberta was a committed Christian who pointed Jane back to her source of strength, Jesus.

Throughout the years of ordeal, Roberta never recommended divorce to Jane, but when Jane went through divorce, Roberta stuck with her. Being knowledgeable about divorce, Roberta was not surprised or put off by Jane's emotional tribulation. Rather, Roberta listened and treated Jane as a valuable person, promoted her faith, and encouraged her regardless of what Roberta thought about Jane's decisions. Roberta provided advice, support, and friendship and was an excellent Christian witness to Jane. Whereas many Christians who divorce experience rejection within their church, become disillusioned with the church, and drop out, Jane remained faithful, which could be attributed largely to the faith working through love that she saw in Roberta.

What Does the Bible Say About Remarriage?

Generally, people agree that remarriage after the *death* of a spouse is biblically permissible (Romans 7:2; 1 Corinthians 7:39) and even encouraged if the surviving spouse is young or if young children are involved (1 Timothy 5:14). Remarriage after divorce is more problematic, and different interpretations exist.[5]

No Remarriage

In one interpretation, no remarriage after divorce is permitted. This view is championed mostly by Roman Catholics, and the authority may be more papal than scriptural. A Protestant-oriented argument for not permitting remarriage is explained in Carl Laney's book, *The Divorce Myth*.[6]

Remarriage Is Permissible if Divorce Was Permissible

In a second view, taken by most theologically conservative Protestant scholars, remarriage is thought to be permissible whenever divorce is scripturally permissible. Consult John Stott's *Marriage and Divorce*[7] and Stanley Ellisen's *Divorce and Remarriage in the Church*[8] as examples of this position. The arguments given for this position are complex, but they include these:

1. In Deuteronomy 24:1–4, Moses allowed for the remarriage of a divorced person.

2. Jesus *implied* that people *would* remarry after divorce and, according to Stott and Ellisen, that if a divorce was the result of adultery, then remarriage was permissible and not itself adulterous.
3. In his argument in 1 Corinthians 7, Paul apparently took remarriage for granted after a spouse's desertion.

A Forgiving God

A third position on remarriage focuses on God's forgiveness. It argues that although remarriage may be wrong, God forgives our wrongs. The permission to remarry, then, depends on the person's confession of the previous divorce as sin and on repentance from the sin. The acid test for a permissible remarriage becomes the discernible presence of a sincere and contrite heart.

Remarriage After Divorce

Most Divorced People Remarry

Most divorced people want to and do remarry soon after their divorce,[9] as do most widows soon after their spouse's death. Remarriages after divorce are not all the same. Each person's circumstances and background are unique; however, some generalizations might be appropriate.

Children Complicate Remarriage

Remarriages are generally more complicated than are first marriages. Many remarriages have children involved, either as living with the newly married couple or visiting them regularly. Few *first* marriages have to worry about what to do with the children on the honeymoon. After the honeymoon, the couple must adjust to each other *and* the children simultaneously.

Whose children are involved? Are the children the husband's with a new stepmother? Are they the wife's with a new stepfather? Or are there children from two marriages—with two sets of rules for child discipline that must be negotiated into a new arrangement?

Memories of the Previous Marriage

In remarriages, memories of the previous spouse flit ghostlike across the marriage. Whereas in first marriage, partners draw upon their parents as positive and negative models for marriage, remarriages often have salient examples of what a good marriage should or should not be.

Turmoil Can Be a Way of Life

The remarried family is usually in constant turmoil. People run this way and that, heading to father's for a special occasion, staying with mother during this holiday because father must take a business trip and the children do not get along well with the stepmother. Schedules, when they can be planned, often crash like dominoes if one person's plans change.

Remarried families are usually complex and often chaotic. There are few expectations about exactly how a remarried family should operate. Is there any wonder that the divorce rate is higher in remarried families than in first-married families? Yet, despite the hardships, many people remarry each year and many forge satisfying marriages. It is merely more difficult than in many first marriages.

Helping a Remarrying Couple

Overcome Their Beliefs About Your Prejudice

Often couples who plan to remarry don't seek help from other Christians because they are concerned that they will be judged. They may have seen others judged or even judged others themselves. Because they expect judgment, want to avoid their ex-spouses, and hope to start afresh, many remarriers change churches. They end friendships, ignore acquaintances, and enter a new social network. Adjusting takes time, so remarrying couples often don't have much social support when marital adjustments are needed.

Remarriers may contact a former friend tentatively, their antenna scanning for judgment or rejection—both for remarrying and for abandoning their church and friends. As helper, your first difficulty, then, is to overcome your friend's prejudice that you will judge and condemn. In the early stages of reestablishing the friendship, listen carefully and show that you understand. Your attentiveness and nonjudgmental attitude will open the door for more openness.

Provide Accurate Information

If you have not been remarried, the remarrying person will assume that you don't understand his or her experience. For the person to listen to your counsel, you must convince him or her that you understand. Understanding requires that you combine accurate listening skills and a knowledge base.

Step Back But Stay in Contact

Couples who marry for the first time often avidly seek information prior to marriage. Most remarrying couples—whether divorced or widowed—believe they know about marriage, especially their own. They do. They don't need much of the mundane advice that first marriers need. Remarriers often have strong opinions about what they want from marriage, know what they will tolerate and what they demand from a good marriage, and don't want advice.

On the other hand, they haven't been married to *this person* before. Living in marriage with a new person inevitably requires adjustment. Unanticipated difficulties arise, and with the winnowing of social support, the remarrying person might seek your help—*if* you are positioned to give it. The optimal position is generally at arm's length. Stay far enough away not to foist your help onto the person, creating possible resistance to you. Stay close enough that the person will want to ask you for needed assistance.

Altogether, acting in faith working through love requires sensitivity to the needs and requests of the person you love and seek to help. The person has gone through pain, disruption, and stress during the divorce or death and bereavement. If divorced, the person may still be in legal conflict with the former spouse. If widowed, the person might be in legal hassles with the former spouse's family-of-origin over distribution of an estate. The remarrying person may not feel like discussing the ex-spouse with the new mate, so you will be needed. You can be an effective agent of adjustment if you are accepting, informed, skilled, and sensitive.

PART THREE

UNDERSTANDING YOURSELF AS A MARRIAGE HELPER

CHAPTER SIX

EVALUATE YOURSELF

"When I am asked to help a friend who has a troubled marriage," a friend once confided to me, "I want to be an expert but know I'm a novice." This "novice" was a professional counselor with five years of post-degree individual counseling experience. She knew a lot about counseling, but marriage counseling made her feel inadequate.

Even knowing we can call on God for help at supporting a friend through marital difficulties is not completely confidence inspiring. Can we discern God's will unerringly in our own lives, much less in the lives of others? The consequences of our mistakes might be high. We don't want our friend to stumble. We don't want to cause a divorce. We want to help, not hurt.

You can help your friend with a troubled marriage regardless of your current knowledge and skills. God can use you if you let Him work through you. However, you can also improve your counseling.

Experienced and Inexperienced Counselors

If you had a problem to solve, who would you rather have help you—an inexperienced or an experienced helper? Most of us would prefer the wisdom of experience to the sheer energy of youth. There is some research support for such a preference. Experienced counselors not only counsel differently from inexperienced counselors,[1] but they also help people get over their problems better.[2] In fact, experts are different from novices in many ways.[3]

- Experts have more knowledge than do novices[4] about people and their psychology, marriage, helping, and marital counseling.
- Experts can remember more information—not only because they have been exposed to more information, but also because they organize the information more helpfully.[5] In helping a friend, novices see each marital problem as unique or focus on the grossest behavior—such as threats of divorce or violence. Experts see the big picture and relate one couple's problems to another couple's problems to get ideas about how to help.
- Experts and novices understand problems differently. Experts consider such things as who is involved and how, what areas of the marriage are most affected and how, and what patterns of marriage-threatening behavior are being repeated. Novices tend to consider less important things, like the partners' personalities, topics of conflict, and potential compromises for disagreements.
- Novices try to solve an ill-defined problem quickly, offering suggestions in rapid succession, hoping one will work. Experts carefully define the problem then make fewer (but better) suggestions for solving it.
- Experts usually use a forward-working problem solving strategy whereas novices use a backward-working strategy.[6] Most experts start with a general plan, put the plan into gear, and accelerate, dealing with the twists and turns as they pop up. They don't always arrive at the destination they aimed at, but they usually make progress. Novices are more concerned with the end point. They ask, "Where do I want to arrive? What would I have to do to move the couple to the end point?" They rigidly pursue the end point, even when the strategy isn't working. In helping a friend, devise a forward-working counseling strategy that allows you to deal with new information as it arises but keeps you focused in the right direction. Develop discernment about when to apply and when not to apply the strategy. Recognize your limitations.
- Experts solve problems better than do novices. Generally, experts in one area are not expert in other areas. For instance, a skilled counselor of individuals must still learn to counsel couples.

Becoming More Expert at Helping Friends with Marital Problems

How Not to Become an Expert

How can you become more expert? Not simply through reading books on a topic, nor through mere experience, nor even through becoming more mature or spiritual. Those actions and qualities are necessary to real expertise at helping, but none is sufficient to make you an expert.

Two Examples

Rahim has counseled friends for ten years as part of a lay counseling program sponsored through his church. His pastor says, "Rahim seems to have a gift for counseling. He started out with no training and frankly he wasn't very good. He jumped in and gave advice right away, and he came across like *the man*—a real authority. Trouble was, nobody listened to him." Rahim's pastor paused and rubbed his chin. "I don't know what changed him. I know the Lord got down in his spirit. I guess it was when his wife died. Rahim came to me six months after her death and asked if I would help him get better at helping couples. He and Jackie had such a good marriage. He wanted others to find the love they had. I met with him monthly, and we talked about the people he was seeing. Over time, he got better—listened more, being a brother instead of the man."

In contrast, Kara received her master's degree in marriage and family counseling at a seminary and counseled professionally for four years. The head of the agency was frustrated. "Kara has achieved a level of competence that she's comfortable with. Once she got comfortable, which she did soon after getting her state license, she didn't improve. She's content to see her clients, watch some of them get better and others not. She always says, 'The client wasn't motivated,' when a client doesn't improve. It's not that she's a poor counselor. She just doesn't get any better. It's wasted potential."

Wiley and Ray found that in professional counseling programs, counseling experience by itself did not predict counseling expertise. Rather, expertise was related to the amount of *supervised* counseling experience a trainee had.[7]

There's nothing magical about having a supervisor. Supervision forces people to think systematically about their counseling and to confront their weaknesses without being able to explain away poor counseling. Supervisors also can see weaknesses that the counselor can't and can suggest improvements.

How to Improve

Asking a supervisor to oversee your counseling is often the best way to force yourself to reflect on your counseling. I suggest that talking about your helping with your own spouse, friend, elder, pastor, or supervisor is the safest way to improve your counseling. However, supervisors aren't always available. There are other ways to reflect on your helping skills and knowledge.

- Get into a training program for lay counseling (see list on pages 16–17). If your church has a program or if a program is run in your city, seek it out.
- Read this book as if it were a post-graduate text. Rather than racing excitedly through the book, underline, write notes to yourself, make lists. Use your reading to think about a particular person or couple you are now helping or someone you helped in the past. *Work* to identify similarities and differences in different marriages.
- Look objectively at what you are doing, what you did, and what you want to do in the future. Relate your actions to outcomes.
- Read other resources. I have summarized several books that can assist—on Christian helping (pages 20–22), on Christian marriage (below), and on marriage counseling (page 76).

Some Books about Christian Marriage

Cormac Burke, *Covenanted Happiness: Love and Commitment in Marriage* (San Francisco: Ignatius Press, 1990).

Les Carter, *The Prodigal Spouse: How To Survive Infidelity* (Nashville: Thomas Nelson, 1990).

William L. Coleman, *Cupid Is Stupid! How to Fall in Love Without Falling on Your Face* (Downers Grove, Ill.: InterVarsity, 1991).

Jim and Sally Conway, *Traits of a Lasting Marriage* (Downers Grove, Ill.: InterVarsity, 1991).

Lawrence J. Crabb, Jr., *The Marriage Builder: A Blueprint for Couples and Counselors* (Grand Rapids: Zondervan, 1982).

James C. Dobson, *Love Must Be Tough: New Hope for Families in Crisis* (Waco, Tex.: Word, 1983).

_________. *Straight Talk to Men and Their Wives* (Waco, Tex.: Word, 1980).

Gregory J. P. Godek, *1001 Ways to Be Romantic* (Boston: Casablanca, 1991).

Lucy and Dennis Guernsey, *Real Life Marriage* (Waco, Tex.: Word, 1987).

Willard F. Harley, Jr., *Love Busters: Overcoming the Habits that Destroy Love* (Tarrytown, N.Y.: Fleming H. Revell, 1992).

_________. *His Needs, Her Needs* (Old Tappan, N.J.: Fleming H. Revell, 1986).

Paul Hauck, *Three Faces of Love* (Philadelphia: Westminster, 1984).

Joyce Huggett, *Creative Conflict: How To Confront and Stay Friends* (Downers Grove, Ill.: InterVarsity, 1984).

_________. *Marriage on the Mend* (Downers Grove, Ill.: InterVarsity, 1988).

Donald M. Joy, *Bonding: Relationships in the Image of God* (Waco, Tex.: Word, 1985).

_________. *Re-Bonding: Preventing and Restoring Damaged Relationships* (Dallas: Word, 1986).

David and Elsie MacKenzie, with Beth Spring, *Still Married, Still Sober: Hope for Your Alcoholic Marriage* (Downers Grove, Ill.: InterVarsity, 1991).

Charles Mylander, *Running the Red Lights: Putting the Brakes on Sexual Temptation* (Ventura, Calif.: Regal, 1986).

Gary Jackson Oliver and H. Norman Wright. *When Anger Hits Home: Taking Care of Your Anger Without Taking It Out on Your Family* (Chicago: Moody, 1992).

Clifford and Joyce Penner, *The Gift of Sex* (Waco, Tex.: Word, 1981).

Gary Smalley and John Trent, *The Language of Love* (Pomona, Calif.: Focus on the Family Publishing, 1988).

Lewis B. Smedes, *Caring and Commitment: Learning to Live the Love We Promise* (San Francisco: Harper & Row, 1988).

R. Paul Stevens, *Married for Good: The Lost Art of Staying Happily Married* (Downers Grove, Ill.: InterVarsity, 1986).

_________. *Marriage Spirituality: Ten Disciplines for Couples Who Love God* (Downers Grove, Ill.: InterVarsity, 1989).

Henry A. Virkler, *Broken Promises: Healing and Preventing Affairs in Christian Marriages* (Dallas: Word, 1992).

Ed Wheat, *How to Save Your Marriage Alone* (Grand Rapids: Zondervan, 1983).

Ed Wheat and Gloria Okes Perkins, *Secret Choices: Personal Decisions that Affect Your Marriage* (Grand Rapids: Zondervan, 1989).

Ed Wheat and Gay Wheat, *Intended for Pleasure: New Approaches to Sexual Pleasure in Christian Marriage* (Old Tappan, N.J.: Fleming H. Revell, 1981).

Petroc and Katherine Willey, *Become What You Are: The Call and Gift of Marriage* (London: HarperCollinsReligious, 1992).

Everett L. Worthington, Jr., *Hope for Troubled Marriages: Overcoming Common Problems and Major Difficulties* (Downers Grove, Ill.: InterVarsity, 1993).

H. Norman Wright, *Communication and Conflict Resolution in Marriage* (Elgin, Ill.: David C. Cook, 1979).

__________. *Romancing Your Marriage* (Ventura, Calif.: Regal, 1987).

__________. *So You're Getting Married* (Ventura, Calif.: Regal, 1985).

Some Books about Christian Marriage Counseling

Lawrence J. Crabb, Jr. *The Marriage Builder: A Blueprint for Couples and Counselors* (Grand Rapids: Zondervan, 1982).

DeLoss D. Friesen and Ruby M. Friesen, *Counseling and Marriage* (Dallas: Word, 1989).

Joyce J. Penner and Clifford L. Penner, *Counseling for Sexual Disorders* (Dallas: Word, 1990).

David A. Thompson, *Counseling and Divorce* (Dallas: Word, 1989).

Everett L. Worthington, Jr., *Counseling Before Marriage* (Dallas: Word, 1990).

__________. *Marriage Counseling: A Christian Approach to Counseling Couples* (Downers Grove, Ill.: InterVarsity, 1989).

H. Norman Wright, *Premarital Counseling: A Guidebook for the Counselor*, revised (Chicago: Moody, 1981).

__________. *Marital Counseling: A Biblical, Behavioral, Cognitive Approach* (San Francisco: Harper & Row, 1981).

- Keep a *confidential* journal. In your journal, concentrate on your own helping—not on the problems of the person you are trying to help. If you mention the person at all, *don't mention him or her by name* and *never show your journal to anyone else.* Also write lessons you learn from reading, ideas about how to help, self-assessments, verses of Scripture that apply to marriage, and other things that excite you.
- Watch others help troubled people. Some videotapes of professional counseling are available. Some lay counselor training programs yoke experienced and inexperienced counselors in teams in which a junior and senior counselor work with a person while other team members observe and discuss the helping. That allows all team members to benefit from multiple approaches and points of view.

Evaluating Yourself

Regardless of your current knowledge or skills, you can become a more expert helper than you now are. The first step is to carefully and accurately evaluate yourself as a person who can help your friend with a marital difficulty. Consider this equation:

$$\text{Personal Qualities} \times \text{Experience} = \text{Knowledge and Skills Applied in Situations}$$

You want to be able to apply the knowledge you have learned and the skills you have developed to benefit a particular friend. Helping a friend with a painful marital problem is like marksmanship with a rifle. When a particular friend asks you for help with a particular problem, you are being asked to direct specific help at a target. The friend does not want a shotgun approach of general advice. The friend wants help that hits the bulls-eye. To direct the help with rifle-like accuracy, aim it precisely.

Write Your Goals

It is tempting to read quickly over this chapter to get on to the new stuff—the stuff you didn't know—rather than dwelling on yourself, which you do know. Yet learning will occur best if you have definite goals for the learning. Years of research have demonstrated that if you *write* specific goals and objectives you will work more, accomplish more of your goals, and apply what you know better than if you leave the goals and objectives as mere thoughts.[8]

If you are serious about becoming a more effective helper, write your strengths and weaknesses as a helper. Building up your weaknesses can then become positive goals, which will focus your energy. Further, those weaknesses can become targets for your prayer, which adds another dimension to improving your ability to help others. I have provided the following graphic to help you evaluate yourself.

A Framework for Self-Evaluation as a Helper of Marital Problems

AREA	STRENGTHS	WEAKNESSES
PERSONAL QUALITIES		
PERSONALITY—(How well do you understand the groups you do and don't belong to? How well do you understand yourself as an individual?)		
SPIRITUAL MATURITY—(Humility? Communication with God? Concern for others more than self?)		
MOTIVATION TO HELP—(Why do you want to help this person? Is it for your benefit or the friend's? Can you discern God's clear leading to help?)		
EXPERIENCES		
FAMILY-OF-ORIGIN—(What portions of your parents' marriage do you want to duplicate? To avoid at all costs? Reflect on the parts of your parents' marriage that you may have picked up unconsciously.)		

AREA	STRENGTHS	WEAKNESSES
OWN ROMANTIC RELATIONSHIPS OR MARRIAGE— (What painful lessons did you learn while dating? What mistakes might you have made in your own marriage but been reluctant to admit to your partner or to yourself? Which parts of your marriage work so well for you that you think others would surely benefit from them?)		
HELPING—(Name some people you've helped. How effective were you? What did you do that was particularly helpful? What did you do that wasn't helpful?)		
KNOWLEDGE AND SKILLS		
MARRIAGE—(How much have you systematically studied marriage from the point of view of psychologists, sociologists, marriage specialists, and theologians?)		
HELPING—(How much have you studied individual counseling? Marital counseling?)		
FOCAL OR TACIT?—(Are your knowledge and skills as a marital helper more focal [requiring explicit attention] or tacit [automatic]?)		
ACCESSIBLE OR INERT?—(Are your knowledge and skills as a marital helper accessible [available in many situations] or inert [only accessible when you are reading about helping]?)		

Personal Qualities

Personality. Personality is the thread of consistency that runs through our lives. Personality organizes our thoughts, emotions, and actions. It gives a sense of connection across situations and through time.

Personality depends on our senses of communalism and individuality. Personality depends on membership in many groups, which give us a sense of belonging. This sense of belonging consists of our gender, ethnic, religious, family, group, career, community, and friendship identities. Sensing that we belong, we also have a sense of being separate, individual.

For example, I am a member of various groups—male, Caucasian of English and Scottish descent, Christian, husband, father, son of my parents, team player, friend, psychologist and writer, participant in the community. But I am also unique. I have thoughts, feelings, and behaviors that are unique. I cry at touching situation comedies, compete at tennis and soccer, draw block diagrams to explain things to my students, read adventure novels, and backpack. I hold my family dear to my heart, above work and play. My love for Kirby is the center of my love for family. I have ambitions that are uniquely combined as my own. I value friends but don't get very excited about money. I want to teach others and see them excited about learning. I want to help others grow in the Lord. I have a strong sense of loyalty and commitment. I want my word to mean something. Although my group identities and my individual thoughts, feelings, and behaviors are not unique in the human race—many people have similar group memberships and thoughts, feelings, and behaviors—their combination is unique to me.

Describe yourself. As I did in the paragraph above, write a short sketch of yourself. To what groups do you belong? What values, thoughts, feelings, and behaviors would you use to describe yourself?

Ask someone close to you to write a similar paragraph about you. Remember, that person has not lived inside your skin. Even a spouse with whom you've lived for thirty years will not have a more accurate picture of you than you do. But the person will have a *different* picture that will help you see yourself as at least one other person does.

Once you have two descriptions of yourself, compare them. Notice first your group membership. Culture—your gender, race, ethnicity, and social class—powerfully affects your identity. Culture is like canoeing a rushing river. We don't notice the current when we are floating with it; but when we paddle against the current, we feel it. When we help someone of different gender, race, ethnicity, or social status than our own, we experience powerful emotions ourselves, or we can trample the exposed toes of the other person without realizing what we are doing. The effective helper becomes aware of his or her group memberships and tries to learn about other groups so that painful miscommunications can be minimized. Some resources, listed below, might help you learn about others.

Some Books to Help You Learn about Others of Non-majority Ethnicity or Culture

D. Augsburger, *Pastoral Counseling Across Cultures* (Philadelphia: Westminster, 1986).

L. G. Baruth and M. L. Manning, *Multicultural Counseling and Psychotherapy: A Life-span Perspective* (New York: Macmillan, 1991).

D. J. Hesselgrave, *Counseling Cross-Culturally: An Introduction to Theory and Practice for Christians* (Grand Rapids: Baker, 1984).

Man Keung Ho, *Family Therapy with Ethnic Minorities* (Newbury Park, Calif.: Sage, 1987).

D. J. Lee, A. L. Nieves, and H. L. Allen, eds. *Ethnic Minorities and Evangelical Christian Colleges* (Lanham, Md.: University Press of America, 1991).

Charles R. Ridley, ed. "Multicultural Counseling," *Journal of Psychology and Christianity* (Special Issue), 11 (1992): 315–99.

Derald Wing Sue and David Sue, *Counseling the Culturally Different: Theory and Practice* (New York: Wiley, 1990).

Assess your individual interests, talents, gifts, and abilities. Are you more comfortable working with people, ideas, or things? Do you feel comfortable when people express their feelings, or do you prefer to keep things on an emotionally level surface? Are you more interested in solving problems or in personal growth and understanding? Are you more active or inactive? More thoughtful or inclined toward operating on automatic pilot? Do you emphasize God's judgment or mercy? Under what conditions? How forgiving are you? Under what conditions? What are your pet peeves? Do you feel emotions well up when people say they want a divorce, intend to remarry, had sex before marriage, engage in oral sex, vote Republican or Democratic, overspend their budget, believe a woman's place is in the home (or in the workplace), once had an affair, think homosexuals should be allowed to serve in the military, oppose abortion, spank their children with a belt, or consume mixed drinks?

If you get emotional at these issues, how will you act if a couple disagrees about the issues? Will you support the partner who favors your position, or will you put aside your feelings to help the couple resolve their differences? Importantly, you don't have to be neutral on the issues. Remain aware of your position so you can see when it interferes with helping.

Spiritual maturity. There is a mysterious spiritual connection between married partners that we can't quite comprehend.[9] When we help people with their marriage, we may have a spiritual impact on them, especially if they identify us as Christians. It is imperative, then, that we take our Christian beliefs, values, and actions seriously. Christianity must be more than a creed for us. It should be a living relationship with the Lord of creation.

We need maturity in the relationship with Christ to help us discern God's hand in the lives of distressed married people. What is spiritual maturity? I can't answer authoritatively, but I believe spiritual maturity involves a sense of humility before God. It acknowledges our need for help, our imperfection, and our moral weakness, and it seeks strength in a relationship with Jesus. Spiritual maturity involves communication. We talk to God, seek His will, and strive to listen to Him. We have achieved a sense of equanimity and our faith is not damaged or upset by disturbing events, failures, catastrophes, and calamities. We have lived in close enough relationship with Jesus for long enough to trust Him, despite what occurs. We think more about meeting others' needs than about how they meet (or, more commonly, don't meet) our needs.

Motivational drive to help others. Just because a person seeks our help does not mean that God wants us to meet his or her needs. We must check the press of circumstances against the witness of the Holy Spirit within, Scripture, and other external signs that suggest that God is calling us as helpers.

When a friend seeks help, we may feel pressured to help. Our natural tendency can be either to delay or advance when we are uncertain of whether to help. Instead of doing what's natural, say, "I don't know if we'll be able to meet often to talk about these problems, but I'm available now. I'd love to hear whatever you'd like to tell me and offer all the help I can. God may not be calling us to work together on this matter, though, so don't tell me anything that you wouldn't feel comfortable having me know right now. OK?"

After your conversation, pray for discernment about whether you are called to continue helping.

Experiences

Your experiences have filtered your personal qualities. Identify the experiences that have had an impact on your ability to help your friend with his or her marriage. These fall generally into three broad headings: experiences in your family-of-origin; in your own dating, marriage, and family life; and in helping.

Experiences with family-of-origin. We learn about marriage in our family-of-origin. Our family-of-origin can control our view of marriage in two ways. We can either want to copy or to avoid what our parents did. Those qualities that we paid explicit attention to in our family tend to be loaded with emotional power. If one parent had a drinking problem, we may become very invested in helping a friend stop drinking and may miss other things that are crucial to improving his or her marriage. What emotionally loaded issues from your family-of-origin might affect your helping?

Experiences in our own marriage-related relationships. We all make mistakes in marriage. Part of the human condition is a reluctance to admit and correct those mistakes. In fact, we usually hide and justify those mistakes. One particularly dangerous way of justifying our own mistakes is to guide others to act the same ways that we acted. *After all,* we think, *if they do it, it must be OK for me.* On the other hand, perhaps we have an excellent marriage. We automatically think that what works for us will work for others. Sometimes it doesn't. What experiences might affect the advice you give?

Experiences with helping. Generally, your experience helping others will become the basis for helping your friend. Helpers tend to think they are more effective than helpees think they are,[10] and helpers repeat mistakes believing them to have helped. Helpers themselves may have received help. If they benefited by straightforward, confrontive advice, they will probably give others straightforward, confrontive advice, which may not help the friend. How have your experiences at helping or receiving help influenced your current helping?

Knowledge and Skills

Your personal qualities and your experiences have interacted to make you what you are today. You undoubtedly have some knowledge and skills at helping, or you would not have been consulted by a friend who is having marital troubles. Having reflected on yourself and your experiences, now assess your knowledge and skills. You need knowledge and skills in two primary areas to effectively help friends with marital problems. You need to know about marriage and helping.

Marriage. To effectively help friends with marital problems, it is helpful to study marriage systematically. Different viewpoints should be sought—those of psychologist, sociologist, marital specialist, and theologian. How would you rate your knowledge of marriage?

Helping. Professional counseling is both a relationship and a technology. As a technology, there are behaviors and interventions that can help clients recover rapidly from troublesome psychological problems. As a relationship, the human contact, love, and emotionality of helping interactions keep counseling exciting and unpredictable. As a friend, you won't practice the technology of counseling, but you will practice the art of effective healing. How would you rate your relationship skills?

Building Expertise You Can Use

We began this chapter discussing experts and novices. Throughout the chapter, you have evaluated yourself as a helper for marital problems. How far along the path to expert are you?

If you have deficits, fill in the holes. However, expertise is not simply a matter of filling all the available holes. If you read all the books ever written on lay counseling, on marriage, on marriage counseling, and on spiritual maturity, you would have filled the information void but still may not be a good counselor. Suppose, though, that you systematically sought experience in counseling individuals and in helping people with their marriages—conducting marriage enrichment groups, leading premarital counseling, working with couples in marital crisis, conducting long-term counseling with individuals and couples who had marital problems. Would you then be an expert?

Not necessarily.

Expertise is not simply acquiring knowledge and using your skills. It is doing so creatively in the spur of the moment. Expertise is forming multiple connections among bits of knowledge and skills that are organized for easy access, and then dealing creatively with a problem that you have not previously encountered. Expert helping is creative innovation. It has a plan, but it recognizes the need to deviate from and even change the plan. Expertise also recognizes mistakes and tries to correct those mistakes rather than plowing ahead like a bulldozer, digging up tender psychological plants and leaving them strewn across a ravaged psychological wasteland.

Expertise can be built through studying what to do, doing it, and systematically reflecting about what you did. It won't happen merely because you've helped many people. Sometimes even relatively inexperienced helpers are more expert than are more experienced ones because the rookies have reflected on what they are doing and the old pros haven't.

Building expertise occurs over time. You probably bought this book not because you want to be an expert helper some day but because you want to help a loved one who is struggling with a troubled marriage now. Nonetheless, you'll help the person, recognize your mistakes, and correct them more if you consciously reflect on yourself and your helping than if you don't.

CHAPTER SEVEN

MISTAKES HELPERS MAKE

Can you recognize mistakes at helping? Nichole couldn't. She made several mistakes in helping Ham and Monica. See if you can detect her mistakes. When you notice something she did wrong, mark it in the margin. At the end of the chapter, I'll reprint this illustration and point out the mistakes I see.

Attempting to Help

Nichole, a single parent of a ten-year-old girl, was a friend of both Ham and Monica, who had been married for twelve years. They had all been members of the same Sunday school class for three years. When it became obvious through their constant bickering that Ham and Monica were having marital strains, Nichole thought she should do something. She liked both partners and didn't want to see them in pain. She and her deceased husband Harris had enjoyed ten years of happy marriage before Harris's death three years earlier. Nichole thought she could help Ham and Monica, so she invited them to dinner.

After dinner, the conversation erupted into a disagreement between Ham and Monica. Nichole said that she had noticed the tensions between the partners, and she asked if she could help. Ham said "No" and Monica said "Yes" simultaneously. Nichole asked Monica to talk about her experience. As Monica talked, she cried.

Ham folded his arms and fumed. Finally, he stormed out, saying, "If you two want to talk, I don't care. But I'm leaving. If you want to stay, Monica, Nichole can bring you home." After Ham left, Nichole and Monica talked for four hours.

Nichole realized that she had made an alliance with Monica. Determined to rebalance her relationship with the couple, she called Ham at work and suggested that they meet for lunch. The luncheon meeting two days later was a disaster. Ham was angry with Monica over numerous faults. He ranted throughout the meal about Monica's inadequacies, finally storming away from the table, leaving Nichole to pay.

Meanwhile, Monica called Nichole daily asking for advice. When Ham moved out one week later, Monica phoned twice each day. Nichole was always supportive, listening to Monica's tales of woe and encouraging her to work on the marriage and stick out the difficult times. Nichole often repeated the story about the rocky first year of her marriage to Harris, when Harris had moved back to his home for a month. Nichole suggested many things Monica could do to improve the marriage, but Monica could never follow the suggestions successfully.

Nichole was increasingly frustrated. In desperation, she asked her midweek Bible study and support group to pray for her and particularly to pray for Monica and Ham. When the members of the group wanted to know what the problem was, Nichole summarized Monica's and Ham's problems. The group prayed for twenty minutes for the couple.

Despite the group's prayers, the marriage continued to deteriorate. Nichole felt frustrated, depressed, and burdened with Monica's constant phoning. Eventually Ham filed for a divorce, left the congregation, and severed his ties with all the people at the church. Monica was consoled by the Sunday school class. When the divorce became final, relief was evident in almost everyone who knew Monica, even though many people had encouraged her to keep trying to make the marriage work.

Detecting Helping Mistakes

It is easy to make mistakes when you are involved in an emotional marital dispute. It is much easier to detect those mistakes as an impassive observer not having to deal with maudlin Monica or horrible Ham. In any helping, some mistakes are too obvious to discuss—giving incorrect psychological information, quoting Scripture out of context, misinterpreting Scripture, or using inappropriate or ineffective relational skills. I'll mention some less obvious problems common to helping friends—both with individual issues and specifically with their marriages.

The John Henry Syndrome

There are two common abuses in helping.[1] On one extreme, the helper learns one style of counseling and rigidly applies it, appropriate or not. I call this the "John Henry syndrome." According to the story, John Henry was a steel-driving man, who pounded steel railroad ties with a big hammer, even when a steam hammer was introduced. Unable to keep up with the steam hammer, John Henry died pounding in nails.

Seat-of-the-Pants Helping

On the other extreme, in seat-of-the-pants helping, the helper does whatever "feels" right, appealing to the leading of the Holy Spirit to justify his or her actions. For the Christian, *all* counseling *should* be led by the Holy Spirit, but sometimes helpers assume that the Holy Spirit does not work through orderly preparation and forethought. He does. Good helping must balance preparation and sensitivity to the leading of the Holy Spirit.

It isn't easy to find the balance between a rigid, formula-driven approach to helping and free-flowing helping. Think through how you can help before talking to your friend; then even though you may have rehearsed what to say, be patient. Since you last talked to your friend, many events may have occurred that make your carefully constructed advice inapplicable.

When I was almost ready to sit for my state licensing exam, I had to prepare a "work sample." I chose a married couple whom I had been counseling for weeks. In the session before I handed in my work sample, I planned to work with the couple on increasing their intimacy. When the session began, though, something didn't seem quite right.

"We had a disagreement this week," Robbie said.

I leaned back. "Oh?" My best tell-me-more "Oh."

"Robbie's parents visited this week," said Sally. "They wanted to take us to Washington, D.C., for the weekend."

"Oh." A statement-of-interest "Oh."

"Sally didn't want to go," said Robbie.

"Oh." A puzzled-but-beginning-to-see-the-conflict "Oh."

"They decided to go without me."

An empathic-I-see-how-that-would-hurt "Oh."

"They wanted to take my baby and leave me alone," said Sally.

"It's my baby too," said Robbie. "And it's their grandchild. They came all the way here to see her, and you wanted to keep her selfishly to yourself."

Sally looked to me. "So I took my baby and locked myself in the car."

"OH." Alarmed, but in control.

"They chased me. These huge adults chased me to the car and stood around the car yelling hateful things while I locked myself inside and held my little baby."

A sinking-feeling-in-the-pit-of-the-stomach "Oh."

"If they broke into the car, I would have called the police."

"Oh." If I'd had bubble gum, I'd have swallowed it.

"For the first time, I think I might want a divorce."

"Me too," said Robbie.

"Ooohhh." A my-psychologist-license-has-just-gone-up-in-flames "Oh." I knew we weren't going to talk about intimacy as I had planned.

I held up my hand, stopping the onslaught. "I need a minute," I said. I put my head down and prayed. Afterward, they resolved the conflict and got the marriage recovery back on track. (P.S., I got my license.)

I always enter a counseling session—whether with a friend or client—with an agenda, though I know that my agenda may be inappropriate five seconds into the session.

Recognizing Your Limitations

Failure to recognize your limitations can be disastrous. When I began a part-time private practice in psychology in the early 1980s, I was confident about helping people conquer depression. I had counseled more than twenty depressed people using a cognitive-behavioral method. All had improved.

One day I received a referral from a local professional—not a therapist—who was spending an inordinate amount of time with one of his clients. The client was depressed, and her demands for psychological help were intruding on the professional help he could give her and his other clients. Would I take her on as a client?

"Glad to," I said, thinking of adding her name to my "success list." What I didn't know, didn't even suspect, was that this woman—

I'll call her Heide—was diagnosable as having a borderline personality disorder. Looking back, I now call this case: Bambi meets Godzilla. (I'm Bambi.)

The borderline personality disorder diagnosis was relatively new in the early 1980s, probably originating in the early 1970s.[2] I had attended a brief seminar once. I should have paid more attention.

People with borderline personality disorders are often depressed and dissatisfied over relationships.[3] They think their counselor is great, terrific, the most wonderful thing since double chocolate ice cream. Except periodically when they think the counselor is horrible, terrible, the epitome of evil. They yell, curse, berate, degrade. What triggers this about-face? Fearing the relationship will end. The relationship with the counselor, with its extreme ups and downs, parallels other relationships. Those flip-flops result in lots of rejection and consequent depression.

During our first six sessions, things were clicking between Heide and me. She felt much happier. I was in love with my own skill and clinical acumen. I told the professional who had referred Heide to me—I'll call him Bob—about Heide's progress, and I advised him to disengage from her. That night, I received a call from Heide. "I checked myself into the psychiatric hospital. Now they won't let me go," she wailed. Threatened by losing her relationship with Bob, Heide had taken drastic action.

One month later, Heide was released from the hospital, and we resumed treatment for depression. Her hospitalization at least broke Bob's over-involvement with her, and that relationship became purely professional.

Counseling went well until the tenth session. I casually mentioned that we had agreed to meet for twelve sessions, so we should begin to plan how Heide was going to maintain her good mood after we ended counseling. The next day, Heide kicked open my office door. "I want you and Bob in this office tomorrow at 12 o'clock sharp!" she screamed, then stalked out.

The next day at 12 (sharp), Heide stood and yelled at Bob and me for an hour and a half. It was the most impressive display of sustained rage I have ever seen—to this day. Eventually, I calmed her down. We terminated counseling after twelve sessions (without bloodshed, which seems a miracle).

Throughout the case, I continually overestimated my effectiveness as a counselor. Proverbs 16:18 says, "Pride goes before destruction, a haughty spirit before a fall." Scripture was correct.

Friends sometimes try to help anyone who has a difficulty. That is not God's will. We must learn to recognize our limitations and not be driven by pride. How do we control pride? We must cultivate a sense of humility, what the Old Testament often calls the "fear of the Lord." Proverbs 9:10 tells us, "The fear of the Lord is the beginning of wisdom, and knowledge of the Holy One is understanding." God must deflate us before He can fill us. He may deflate us by showing us our inadequacies. Sometimes He allows us to fail at our grand schemes. At other times, we rush ahead of Him, losing our peace and forfeiting the power that comes about when we are yoked to Him. At times, He gives us an emotional sense of how it would be without Him. We feel cut loose from our roots, alone, and afraid. We sense our loneliness and our lack of meaning apart from Him. That is the fear of the Lord. It defeats pride and turns our attention back to Jesus Christ, our Savior.

Proper humility is reflected in Philippians 2:3, which says, "Do nothing out of selfish ambition or vain conceit, but in humility consider others better than yourselves." It doesn't say to consider ourselves worse than others. It says to focus on others. Value others. Esteem others. Look for ways to serve others. This is love.

The practical implication of recognizing your limitations is that you won't want to be a Lone Ranger helper. You'll recognize when you need to consult your pastor or someone with a more objective view on a problem. On the other hand, you'll carefully examine your motives to ensure that you sincerely want and need help and aren't merely gossiping.

Supervision

For competent helping, friends should *arrange supervision.* As Christians, who carry the name of Christ as a badge to the world, we want to be as competent as possible at what we do. That means we should seek supervision, continue to learn about helping, and help only if we can do so without letting our own troubles interfere with helping.

Referral

We should also refer our friend to a professional if we suspect that we can't handle the person's problem. Referral is not a defeat. Jesus is capable of healing a person of whatever ails him or her. Referral may seem to be an admission that the counselor is giving up on

Jesus—a statement of unbelief. It isn't. Jesus demonstrated many ways of healing the hurting. At times, he commanded the illness to end, pronounced the person already healed, stuck His fingers in people's ears, spit on their tongues, put mud on their eyes, and sent others to minister in His name. Referral can be God directing a hurting person to the place He has selected for their healing. Eagerly refer when you reach your limits in competence. For friends, this means honestly evaluating your limitations and not trying to help someone you aren't capable of helping. Be aware of the danger signs of psychological problems that could occur in a marital difficulty, such as depression, suicide, alcoholism, and violence. Compile a list of Christian and perhaps even non-Christian professionals to whom you can refer.

Emphasizing Your Strengths

Don't try to formally assess, diagnose, or use sophisticated conceptualizations and professional interventions. Instead, emphasize your strengths. *Listen* to friends with sincere empathy. Provide *emotional support* in crises. Give *sound advice.* Emphasize building those skills. Seek to love and help your friend and reflect on what you do, and your helping skills will improve.

Confidentiality

One day, I heard a conversation drifting through the hallway of our building at work. The conversation concerned a client who was particularly troublesome for a student counselor. The student was asking another graduate student counselor for advice. There's nothing wrong with getting good advice about how to help someone better. The problem was soliciting the advice in our building lobby. I saw red. My eyes narrowed. My beard frizzed. Both hairs on my head stood straight up. I hustled downstairs to silence the public discussion about a client.

The students had excellent motives in discussing the client. They wanted to help her. But they violated the client's confidentiality, and they shouldn't do that even if their motives are good.

By the time students graduate with a Ph.D. from our program in counseling psychology, they have been sensitized for five to seven years to the need to maintain confidentiality. Yet, sometimes they still slip up.

Christians are under opposite pressures. Christians are expected to speak their concerns openly so that others can pray with them.

When you are helping a friend who has marital problems—especially if you are frustrated with the progress—you might phone another person to enlist his or her prayer support for your friend's trials or bring up the concern at a weekly prayer meeting so that the group can pray for the troubled individual. You don't feel insensitive or like a gossip; your motives are excellent. But as with the two students, a confidence revealed in private could become public knowledge if you reveal the identity or the details of the problem (see following graphic).

When Is Passing Information Helpful and When Is It Gossip?

Gossiping is revealing personal information about a person that:

- does not result in direct help (e.g., advice, prayer, other support) for the person. [Note, though, that it's easy to justify gossip as "a prayer request."]
- may embarrass, demean, or devalue the person
- the person would not want others to know (even if the information is helpful or valuing)

You can probably tell when you are gossiping if:

- you are as concerned (or more concerned) about looking good as a helper as about helping your friend
- you would be unwilling to reveal the same information if your friend were standing in the room overhearing it
- you can't think of a *compelling* reason that you are revealing information about your friend (such as, you are worried that your friend may actually harm himself or herself; you honestly do not know what to do to help, and the person with whom you are talking can reasonably be expected to provide information or wisdom that you don't have; or another compelling reason)

If you believe you must violate a confidence:

- if possible, ask your friend if it is OK to discuss information about his or her situation with a pastor or other trusted person; abide by your friend's wishes
- know the person in whom you are confiding; can you trust that person not to pass the information to another?

- set the ground rules up front; don't pass on the information unless you ask the consultant to keep confidence; don't simply assume that the consultant will do so
- don't identify your friend to the person you are consulting, and don't give enough information (or disguise what you give) so that your friend could be identified (sometimes this is impossible; if the friend will be identified, think hard whether the benefits outweigh the costs; they usually don't); never tell identifying information in a group
- never pass on secondhand information (particularly difficult when dealing with marriages when you have only one partner's point of view)

It's not always this easy or clear to determine whether a confidentiality has been betrayed. For example, suppose that through conversations with Melanie, you know that she is having an affair with a co-worker. One day, John (Melanie's husband) says that he suspects the affair and if he finds out for sure, he will shoot them both. He sounds deadly serious. What do you do? Or suppose you become convinced that Meg's husband Daniel has, on several occasions, hit her and her children in the face and head. What do you do about that? In both cases, you have obtained information in confidence, but should it remain a confidence?

Let's take the first instance, the suspicion of a potential murder. In 1969, Prosenjit Poddar, a student at the University of California-Berkeley told his counselor, named Moore, that he planned to kill a woman, whose identity the therapist knew, Tatiana Tarasoff. Although the therapist informed the campus police and suggested that the student be questioned—which he was—the therapist didn't tell Tatiana Tarasoff. Poddar murdered her. Her parents sued Moore (and a host of others) for failure to warn the victim. In the subsequent case, *Tarasoff v. Regents of the University of California,* the therapist was held liable for his failure to inform Ms. Tarasoff.[4] The court established three conditions necessary to hold the counselor legally liable. First, a special relationship, such as counseling or psychotherapy, must exist between a person and either victim or perpetrator of the crime. Second, it must be reasonable to expect that a crime will be committed. Third, if an intended victim is identifiable, then the counselor has the duty to warn the potential victim.

Let's analyze what this means for you. Friendship probably doesn't qualify as a "special relationship" under the guidelines established by the *Tarasoff* case, and friends aren't expected to be proficient at evaluating the possibility of violence. However, sometimes even an untrained person might reasonably expect a crime to be committed.

Your actions in suspected spouse and child abuse also aren't clearly prescribed. In most states, all citizens have the responsibility to report suspected child (but not spouse) abuse and neglect. "Willfully" and "knowingly" failing to report such abuse is usually a legal misdemeanor. In practice, few such cases are prosecuted because it is difficult to prove that the person "willfully" and "knowingly" failed to report the abuse. The case of Meg and Dan that we are considering is murkier because the friend did not *see* evidence of child abuse. Rather, the report of abuse comes from an aggrieved spouse, who might exaggerate or lie about the "abuse." Although the abuse may be happening, there is no *legal* duty to report it. In another California case, though, *Hedlund v. Superior Court,* the court found that a paraprofessional counselor had a duty to warn of potential violence.[5]

These difficult cases pit the principle of confidentiality against the moral imperative to warn potential victims. Courts have repeatedly decided that confidentiality must give way to potential harm, even if it destroys a counselor-client relationship. For friends, the best rule of thumb is this: if you are unsure what you should do, consult with someone who has more experience, usually a pastor. Assure yourself and your pastor that you are not gossiping. Be sure that your motivation is to clarify a puzzling and potentially dangerous situation. Often your pastor may say that you need to get more information from the participants before deciding what to do. In the end, though, if the risk of danger seems great, you may decide to breach confidentiality. This will almost certainly have adverse consequences for the helping relationship. Explore the consequences of your decision carefully before you act.

Finding the Right Level of Help

It is difficult to find the right balance between giving too much or too little help. Sometimes we assume that people want suggestions about how to solve their problems when they want only to be listened to. On the other hand, we may be quite empathic and supportive, while the friend wants specific suggestions.

The other end of the teeter-totter concerns how much help your friend asks of you. Sometimes you will feel burdened under the weight of constant demands for support. You may feel that your friend must believe that you have nothing to do except minister to him or her. Or your friend may want only a little understanding while you want to do some heavy-duty helping.

Avoid misunderstandings about the amount and type of help desired by asking directly, "Could you tell me exactly how I can help you?" Despite having asked, be tentative in your action. People in emotional turmoil may not know what they want. They are stirred up inside and want to feel less stirred up, but they don't know how you can help. They may say, "Answer my questions," but they may actually need to vent emotions or to clarify their thinking. Observe the way that the person accepts, or doesn't accept, the help you offer and be willing to modify your plans.

Getting Caught in Game-Playing

Sometimes people ask for help but seem not to want it. They want desperately to get over their problems but are at the same time receiving a payoff from having the problem. The Transactional Analysts[6] most clearly identified the patterns that usually occur in this "game-playing." The "victim" seeks help. When the helper tries to help, the victim gratefully thanks the rescuer and then says, "Yes, but—" by either giving a reason why the help won't work or trying the suggested solution and failing. The rescuer keeps trying suggestions until he or she tires of this repeated frustration. The victim really wants to get better, but he or she also wants the attention and support that comes with being a victim. The rescuer really wants the victim to get better, but he or she also wants the feelings of power and helpfulness that come in being in the rescuer role.

Detecting Mistakes in Helping with Marriage Problems

Marital Projection

"Marital projection" is the tendency to think that our experience fits others, which may or may not be true. Learn to recognize when you are projecting. Here are some tip-offs.

- Getting emotionally involved over whether your friend follows your advice. If you are strongly invested, you usually are justifying your own experience or are in a power struggle.

- Being *positive* your suggestion will work because it worked for you.
- Continuing to believe your helping is wise even if a supervisor disagrees.
- Suggesting many specific solutions to your friend's problems, which could mean you're too ego-involved.

To avoid marital projection, stick to the basics of helping. Listen attentively and repeat key elements of what your friend says so he or she can know that you understand. Support your friend in any attempts he or she makes to change, especially if you think the change will positively affect the marriage. Give advice only after hearing the entire story and only if your friend wants your advice. Perhaps your best defense against projecting your needs, problems, and solutions on the help-seeker is to arrange some supervision.

Empathy

When you help an individual about a personal, emotional problem, empathy works to your advantage. However, with marital disruption, your empathy can cause unintended complications.

Barbara's sister, Bonnie, phoned. The conversation lasted for fifteen minutes—longer than usual. Finally, Barbara said, "Well, Bon, I need to be running."

"We're thinking of splitting up," Bonnie said. She sounded nonchalant, but her voice had a tremor that wasn't usually there.

"What's going on?" asked Barbara. "I knew you were having problems, but I didn't expect divorce."

"He doesn't love me, Babs." Bonnie paused.

"Why do you say that?"

"He stays out three nights a week with his friends. When we go out, we're always with other people, and he ignores me all night."

"How can he ignore you? You're precious. He must be a dolt."

"Thanks, Babs. You've always been supportive. I wish Gary felt the same. He doesn't ever ask how I'm doing or start a conversation. He treats me like I'm not there."

When the phone call ended, Barbara fumed, knocking pots and pans together. After a while, Randall walked in. "Sounds like dueling drums in here," he said. "What's up?"

"Aw, that idiot Gary treats Bonnie like dirt. He ignores her. That guy doesn't realize what a treasure he has."

"You sound pretty upset at him."

"I am. He goes out with his friends and leaves her at home. He doesn't ask her about her day. You always ask about me." Barbara gave Randall a hug. "He never talks to her. Bonnie and he are thinking about divorce. I don't want my sister to be a statistic. I'd like to shake some sense into Gary."

"What's his gripe? Is he upset about something Bonnie does?"

"I didn't think to ask. I was so angry at Gary."

"I love your sister. You know that. But she's awfully passive sometimes. Even you must draw her out. She doesn't volunteer what's bothering her. Maybe he doesn't know how upset she is."

"You could be right. I know there's always another side, but I get so wrapped up in what's happening to Bonnie that I lose my perspective sometimes."

Barbara has used a form of supervision to help Bonnie better when they talk again. Instead of becoming wrapped up in Bonnie's story, she got help from Randall, who was not as intimately involved with the problem. It helped her gain objectivity.

Gender Bias

Even if you can see both partners at the same time, you may find that you understand one partner better than the other. Almost always you discover that the person of the same sex as you makes more sense than the partner of the other sex.

Even if you can keep your bias completely controlled, the partners often don't believe that you are unbiased. The other-sex partner might believe that you are in league with his or her partner. This is especially true if you suggest that the other-sex partner change an ongoing habit. The same-sex partner might believe that he or she has a special ally who will sympathize with his or her thinking. If you suggest that *that* partner change a habit, he or she feels betrayed.

When partners in chronic conflict discuss their difficulties with a third party, they want to tell the things that the partner has done to wrong or hurt them. They want to "triangulate" the third person, pulling him or her onto their side of the argument, which they think will somehow force the other person to change. Avoid being triangulated by affirming both people, occasionally making a statement that differs from either spouse's position (called making a "self-statement"), and by focusing the discussion on solving difficulties, not complaining about the partner.

Sexual Attraction

Judith was a vibrant, beautiful, twenty-six-year-old woman until disaster reduced her to a depressed, aggrieved woman. Judith's husband was having a blatant affair with the church secretary. Judith sought counseling from her pastor. Judith was vulnerable, disappointed in a husband who wouldn't listen to or respect her. In the pastor, she found all the qualities missing in her husband—a faithful Christian, a mature counselor, someone she could rely on. The pastor found a woman who needed him, made him feel powerful and wise, and listened to his advice and opinions. They married.

The marriage seemed to be made in heaven, but three years later, Judith and the pastor divorced. The marriage had been made not in heaven but in the counseling room.

But I'll never be sexually attracted to someone I'm counseling, you may think. *I'm happily married. My faith is strong. I've weathered temptations before. It'll never happen to me.*

James T. Berry surveyed 100 pastors in Virginia.[7] Their mean age was 48 years old, number of years married was 17.9, and number of years in the ministry was 15.7. Of the 100 pastors, 71 reported some level of sexual attraction to a parishioner—34 currently and 37 to a previous parishioner. (Remember about half of these pastors were over fifty.) Of those 71 pastors, 11% had had sexual intercourse with the person, 9% had had oral sex, 14% had caressed the genitals of the person, and 25% had kissed the person. If such a high level of sexual attraction and behavior can occur in pastors, it can also occur with friends—even strong Christians with high morals.

Instead of relying on your Christian beliefs and moral restraint to prevent unwanted sexual attraction, supplement those with concrete steps to reduce the chances of the attraction.

- Help only same-sex friends, if possible.
- If you help an other-sex friend, keep clear boundaries. Agree on times for helping and stick to the task. Don't socialize or meet privately.
- Don't touch the person. Sometimes a supportive hug or touch can be misinterpreted.
- Keep doors open when possible.
- Invite more than one helper (Mark 6:7). Having two counselors protects the helper's and help-seeker's reputations.

- Even better, help jointly with your own spouse.
- Help by phone.
- Invite a supervisor to oversee your helping relationship.

Being Too Passive

Don't be passive. If you are helping an individual, you generally don't worry about being passive. When your friend tires of talking, he or she stops and you say or do something. When you are helping a couple, that isn't true. When the husband stops talking, the wife starts. Back and forth. They have argued for years and when they get rolling, they can steamroll a friend. Interrupting arguments of a conflicted couple can be like trying to stop a flood by holding up your hand. You'll get swamped. Intervene before they get flowing.

Nichole with Ham and Monica Revisited

I have reprinted the case I began the chapter with. I have included some comments about Nichole's mistakes.

Nichole, a single parent of a ten-year-old girl, was a friend of both Ham and Monica, who had been married for twelve years. They had all been members of the same Sunday school class for three years. When it became obvious through their constant bickering that Ham and Monica were having marital strains, Nichole thought she should do something. She liked both partners and didn't want to see them in pain. She and her deceased husband Harris had enjoyed ten years of happy marriage before Harris's death three years earlier. Nichole thought she could help Ham and Monica, so she invited them to dinner.

Nichole is trying to help the couple without finding whether they would like her help. She may well find that they are not interested. She may also be assuming that she can use the experiences in her marriage to directly help the marriage of Ham and Monica.

After dinner, the conversation erupted into a disagreement between Ham and Monica. Nichole said that she had noticed the tensions between the partners, and she asked if she could help. Ham said "No" and Monica said "Yes" simultaneously. Nichole asked Monica to talk about her experience. As Monica talked, she cried. Ham folded his arms and fumed. Finally, he stormed out, saying, "If you two want to talk, I don't care. But I'm leaving. If you want to stay, Monica, Nichole can bring you home." After Ham left, Nichole and Monica talked for four hours.

When Monica and Ham disagreed about whether they wanted to talk about the problems, Nichole should have asked Ham if he minded telling why he didn't want to talk about them. Perhaps his objections could have been answered. At a minimum, Nichole might have asked whether she and Monica could talk about the problems—either at the present or at some later date. Nichole inadvertently sided with Monica, angering Ham more than he already was and creating barriers to later communication.

Nichole realized that she had made an alliance with Monica. Determined to rebalance her relationship with the couple, she called Ham at work and suggested that they meet for lunch.

Making a luncheon date with a troubled partner is not a good idea. The date could have been misunderstood by Monica, Ham, or others.

The luncheon meeting two days later was a disaster. Ham was angry with Monica over numerous faults. He ranted throughout the meal about Monica's inadequacies, finally storming away from the table, leaving Nichole to pay.

Nichole's mistakes are difficult to determine, but getting stuck with the bill is a dead giveaway that she made some. Nichole probably allowed the discussion to stay too negative. If negative affect is constant, productive change in the marriage will rarely happen.

Meanwhile, Monica called Nichole daily asking for advice. When Ham moved out one week later, Monica phoned twice each day. Nichole was always supportive, listening to Monica's tales of woe and encouraging her to work on the marriage and stick out the difficult times.

Nichole needs to set limits. Monica is encroaching into Nichole's home-life. Further, Nichole may be too supportive, allowing Monica to think she is completely right.

Nichole often repeated the story about the rocky first year of her marriage to Harris, when Harris had moved back to his home for a month.

As we suspected earlier, Nichole is apparently assuming that her marriage experience will be Monica's experience. Not likely. A marital disruption in Nichole's first year of marriage is different than a separation in Monica's twelfth year.

Nichole suggested many things Monica could do to improve the marriage, but Monica could never follow the suggestions successfully.

It sounds as if Monica may be playing the game "Why Don't You; Yes, But." If Monica is, Nichole should stop making specific suggestions but continue to support Monica.

Nichole was increasingly frustrated. In desperation, she asked her midweek Bible study and support group to pray for her and particularly to pray for Monica and Ham. When the members of the group wanted to know what the problem was, Nichole summarized Monica's and Ham's problems. The group prayed for twenty minutes for the couple.

Nichole has violated Monica's confidentiality. There was no need to identify the person nor to give specifics of the marital troubles to seek prayer for Monica or for herself.

Despite the group's prayers, the marriage continued to deteriorate. Nichole felt frustrated, depressed, and burdened with Monica's constant phoning. Eventually Ham filed for a divorce, left the congregation, and severed his ties with all the people at the church. Monica was consoled by the Sunday school class. When the divorce became final, relief was evident in almost everyone who knew Monica, even though many people had encouraged her to keep trying to make the marriage work.

Throughout the episode, Nichole did not seek consultation about how she could have helped better. She should have consulted her pastor.

CHAPTER EIGHT

BECOME A BETTER HELPER

Learning happens one event at a time.

Learning occurs best when we concentrate on one event and perform it as well as we can. Improvement is solidified if we reflect on what we did. The practical implication is this: Concentrate on helping the loved one who has sought your assistance.

Ways to Help

Practical Assistance

Sometimes the best way you can help a needy friend is by providing practical assistance. A friend might need food, a helping hand with cleaning, child care, or the use of your vehicle. Providing mundane service can be a gift from God through you to your friend. The church is Jesus' body, a physical way that Jesus works in people's lives.

Prayer

Prayer is not just a psychological comfort. Prayer has great power. Robson Gomes, a friend from Brazil, once described a rainy Sunday in Brazil when he was scheduled to give a sermon. Dressed in his suit, he drove through torrential rain. Water had collected a foot deep in the streets. He drove through a deep puddle and the car stalled.

There sat Robson, rain falling in sheets, car sitting in a foot-deep puddle. "RRRuuuu. RRRuuuu," ground the stalled motor.

"Oh, Lord," prayed Robson, "You know the congregation is counting on me to conduct their service. Lord, You know that there is no time to spare. I need Your help."

Down the street came a group of large men, jogging in rain so heavy that Robson could hardly see them. One waved, smiled, and nodded to Robson, and the entire group pushed Robson's car from the puddle. Robson turned the ignition. "Varoom," the motor roared to life. The men smiled and resumed their jogging, and away Robson sped—on time to the church service.

"I'm convinced that God sent angels to rescue me," said Robson. Prayer has enormous power to bring about the unexpected.

Resources

Resources for self-help now come in a variety of packages: self-help books, audiocassettes, videocassettes, and lectures. The most widely available resources at present are self-help books.

Some people just like books. Others have a hard time learning from teachers because they have control issues, but they have no trouble learning from books. You can help by providing resources for people's self-help. A vast number of self-help books exist. By one estimate, more than 2,000 are published each year.[1] Quackenbush has provided a bibliography of 271 self-help books frequently recommended by professional therapists.[2] A survey of professional therapists in the Seattle area found that about 88 percent of them recommended self-help books to some patients.[3] Halliday surveyed one hundred psychotherapy clients about their use of self-help books to supplement counseling.[4] Forty-three said they read a self-help book about their difficulty. Each was asked to recall specific ways that the self-help book caused distress, was beneficial, both, or neither. Most thought the book was beneficial (see graphic, page 105).

Self-help books vary in quality. If you recommend a book, you probably should have read the book so you can discuss its contents with the person you are helping. Help the person evaluate the quality of the advice.

- What are the author's credentials?
- Is the book's advice consistent with Scripture? Not every book needs to be derived from Scripture to have merit. Yet books that contradict Scripture should not be used.

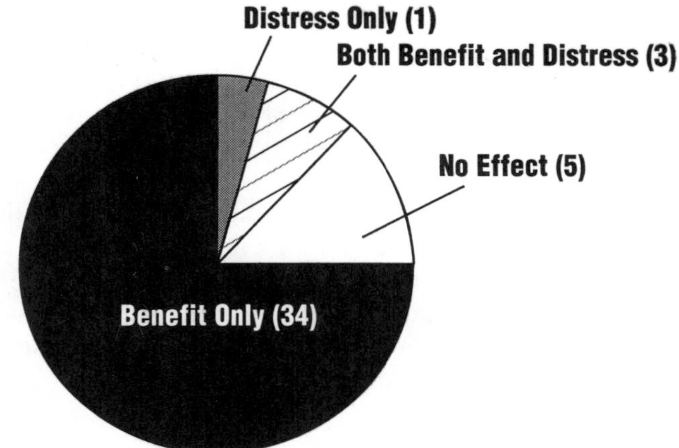

Do Self-Help Books Help?

Halliday (1991) reported that of 100 clients, 43 read self-help books about their problems. The clients rated whether the books were beneficial, distressing, both, or neither.

- Is the book well documented? Rather than place confidence in an author's authoritative pronouncements about truth, counsel your friend to look at the references and determine the sources of information that are used. Are scientific studies used? Are they current? Are other books used as sources? What is the quality of the other books? Is the Bible quoted? Are Bible texts quoted in context, or does the author misuse Scripture?
- Is the writing clear and logical, or is it nebulous and filled with vague psychological slang that appears to be good advice but can mean virtually anything?
- What does the author promise? Are successes discussed but problems never mentioned? Does the author imply that success is assured?
- Are data reported about the effectiveness of the method that is recommended? Are scientific studies reported? Are undocumented success rates claimed? Does the author merely cite testimonials?

Information

Provide information. Often marital problems are due to simple lack of information—especially in the early stages of marriage. For example, one newly wedded couple, both virgins when they married, had difficulty with their sex life. They had heard of "foreplay" but didn't know what it was. In talking with another couple who had been married for several years, the young couple found some ways of stimulating each other prior to intromission that made their sex life not only more fun but also less painful and more satisfying.

For newly wedded partners, more experienced married couples can provide a lot of information that can head off difficulties before they get to be big enough to be called "problems." Even for more experienced couples, when they reach a new stage of life—having a first child, dealing with a toddler, negotiating the school system, coping with children in middle school, helping their high school senior select a college—more experienced parents can provide valuable information.

Charles Hummel, former president of Barrington College and director of faculty ministries for InterVarsity Christian Fellowship, visited Richmond to give faculty symposia at Virginia Commonwealth University and the University of Richmond. We were privileged to have him stay at our home. I mentioned that I didn't know to which college Kirby and I were going to send Christen, our (then) ninth-grade daughter, when she graduated. Charles laughed and said, "Ev, you probably won't *send* Christen anywhere. When they become high school seniors, they have a mind of their own." That casual, offhand comment changed my way of looking at my college-bound daughter, and it probably helped prevent conflict during Christen's senior year in high school.

Interaction

Help through interacting with your friend. Listen to your friend as he or she wrestles with difficulties, help clarify thinking about the marriage, provide support and emotional nurturance, make suggestions and give advice, and follow up on the relationship to see how things came out. Through those interactions, you convey an unmistakable message to your friend apart from any specific help you provide. You say, "I value you. I care." That message liberates and empowers. We all want unconditional love (Proverbs 19:22a), and by your willingness to listen, you provide a glimpse of that love.

How Do We Learn Interaction Skills?

Helping is essentially discipleship training. Disciples learn faith working through love. By studying how Jesus trained His disciples during His three years of public ministry, we can learn how to help better.

Jesus selected the disciples and demonstrated how God's power could work through a person (Himself). For example, in Matthew 4, He called Simon Peter, Andrew, James, and John (verses 18–22). Immediately, "he went about all Galilee, teaching in their synagogues and preaching the gospel of the kingdom and healing every disease and every infirmity among the people" (verse 23 RSV). He explained principles of the kingdom of God (Matthew 5:1–7:29, the Sermon on the Mount). He preferred parables and analogies (Matthew 13:3–10), which made the disciples struggle to figure out what He meant, but eventually, He explained the principles to His disciples in straightforward language (Matthew 13:18–23).

He often illustrated His teaching with miracles (Matthew 8:1–3; 5–13; 14–17). He placed the disciples in real-life situations and quizzed them about what they should do if living a life of faith. For example, in John 6:1–14, Jesus illustrated His claim to be the bread of life (John 6:35) by feeding a crowd on five barley loaves and two fish. In doing so, He tested Philip (6:6) without requiring Philip to actually use his faith. Eventually, Jesus sent the disciples into real-life situations. "And he called to him his twelve disciples and gave them authority over unclean spirits, to cast them out, and to heal every disease and every infirmity. . . . These twelve Jesus sent out" (Matthew 10:1, 5a RSV; see also Luke 9:1–6; and see Luke 10:1–17 for sending out the seventy).

Learning happens one event at a time. However, Jesus provided a sequence of single events that promoted systematic learning in His disciples. You can learn to be a better helper in the same way. Although you can learn to help others without receiving formal training, you'll learn more efficiently if you learn systematically.

Learn the Fundamentals

First, learn fundamental helping skills. The most fundamental skill is active listening. Active listening involves reflecting what a person says through

- repeating short phrases that encourage the person to continue to talk (i.e., "He hurt your feelings?");
- summarizing the essence of a statement (i.e., "It sounds like you're saying that he didn't realize he was doing it, but it still hurt");

- summarizing the amount and type of emotion being felt (i.e., "So it made you absolutely furious");
- paraphrasing the person (i.e., "You wanted to lash out, to hurt back");
- stopping the person at intervals and summarizing the main points of the person's story (i.e., "Let me see if I have all of this straight. When he told you he was too tired to make love, you took it as rejecting you. You were hurt and angry, and you wanted to hurt back. Is that it?").

Many books describe active listening skills thoroughly and illustrate them with longer conversations.[5] Review those skills.

Another fundamental skill involves learning to rethink problems helpfully. Thinking of marriage difficulties as being due to failures in faith working through love is an example of rethinking marriage problems. Still another fundamental skill involves formulating action plans which are based on the new way of thinking about the problem. Planning ways to promote intimacy, communication, problem solving, positive thinking, or forgiveness are examples of formulating action plans.[6]

Practice in Lifelike and Real Situations

Role-playing is an excellent way to gain experience quickly. There is great benefit in having several people meet together, following the same book or program, and learning to improve their helping skills, for a group can provide chances to build and practice skills without risking harmful effects on troubled help seekers. If your church does not have such a program in place, see your pastor about whether there might be sufficient interest to start one.

You, of course, might be asked to spearhead the group, which often happens to the one who suggests a new program. If you are asked to help, don't be daunted. Contact the various ministries (listed on pages 16–17) to see what kind of help they can lend. While waiting on responses, contact people whom you and your pastor think might be interested in the group and might be good helpers. Most people who have begun helper groups have found it advisable to screen people prior to their being allowed to help others as part of a lay counseling team associated with the church.

Church-based lay counseling differs from friendship helping. Anyone interested in improving his or her helping skills should be allowed to join the group, understanding that not everyone will necessarily become a church-certified lay counselor. Most people *do* help their friends with psychological, marital, and family problems, so almost everyone can benefit from being in a helping-skills group. Such a group can only strengthen the body of Christ as servants (Romans 12:7; Ephesians 4:1–16), encouragers (2 Corinthians 1:3–7), ministers of love (John 13:34–35; Romans 12:9–10), sharers of burdens (Galatians 6:1–2), exhorters (Romans 15:14; Hebrews 3:13), and comforters (Romans 12:8; 1 Thessalonians 5:14).

Recruit volunteers and call them together to decide on your group's goals. Select books or a curriculum to study together, and enlist the assistance of your pastor or a trained counselor to oversee the group. If all those tasks seem overwhelming, don't be discouraged. Shelley Chapin provides guidelines for establishing such a group in your church.[7] Draw on her book and those of others for guidance.[8]

Who Are Your Teachers of Helping?

God

We each learn from a variety of teachers. Jesus brings teachers across our path and readies our hearts to receive the teaching that is beneficial for us. The Holy Spirit prompts and teaches us.

Reading, Talking, Thinking

Other teachers are also important. Reading can teach us, as can talking with experienced helpers about marriage or helping. We can benefit by thinking about our own and others' marriages, especially if we put our thinking into words through conversation or writing.

Observing Helpers in Action

Observe counseling and reflect on it. Read case studies, especially those with dialogue. Gary Collins published *Case Studies in Christian Counseling*,[9] in which nine professional counselors describe cases and provide examples of dialogue from counseling sessions. Reading the cases and studying the dialogues help you see how counseling actually occurs.

Some videotape demonstrations of counseling are available, but they are hard to come by unless you have access to a training program for counselors. If you wish to learn more about helping your friend, find and watch such tapes.

Watch others counsel. I have learned as much watching Kirby talk with friends as I have through my professional education. Kirby is a natural helper who interacts with friends in love. She is sensitive and yet focused in giving help. She tirelessly listens and empathizes with friends.

"I don't feel ready to help someone with a marriage problem." Should you try to help someone if you don't feel competent to help? That isn't an easy question to answer. It has two sides.

On one hand, you know yourself best. If you lack confidence, take yourself seriously. The first rule of helping—medical or psychological—is "Do no harm." That maxim must guide you. Whenever you are unsure of your advice, err on the conservative side rather than forge ahead and expect God to repair your damage. If you are unsure: first, don't act; second, seek supervision or consultation.

On the other hand, most of us never feel completely qualified to help. Help-seekers have a disconcerting way of doing the unexpected and throwing new situations, puzzles, and dilemmas at us. Only someone who is foolhardy glibly tries to help a wounded person. Helping, more than most activities, builds humility because we so often fall short of the glory of God in our response to the person, in our ability to love, in our willingness to think clearly and objectively, and in our reliance on God to intervene in the person's life and in our own life. Yet, we are called repeatedly through the Scriptures to help others, and if we are sure we can do so without causing harm, we should courageously answer the Lord's call.

In recognizing our competencies, limitations, and utter dependence on God, we can embark on a path to self-improvement in helping. We can provide information at the level appropriate for the person asking for help—through practical assistance, prayer, resources, information, and personal interaction. We can learn from our experiences—seeking to improve the fundamentals and to find situations where we can practice our helping skills under realistic conditions. We can learn from our teachers—from the Holy Spirit, from reading, talking, and thinking about marriage, from observation of talented friends, or observation of professionals on videotape or within a team. Armed with the basic helping skills, we can turn our attention to marriage and marital problems, which we shall do in the following chapters.

PART FOUR

UNDERSTANDING HOW TO START HELPING WITH MARRIAGE PROBLEMS

CHAPTER NINE

BIRD'S-EYE VIEW OF HELPING

This past Christmas, I was on a seven-mile walk in a strange neighborhood. Really striding out. Making time.

Walking toward me I saw a woman, moving fast. We approached like trains on parallel tracks. I expected the eee-oooo sound of the Doppler effect as we passed each other.

Suddenly, she was walking beside me, matching me stride for stride. I looked at her out of the corner of my eye. Nope, I still didn't know her.

"You're a runner?" she asked.

"I run a little."

"My doctor said I can't run anymore. I have a bladder condition."

"Oh?"

She filled me in on her bladder condition in detail. It was fascinating. I had no clue who she was.

"I'm addicted," she said.

Ah, at last, I thought, *this explains how a stranger can confide about her bladder condition.*

"I'm addicted to running. I've run consistently, five miles a day, six days a week, for three years. I can't do without it."

Drat, I thought, *there goes the addiction theory.* "It does get in your blood," I said.

"My husband doesn't understand how addicting running is, how I *need* it—physically and psychologically. Now the doctor won't let me run. I'll die."

"It sounds like it's really important to you." (I can't help it. Sometimes I just talk like a counselor.)

"It is! I get so disgusted with my husband. He doesn't try to understand. He doesn't run. He can't know how important it is. But *you* know how important running is, don't you?"

"Um," I said. (This is known among highly trained and super-skilled professionals as a non-committal grunt. It's known by everyone else as a gutless response.)

"We argue over it. Then the arguments spread into other areas—money, responsibilities around the house, all of the normal marriage things."

She then told me all about the normal marriage things that they argued about. After four blocks of huffing and puffing, she wound down. I secretly checked to make sure I hadn't worn my counselor's uniform by mistake.

"What should I do about the running? Should I get a second opinion about the bladder problem? How can I make my husband understand how important running is? How can we get past this continual arguing?"

"It sounds as if not being able to run bothers you, but your troubles with your husband bother you even more." She nodded. "I think you want to feel valued, and when your husband hasn't made what you consider to be enough effort to understand your love of running, you feel a little unloved."

"A lot unloved," she said hoarsely.

"That seems at the crux of the marital problems. Let me ask you, though, a tough question. Sometimes husbands and wives argue because they both feel unvalued or unloved. Has your running, or maybe something you've done, made your husband feel devalued or unloved, like you've felt?"

"I *know* he feels that way! I get real enthusiastic about whatever I do and throw myself into it. He's always complained that I ignore him by running, talking with runners, reading about running, and living running. I never really thought of it before, but we have both felt like the other didn't care as much as we used to. I guess the arguments came from that."

"If that's true," I said, "then this bladder problem—difficult as it is for you to cope with because you love running so much—might be a blessing in disguise as far as rebuilding the love between your husband and yourself."

"You're right. I can enjoy walking or low-impact aerobics eventually." Her lip curled at the thought. "But I need to get our love back. Maybe I should apologize for neglecting him."

"That might help him see that you want to rebuild your love."

"Right. I'll do it!"

I gave another suggestion or two. By that time, we had reached a crossroads. The light was red, so we pulled up to wait to cross the highway.

She extended her hand and I took it. "Thank you, sir, for being so understanding. You've been very helpful." She pumped my hand once, firmly, and strode off in the opposite direction.

Granted, that was an unusual instance of helping, but (in spite of my attempts to make it sound a bit more humorous than it was) it appeared to help the woman. She picked a safe stranger who looked as if he might hold similar interests. I later realized that I had my Richmond Marathon baseball hat screwed down over my eyebrows—the hat Kirby got me at a yard sale (I feel like an impostor)—so she mistook me for a runner. She unburdened herself in safety, took my advice and encouragement, and left (arms pumping).

Even this unusual helping episode embodied most of the elements of helping. In this chapter, I'll discuss types of helping and give an overview of how helping is carried out.

Effective Versus Ineffective Helpers

There *are* effective ways to help others with their marriage. Research has shown that effective marriage therapists differ from ineffective marriage therapists in several ways. Effective therapists *have better general helping skills than ineffective therapists*.[1] So, if you have learned how to help people effectively—that is, to care about them, to allow them to feel valued, to empathically understand their experience and communicate to them that you understand, to treat them with respect—then most people will listen to your advice about their marriage. Using good helping skills is the prerequisite for effective marital counseling.

An effective marital therapist also *helps the person or couple feel that the therapist will not let destructive arguments occur in the therapist's presence*.[2] A good marriage counselor can help the couple talk in a self-controlled way and can interrupt tactfully whenever things threaten to get out of hand.

Effective helpers also *understand marriage, marital stresses, and divorce better than ineffective helpers*.[3] But understanding isn't enough. Effective marriage counselors draw on that understanding *to help people try changes that are likely to help their marriage.*

Stages of Counseling

An Example of Friendship Helping

Helping friends follows the same path as does professional counseling. For example, I was recently working in the yard when Kirby called me inside to talk with our friend Sandra. Sandra had just had an argument with her husband of six years, Mark. Kirby had given her some excellent counsel and had suggested that perhaps I might give Sandra other ideas.

While Kirby stayed in the room and sometimes contributed other ideas, I talked with Sandra for about an hour. Even though I am a professional marriage counselor, I was doing friendship helping with Sandra, not professional counseling, because the helping was limited to one conversation and our relationship was not a formal, professional one.

Sandra described the recent argument. Mark had said, "Let's go to the mountains for a picnic. I bought some potato chips, cold cuts, ice, and sodas."

Sandra said that she couldn't take off that day because she was in the middle of some projects. She also said that the next day, Sunday, wouldn't be possible either. Then, she simply said, "Mark, I wish you wouldn't spend money without asking me first. We're having a hard time keeping to our budget, and when you spend money on perishables that we don't need and that will spoil, it doesn't help our finances."

Mark argued that the mountains were nice and that he was trying to be romantic. Then he added, "You're a workaholic. You have to let your hair down occasionally."

Sandra said that the argument progressed along "typical" lines. She had told Mark that he was "irresponsible." She added, "He's so spontaneous. I *used* to think that was a virtue. Ha! I keep the financial records. He wastes money on any scheme that comes along. That's *not* a virtue."

I asked how Mark criticized her. She said, "He calls me 'too logical' and 'overcontrolled.' He says I'm a workaholic who has forgotten how to have fun. But *someone's* got to take life seriously. If I left it to him, we'd starve."

When I asked how frequently they argued, Sandra mentioned three almost identical arguments. Sandra viewed the problem as one in which her and Mark's *personalities* were at odds, which suggested little hope of changing. I tried to get her to think of the problem differently.

I asked, "Have you tried to convince Mark that he needed to change his personality, to become more responsible?"

She almost shouted, "All the time!"

"How about him? Has he ever tried to get you to change?"

She laughed. "At least as often."

"It sounds as if you two are engaged in a battle to try to get the other person to see things your way."

"Yeah, we do that all the time."

She was beginning to think of their problem differently—more as a power struggle and less as Mark's personality problem. So I asked whether she could remember other times when they had had such a power struggle.

She described several. When she finished, I observed that both she and Mark saw things only from their own point of view. "As long as that occurs," I added, "there'll never be a winner." She nodded. Then I said, "I assume you want to resolve your differences with Mark rather than win the battle over whether your problem or his is responsible for the arguments. Is that right?" When she said yes, I asked her what she could do if she found herself in such a power struggle again.

She made several good suggestions—such as trying to see things from his point of view, not thinking of the problem as unsolvable, and bending rather than holding out for her way. But then she asked how she could learn to resolve the differences when they were already involved in a power struggle. "It doesn't seem like we can avoid power struggles if our history is any clue."

I suggested that she read the popular book, *Getting To Yes: Negotiating Agreement Without Giving In*,[4] by Roger Fisher and William Ury.

Sandra said, "I'll buy it and make Mark read it."

I had visions of another power struggle brewing.

I said, "You'll enjoy it, but I wouldn't try to persuade Mark to read it. If you're indeed in a power struggle, then your attempt to impose help might backfire. Why don't you read it but wait and see if Mark spontaneously asks about it? Then he can decide to read it without feeling controlled."

Stages of Friendship Counseling

In my brief time with Sandra, our conversation followed the same pattern as *any* effective helping. I discussed the pattern in my book for lay counselors, *When Someone Asks for Help,* and I applied the method to helping people who had problems with self-esteem, self-control, depression, anxiety, and loneliness in *How to Help the Hurting.*[5]

Those six stages are as follows:

1. Understanding the problem from your friend's point of view and communicating that you understand;
2. Helping your friend think differently about the problem;
3. Planning helpful actions and motivating your friend to try out plans;
4. Supporting efforts to change;
5. Following your friend to see how he or she implemented the action plans; and
6. Disengaging from the helping role.

Applications

In this chapter, I have tried to help you understand stages of friendship helping. I have used these same helping stages within this chapter. At the beginning of the chapter, I tried to show that I understand some of the practical problems that you might face in trying to help others. That's stage one. I have also tried to move beyond the understanding you had originally and give you a new perspective (i.e., that there are six stages). That's stage two. The new perspective should allow you to think systematically about your helping so you can be more effective. I gave some examples to demonstrate ways to help better. That's stage three, planning specific actions. Throughout coming chapters, I hope to suggest many other ideas that you might translate into action. As you work through the book, you will, of course, be supported by prayer and through your reading. That's stage four. Also within the book are questions for you to test yourself, which provide feedback to you about how well you understand what you have learned. That's stage five. Finally, having completed the book, you will move into responsible helping, which is stage six.

My interaction with my instant "friend," the runner, went through these stages of helping, too. I listened to her and helped her feel that I understood her problems (Stage 1). Then I guided her toward thinking about the problem differently. In her case, I helped her see that both she and her husband might have felt devalued by the other one's behavior (Stage 2). That led to her making some action plans (Stage 3)—trying low-impact aerobics or walking, and apologizing to her husband about neglecting him. In this brief encounter, I couldn't support her efforts to change (Stage 4) or follow up to see how well her plans worked (Stage 5). However, we did manage a successful termination (Stage 6) as she scurried off into the sunset—walking, not running.

CHAPTER TEN

HAVE A POSITIVE ATTITUDE

Helen and Richard's marriage was on the rocks. In desperation they sought counseling. Here are some excerpts from the first session.

"Change is hopeless. I don't know how to change or where to begin. Our marriage is so bad that it's pointless to try."

"We have a zero balance in our love account. I'm afraid of overdrawing. Our marriage is totally negative."

"I'm afraid to change but terrified that we won't change."

"We have a very giving marriage. We give pain for pain, anger for anger, and distress for distress. He gives me the works, and I give him the cold shoulder."

"We hurt each other often, and we live by inviolable rules: Never say you're sorry. If you must, don't mean it. Even if you mean it, resent the partner for making you apologize. Oh, yes, there's one more. Remember hurts forever. You never know when you can use them against her."

A Positive Attitude for Couples

For a troubled marriage to change, at least one partner must believe that the marriage can change. As a friend, you will help most effectively if both spouses can work in concert; but one spouse alone can positively affect the marriage.

How Not to Promote Change

"Helen, you and Richard have some bad attitudes about marriage. You must change them if you want a better marriage."

Suppose you were Helen. Would you change your attitudes because someone told you to? Almost no one will respond to a straightforward suggestion to change.

Nor will most people respond well to coercion. Pastors, counselors, and friends who try to force a friend to change by quoting Scripture, threatening with hellfire and brimstone, or withdrawing love will usually succeed only in making the person angrily avoid them.

When Does Love Grow?

Ask your friend to recall when love for the partner grew.

The love between Kirby and me grew when we attended a marriage enrichment workshop soon after our marriage. Discussing struggles with other couples helped us handle a rough first year of marriage and provided positive goals. Our love spurted ahead when we camped and hiked every weekend one summer. It soared when we traveled to Hawaii, Japan, Thailand, and Europe. Traveling wasn't all fun, but the struggles and the good times drew us closer. Recently, family camping trips, walks, and special meals as a couple have bonded us more firmly.

Breaks from routine have energized our marriage. The time we laboriously and sacrificially wrenched from our busy schedules to be together has yielded dividends. The extra effort of doing new things has refreshed us. Change has challenged us. To meet the demands of change, we had to obtain and maintain a positive attitude toward change.

When you ask your friend to reflect on times when love grew, you not only focus the person's attention on the more positive times of marriage, but you give ideas about how to regain those positive times. The couple can get away, try different behaviors, go places, do things together that were fun, and thus recapture the magic. Keep in mind that the things you enjoy will not work for everyone. Your family's dream of backpacking through the Grand Canyon may be a nightmare for a couple who rediscovers romance spending their vacations working in the backyard garden.

Change Requires Effort

Most positive change won't just happen to marriages. It is made to happen through the efforts of committed couples who are willing to risk their time and energy to improve their marriage. Improvement comes from a positive attitude toward change. Thus, help your friend think more positively about his or her marriage.

Some Attitudes to Promote

Change Is Worth the Risk

Anytime partners try to change their marriage, things could get worse or better. *If we try and fail,* they think, *we'll be worse off than if we hadn't tried.* But if partners don't try to improve, their marriage *will* run downhill. Marriages are like gardens. They don't produce vegetables without the work of gardening.

It's worth the risk of trying to improve. About 80 percent of the people who seek counseling with marital problems patch up their marriage, which suggests that even seriously troubled marriages can be healed if partners work at it.

Change Takes Time and Hard Work

Marriage is like playing tennis. A person can read books, watch videotapes, watch live matches, and generate enormous enthusiasm about playing tennis without improving his or her game. Life skills must be changed through living. Marriage skills must be lived to be learned.

Focus on Solutions Rather than Problems

To improve my tennis skills, I must learn to hit strokes correctly. Knowing that I am hitting incorrectly will not tell me how to hit correctly. When marital problems develop, knowing one has problems doesn't solve the problems. Yet, most troubled couples spend 95 percent of their time and effort focusing on problems and 5 percent focusing on solutions. Each couple needs to develop an attitude that will reverse this—5 percent focus on problems and 95 percent on finding solutions.

This can only be done if each person feels heard and valued. Help partners listen carefully to each other and repeat enough back that the spouse can tell whether or not his or her point of view and feelings are understood.

Compartmentalize the Pain

When we smash a thumb, we think of nothing else all day. Life is a smashed-thumb experience. We whack and thwack the thumb throughout the day. We forget that the remainder of our body is working because the thumb aches so terribly.

When a marriage has trouble, couples feel as if it hurts all over. In parts of the marriage, love still blossoms, yet the blossoms are overlooked by people in pain who are searching for its source. To heal the marriage, partners need to compartmentalize the pain, then reduce the size of the compartment.

Do More of What Works

In marriage, each couple has found things that work for them—pet phrases, looks, ways to make love, be intimate, avoid arguments. Promote this attitude: *Find the positive and do more of it.* Ask, "When was the last time things went well in your marriage? How did you make that happen? How did you react to your spouse?" Have the person discuss these memories with his or her spouse and try to recreate the positive experiences.

Don't Expect Perfection

We all agree that no one is perfect, yet many people live as if they expected perfection from themselves or their spouses. Perfectionism bursts forth when couples are having marital troubles. When marriage coasts smoothly, partners accept imperfection without a blink. When marriage hits the rocks, they search for the smallest pebble. Help the person look down the road to smoother streets. Don't minimize the current bumps, but remind him or her of new pavement ahead.

Be Your Own Repair Crew

How can the couple anticipate smooth biking ahead? Someone must fix the street. People expect their partner to fix the street—especially the potholes the partner caused. They are *afraid* to get off the bike and fix the potholes in their path—regardless of who caused them. Instead, they coerce their partners to work. That takes effort, so they see themselves as virtuous. *They* are working hard on the marriage. But their coercion is merely digging more potholes.

Help your friend stop:

- looking at the partner's faults;
- thinking the partner has evil motives;
- looking at the partner's nasty personality;
- looking at the bad things the partner did in the past and is continuing to do even now;
- searching for the partner's failures;
- accumulating evidence to show he or she is right and the partner is wrong;
- criticizing the partner's behavior;
- documenting the partner's failure to work at the marriage;
- pointing out the partner's unwillingness to carry a fair share of the load;
- calling attention to the partner's insensitivity and selfishness.

Help your friend start:

- examining his or her willingness to show love;
- working to improve the marriage;
- striving to show faith in the marriage and faith in God to change both partners' hearts.

Be First to Repair

"I've tried and tried to change our marriage, and it hasn't done any good. I don't believe my wife wants to change. I'm not going to put myself on the line again until I have concrete evidence that she is willing to change." This husband will wait a long time. If a spouse waits to see evidence of the partner's changing, he or she will never see it. Each person is blinded to what his or her mind is set against. Spouses whose minds are already made up that their partners aren't trying won't see change when it is before their eyes.

To make marital changes, your friend must change first. "I've tried many times before." Good, try again. Change won't happen by itself.

Be Patient

Couples feel trapped in a stagnant marriage. They see only more of the same hum-drum boredom. They decide to change, but at first they seem to get nowhere. Finally, change begins. Slowly. Agonizingly. Three steps forward, two backward. This uneven progress tests the permanency of change and the sincerity of the partners in being committed to change the marriage. Usually, it tests their patience too. After much work, though, progress actually becomes visible, until new arenas of freedom are opened to the couple. Through it all, patience and faith are the sustaining virtues.

Look to God

God wants marriage not only to survive but to mirror the joy of a spiritual relationship between Christ and the church and between the believer and Jesus. We cannot make marriage change on our own. We must rely on God. Change in marriage is fundamentally receiving a new heart. A troubled couple, like a troubled individual, has worked its way into a predicament in which the husband and wife deserve nothing except the death of the relationship. Yet Jesus' table is a table of restoration. Only by coming to Jesus' table can they hope to repair their marriage.

Without God, they may put a bandage on the marriage, but the wound lingers. Unless the Lord in His mercy heals the wound, it will not heal.

A Positive Attitude for You, the Helper

Your Negative Attitudes

I hear nothing but complaints. A negative attitude permeates a troubled marriage. As you try to help a troubled spouse, you will hear a lot about the difficulties. It's easy to get swept into the negativity and to feel that your helping is going nowhere. Focus the spouse on the positive and you'll soon start to hear more positive comments from the person. Generally, the negative thinking and complaints will not simply disappear, but they will lessen in frequency over time.

I don't have time. A person in a troubled marriage has an important aspect of his or her life imperiled. Sensing the threat directly, that person will almost always have more energy and time to discuss the problem than you have to listen. Listen patiently but set firm limits about the number of phone calls or visits that you can take without losing your own mental health. If you overextend yourself by helping, you will be less effective as a helper and in your own life.

This is too hard. I recently sat in an adult Sunday school class while an older adult talked nonstop for fifteen minutes about his physical problems, difficulties getting a job, inability to receive money from welfare and Medicaid for treatment, mental problems, concern about the care of his aging parents, and numerous other problems. Everyone was reduced to hopelessness listening to his tales of woe. *This is too hard,* I thought. *I'm a professional. I should be able to help him.* But I couldn't. At times, we all feel inadequate. Problems seem too much, sorrows too great. We are paralyzed with inaction. At those times, remind yourself that you don't have to instantly answer every difficulty. Over time, answers may emerge. Your main responsibility is to support your friend. Later you can think about solutions.

I'm not good enough. Some situations can be absolutely overwhelming. We can conclude not only that this problem is too hard but that we're not good enough to help. Heed that message. Feeling unable to help the person opens us to seek the help we need. That help will come through Jesus' intervention, if we ask in prayer. Yet, Jesus may help by providing another friend who can help, guiding us toward professional assistance, or aiming us at someone with whom to consult. Sometimes, the Lord will provide a way to help directly. Knowing our limitations opens us for help from the Lord.

Build Positive Attitudes in Yourself

The attitudes that you try to cultivate in the person seeking your help are the same ones you need to develop in your provision of the help.

Work together. In the same way that a couple will be more likely to solve their marital problems if they work together and if they join their wills to God's, you can help better if you work with your friend and align your wills to God's. It is tempting to see problems from your own point of view and charge off doing your own thing. However, strive for a mutual understanding of the difficulties with your friend and submit the problems in prayer to the Lord. Only through discernment of God's will will you truly succeed at helping.

Change is worth the risk. Helping puts a person's ego on the line. It's less risky to one's ego, especially when a problem is difficult, when the helper feels inadequate, or when helping doesn't produce fruit, to avoid helping or to find other things to do. The problem won't simply repair itself. Stick with it.

Change takes time and hard work. Like couples, helpers want instant solutions. Yet, helping is hard work. It involves ups and downs and substantial time. Keep your perspective and stay motivated to help.

Focus on solutions, not problems. When you hear complaints every time you talk to someone, it is easy to focus on the problems. Problem-focus will overwhelm you. Instead, balance listening and supporting the person with helping think of solutions. Define roadblocks to effective helping. Rather than complaining or grumbling that the person isn't motivated to change, work toward solutions that help promote change.

Compartmentalize. The helping relationship can consume your time, energy, and emotion. To help effectively, keep a balance. Make time for your other relationships and needs.

I knew a pastor years ago who was one of the most unselfish, giving men ever. Whenever anyone called, regardless of his own or his family's plans, he would help. He constantly felt overwhelmed and overcommitted, and his family life was a wreck. He had not learned to compartmentalize his helping.

Do more of what works. If your attempts to help don't succeed, do something else. If it works, do more of it.

Don't expect perfection. Rather than scolding yourself for not being perfect, be kind to yourself. Allow yourself the freedom to make mistakes at helping. Few mistakes that a helper can make have serious consequences for the person you're helping. If you have any doubt, though, seek consultation before you recommend something that might be harmful.

Be your own repair crew. Learn from your mistakes so you can repair them and avoid future mistakes.

Be patient. The person in a troubled marriage got there over several years. You can say nothing that will instantaneously end the marriage turmoil. Change takes time. Be patient with the person you are helping and with yourself.

Look to God. God not only knows what must be done to help the other person, but He also knows what you need to make you a better disciple of Jesus Christ. God provided a person for you to help to mold your character. Look to God to see what He is teaching you.

A positive attitude is vital to you as a helper and to those you try to help. It isn't power of positive thinking or New Age mental self-delusion. Rather, a positive attitude is a practical expression of faith working through love. A positive attitude is an external sign of the power of discipleship working within. It is learning that not everything turns out as we might wish, but we can still trust the Lord. "The Lord gave and the Lord has taken away; may the name of the Lord be praised" (Job 1:21b).

CHAPTER ELEVEN

USE YOUR OWN MARRIAGE AS A POSITIVE MODEL

"Why can't I do it? Jimmy does it," I wailed repeatedly throughout my early years.

My mother would simply look at me. "Copy the good things people do. Don't copy the bad things."

From newborn infancy, we are designed to copy others' behavior. We learn how and when to behave by copying others. We learn what we should be afraid of, and when not to be afraid, by copying others. When children are exposed to adults who talk one way but act another—such as saying, "It's good for you to eat your spinach," but not eating any spinach themselves—the children learn quickly also to talk a good game but not play the game themselves.

Having a good model is extremely important in growing up. Norman Garmazy studied children he called "indestructibles."[1] These children were reared with poor environments, broken homes, welfare, crime, few rewards for staying in school, and little encouragement for to become productive adults. Yet the "indestructibles" were exceptionally well adjusted. How did they develop positively in spite of their poor environment? Almost every "indestructible" had a person who served as an excellent role model. It might have been an older child, a sport coach, a pastor, or a neighbor; but the children overcame horrible backgrounds by observing a good model and copying the good behavior.

What Is a Good Model?

A good model is usually someone who has attributes we value. The model might be attractive, intelligent, successful at business, or powerful. The key element is that a model is strong in some way that we would like to be strong.

In addition, a model is someone with whom we can identify. The model might be similar to us in important ways or might be like we *would like to be.* Regardless, there must be a sense of identification.

Good models show us how to do the right behavior at the right time. When we are primed to learn, if a good model steps forward and shows us how to deal with a situation, we absorb the behavior like a cultivated garden soaks up a long, slow rain.

A good model also shows us that the desirable behavior will probably be rewarded. The model might experience external rewards of praise, gifts, affection, or money, or internal rewards of godly character. Rewards we cherish have the most impact on us.

Your Marriage Can Be a Good Model

In the Right Place at the Right Time

If you have attributes your friend values, have qualities that he or she can identify with, show how to deal with a problem that is relevant, and demonstrate that good behavior will be rewarded, then you can be a powerful model. Usually, a friend struggling with marital difficulties has his or her psychological radar active to detect a good marital model; if you have a helping, loving, caring relationship with the friend, you can be that model. Even if you are not married, you can draw on your experience with your family or with other families you know well to suggest good models that your friend can copy.

The timing is right. A friend in pain over marital trouble looks for solutions. He or she wants to see how to produce positive personal qualities and to receive the rewards of love in action. If your marriage radiates faith working through love and if you have personal qualities that your friend can admire and identify with, then your friend may copy your solutions. That is an awesome responsibility but a wonderful opportunity to use your marriage as a witness for the Lord.

Examining Your Own Marriage to See What You Model Well

Using modeling effectively in counseling. To be an effective model, point out explicitly what your friend might learn from you. Without your pointing to noteworthy behavior, your friend may focus on your clothes, your hairstyle, the way you talk, or even some behaviors you aren't very proud of. (We all seem to have some of those.) For example, to promote modeling, say, "Notice the way we communicate. After we've talked for a while, we'll discuss what you observed."

Using your marriage as an effective model of marriage. Even if your marriage is perfect for you, it won't fit anyone else. But even if your marriage isn't perfect, it has some strong parts. If copied by your friend, those strengths could help. To discern which parts of your marriage can help others, determine what others see in your marriage. Determine your marriage's strengths and weaknesses. The scriptural pattern for marriage is to demonstrate faith working through love. Do you model faith? Do you rely on the Lord? What would others say about your faith? Can they see it? Do you model work? Do you think about your marriage, child rearing, job, and duties at church and then carry out the fruits of your thinking by systematically working? Do you strive to live your faith and love in every relationship? Do you do the work of prayer, Bible study, daily devotions? Would others describe you as a hard worker? Do you model love? Do you see the value in others and let them know what you see? Do you criticize and devalue others? Do you point out the positive, hoping to build up the other person by showing what you value? Do you put down others, especially when you are feeling incompetent or discouraged? Do you treat the hard-to-love people you meet with love just as you do the easy-to-love people?

Faith working through love in your marriage. How does the pattern of Christian discipleship show up in your marriage? Can someone see plainly how you are living out Christian discipline?

Think of specific times when you and your spouse showed a good example of faith, of working on your marriage, of valuing love. Every professional counselor uses stories and analogies in his or her counseling. Those stories aren't spontaneous. They're prepared ahead of time, so they can be examined to see whether the stories are actually helpful. Prepare several examples where you demonstrated faith working through love and *write them in your journal* so that you have the examples ready when you need them. (In fact, if you write those stories *now,* you'll be sure they are done. If you put them off until later, you may forget.)

When You Examine Your Own Marriage

When you examine your marriage, you may see parts that you are not happy with. Don't condemn yourself for your sins or imperfections. Confess them to the Lord and receive forgiveness. In psychology, self-examination is often an end in itself or is thought to promote growth. In Christianity, though, self-examination should lead to confession, repentance, and forgiveness, which frees us to be better disciples of Christ.

When to Use Your Marriage as a Model

You can use your marriage as a model for your friend at any time, but three times are particularly powerful. Use modeling to attract friends who need help, to make a point during helping, and to inspire and educate people who merely see you casually.

To Attract Help-Seekers

Be a magnet. Your marriage is a magnet, attracting people who want your help. People with strained marriages search for relief. They want to believe in marriage, but they can't seem to make a difference in their own marriages. So they look for friends whose marriages are successful and ask them questions. If your marriage is functioning well, you are likely to be asked for help.

Listen, then question. After listening to the person's story, ask your friend what he or she would like you to do. That may elicit a comment such as, "You and your wife always seem so affectionate. How do you keep the romance alive after being married so long?" Or, "You and your husband seem to work together so well at dealing with your children. I can't seem to agree with my husband on how to discipline the children and wondered what your secret was."

Get the specifics. Specific comments from your friend reveal what he or she is primed to copy. Listen and use your marriage to affect the parts of the marriage that your friend wants to change.

During Helping

Promote memory. Throughout your helping, use examples to cement your main points into your friend's memory. Public speakers illustrate their talks with stories, examples, jokes, and concrete illustrations. Writers pen anecdotes, interviews, and dialogues to make the story come alive. Your most vivid stories will describe your own experiences. Those stories have the ring of truth because they actually happened to you, and your friend can look at your life to see that the stories are valid.

Stay humble. Don't treat your story as THE ANSWER, which comes across as bragging and drives friends away.

Select stories well. People seeking help don't want the conversation to focus on you. They want to talk about their troubles. So keep a balance. Only use personal examples to make an important point, not as the basis for your conversation.

Don't seek to make carbon copies. Don't try to make others' marriages similar to your own. Each person's marriage is different. Still, pick illustrations from your marriage that speak to your troubled friend.

An example. Fromma and Leo had been married only weeks when Fromma appeared on Gina's doorstep. The disagreement over the trash (see chapter 5) hadn't even come up yet. Over coffee, Fromma complained of differences between her and Leo. The latest difference was Leo's preoccupation with basketball. He had always played pick-up basketball, but his games hadn't intruded on his and Fromma's relationship. That morning, Leo and Fromma had argued over Leo's adamant statement that he was entering a two-on-two tournament the following month.

"I didn't know he was so eaten up with basketball. It's more important than I am. He just isn't the man I married," she concluded. "I feel duped. I want my money back—if I only thought that was possible."

Gina examined her cup. "I know it's not the same," she said tentatively, "but when Nick and I married, we had some misunderstandings too. Through our three years of dating, he seemed so laid back and relaxed. We'd go on weekend trips and just do things spontaneously. Then, one month after we married, I suggested that we go to the mountains for a picnic. He got agitated and started pacing around the house. I guess he was under a lot of stress, but it scared me with him pacing and wringing his hands."

Gina looked up into Fromma's eyes. "He told me he didn't have time to go to the mountains. By one month of marriage, I could see that he was a lot more ambitious and committed to his work than I had thought while we dated. The refusal to go to the mountains seemed like a major rejection—one that confirmed my biggest fear: he didn't love me and he had pretended to treat me as important to lure me into marriage. I thought he had run up his true colors on the flagpole."

Gina paused. "What'd you do?" asked Fromma.

"Oh, I did what you're doing. We talked about it but didn't resolve anything. I finally went to see a friend. She told me about her many disillusionments in her first year of marriage. After that I didn't feel so bad. Turned out almost everyone I talked to after that had been disillusioned in their first year. At least I had company."

"I guess I have been feeling like I was the only one ever to be disillusioned in marriage. It isn't easy, though, and I don't like it. Not a bit."

"I didn't like it either. No one does. It's like planning a vacation to Mexico for years and getting on the wrong plane, which ends up in Switzerland. It's a shock, but Switzerland is interesting too."

"That's how I feel. I got on the wrong plane, which landed in Podunk. The most interesting part of Podunk is sitting on the porch, drinking sweet tea, and listening to the bug zapper."

"Disillusionments are common during the first year. Most people get over them because they eventually discover that the person they married is still a valuable person. Did you discover any positive parts of Leo that you didn't know before?"

Fromma paused, then smiled. "Funny. He's so sentimental. He reads poetry. I never knew that before we got married. In fact, he even wrote me a poem the other day."

"It sounds like you have a lot to discover about him and that you've merely touched the surface. You'll find both positive and negative as you get to know each other—if you keep your perspective and don't focus on the negative."

Your Daily Witness

People see you as a couple and see how you talk to each other. Your daily behavior gives a clear picture of what marriage can be. Kirby and I don't *try* to "show off" our marriage in public. Nonetheless, we love each other and we show each other. Sometimes others observe this. We lead a newly married couples group and were surprised when several couples commented on my putting my arm around Kirby in church. They noticed the way we exchange smiles and catch each other's eye even when we are across the room from each other. We were both surprised and moved—I confess: I got misty and choked up—when one talented young couple dedicated a love song to us in a recent talent show. Acting lovey-dovey isn't something we do for show. It's something we do for each other. But I'm glad people are blessed by seeing it.

How to Use Your Marriage as a Model

Follow these principles to use your marriage as an effective model.

Principles

Don't tell war stories. Look for the positive. Everyone has both positive and negative stories they could tell about marriage. There may be times for telling the negative—such as if you or someone you know faced a trial and emerged victorious—but when a friend is looking for help isn't the time for a story with an unhappy ending. Your focus on negative events could make the friend lose faith that the problems can be dealt with. It could demotivate the friend from working to change the marriage. It could erode the sense of love in the friend's marriage by making it seem that failures in love are everywhere—even in relationships that the person considers good (like yours).

Be efficient. Point out only one thing to look for at a time. In the example above, Gina related only one example of her early disillusionment—one that had a positive ending. After she had told the story, she summarized the lesson she was making rather than trusting that Fromma would pick out the right lesson. She said, "It's like planning a vacation to Mexico for years and getting on the wrong plane, which ends up in Switzerland. It's a shock, but Switzerland is interesting too. . . . Disillusionments are common during the first year. Most people get over them because they eventually discover that the person they married is still a valuable person." Like Gina, aim your story at a single point, then make your point clearly.

Types of Models

You may think that your marriage cannot be a model for others unless you have a perfect marriage. Not true. For almost everyone, parts of marriage work well. If you tell your friend about those parts, you are using what psychologists call a mastery model.

You can also serve as a positive model even when things go wrong. If you deal with mistakes or failures, you can serve as a coping model. If your faith is challenged and you battle through, you show how to manage crisis. If you begin marriage by devaluing your partner but later learn how to value him or her, again you serve as a coping model. Sometimes people can identify more with a coping model than with a mastery model.

Even if you don't feel that you have mastery over some aspect of your marriage, you can still model growth. A growth model may not have problems to deal with but can give evidence of growth in faith or love that can inspire others to greater growth.

Modeling Good Behavior: Some Examples

As Gina's relationship with Fromma grew, Gina confided more about her marriage, which gave Fromma many ideas to apply in her marriage. Here are some excerpts from later conversations. Importantly, Gina didn't often self-disclose; so when she did, Fromma listened and learned.

Closeness

Fromma said, "Leo and I have different needs for intimacy. I think it's because of the work we do. I work with many women, and we talk throughout the day. Sometimes, I feel as if I'm talked out when I come home. Leo's work as a design engineer is mostly asocial; so when he gets home, he wants to talk and talk."

Gina smiled. "Sounds like you have similar needs for intimacy, but you meet your needs in different places."

Fromma said, "I guess you're right. But I can't do anything about my job, and he can't change his either, so we're stuck."

"Early in our marriage, Nick and I ran into something like this. After Nicky's birth, I had a hard time adjusting to life at home. Instead of relating to adults, I related to dirty diapers and a crying infant all day. By the time Nick got home, I was ready for a cage. I was all over him like a wet blanket as soon as he stepped in the house."

"I guess he felt like I'm feeling now," said Fromma.

"It sounds similar. Nick couldn't change his job, and we agreed that my staying home with Nicky was best, so we felt stuck. After a while, though, Nick began to fiddle with his schedule. He told some of his work buddies that he was under pressure, and he spent more time working and less time chatting while at work. He also withdrew from two church committees so he didn't socialize so much when he wasn't at work. I felt guilty at first, like I was making him change his whole life because I needed time together. He reassured me, though, that he *wanted* to be with me more than he wanted to be with his work buddies or to serve on church committees. It meant a lot. After six months, we had settled into a new routine and felt balanced again."

Respectful Conflict

Fromma was in tears. She and Leo had an argument during the morning as Leo left for a business trip to Boston, so they didn't resolve their differences. After Fromma returned from work, she dropped by Gina's and described the situation, which brought on the tears.

"What I hate the worst," Fromma said, "is the way I yelled at him. I was frustrated that his plane was about to leave and we couldn't agree, so I blurted out some insult about him caring more about his job than about me. He got angry and told me to knock it off. I ran to the bedroom and locked the door. He stood at the door and called, but I wouldn't answer. Finally, he had to go. I felt like I was doing wrong, but I felt angry and wanted to hurt him at the same time. Does that make sense?"

Gina nodded.

"After he went to the car, I ran out, but he had already left. Now, I worry. What if his plane wrecks? I'd never forgive myself for being such a jerk. Have you ever done anything like that, Gina?"

Gina thought. "Not exactly. Nick and I have had disagreements. As stress goes up and available time decreases, aggravations increase. After we noticed this, we started telling each other when we were under stress. If something big comes up, instead of dropping it on the other person at a pressure-filled time, we say, 'I really need to go on a walk.' We talk a lot when we walk around the neighborhood. Anyway, once one of us requests a walk, the other might say, 'I'm under a lot of pressure now, but I have a deadline this week, so we can walk on Friday. Can it wait until then?' That's the way we deal with last-minute conflicts. It works for us."

Working on the Marriage

"We've lost the romance," said Fromma after a year of marriage. "During the first year, we did a lot of romantic things. He wrote poems to me, took me out to eat, went to Virginia Beach. Both of us were so spontaneous. Now, we hardly ever do anything."

"You're disappointed."

"I am. I always dreamed of a romantic marriage, forever fresh. You and Nick seem to have a romantic marriage. How do you do it?"

"I've never thought much about it. We work at it. Nick takes time to think about our marriage, and I really appreciate him for that. He remembers the special days—our anniversary, my birthday, Valentine's Day, Mother's Day—and he does something special. But he also does creative things."

"Like what?"

Gina hesitated. "I know you'll think this is crazy, but it was so funny at the time. Listen, you can't ever tell anybody that I told you this. Nick would die. Anyway, last month, I came home from grocery shopping. I always shop for groceries on Tuesdays. When I walked in with an arm full of groceries, he was standing in the middle of the living room wearing nothing but clear plastic wrap. He said he had read about someone recommending it for wives, and he thought he'd give it a try. After I got over my shock, we both laughed for twenty minutes. Anyway, it was a surprise. He stayed home over lunch too, so we had some special time while the kids were in school."

"I can't see Leo doing that."

"I couldn't imagine Nick doing it either. That's why it was such a good idea. It took me off guard. He worked extra that afternoon to make up for lost time, of course, but knowing he's willing to do things like that makes me happy."

"Maybe I ought to try the plastic wrap gambit. Show up at Leo's office in a raincoat and plastic. What do you think?"

Gina smiled. "I don't think there's a patent on the idea. Whatever you do, if it's special and shows you've thought about it, it says to Leo that you think he's important. I'm not good at coming up with the zany ideas like Nick does, but I keep my eye out for sexy nighties, and I surprise Nick by wearing those some nights."

Fromma laughed. "You both work on keeping your marriage alive."

"That's important. It won't stay alive unless you put in effort."

Summary

Gina and Nick didn't have a perfect marriage, but they worked hard to make it as good as possible. In helping Fromma, Gina used some things she and Nick did to suggest ways that Fromma could help her marriage. Gina used her marriage effectively.

- She presented both a mastery and a coping model at times.
- She used occasional stories about her marriage and only when those stories fit into the conversation.
- She didn't try to present her marriage as perfect, and she clearly pointed out ways that Fromma could learn.
- She listened carefully to what Fromma said so the advice she gave would be well targeted.

Fromma and Leo were beginning a voyage that Gina and Nick had begun earlier. The first year was turbulent. Gina's skilled use of her experiences probably helped Fromma avoid even rockier parts of the marital journey—at least to the extent that she copied the good things and not the bad things.

CHAPTER TWELVE

STAY COOL IN MARITAL CRISES

"Leo and I are going to get a divorce," said Fromma, and the thin line of control crumbled. She wept loudly, shoulders bobbing so that the tea Gina had offered her when she showed up at ten o'clock sloshed unnoticed on her nightclothes.

Nick had gone back to bed, but Gina was afraid that Fromma's wails would wake Nick and the children.

"Let me take that," said Gina, trying to rescue the cup and saucer before they completely emptied.

"I feel like—" Fromma gave a violent hiccup, "the lowest form of life on planet earth." Fromma held onto the cup, creating a minor tug-of-war between herself and Gina.

Gina finally pulled the cup free. Fromma wiped her dripping nose with her fingers, then wiped her hand on her nightgown.

Gina scurried to the table and jerked tissues from the box. Fromma ran her hands through her hair and pulled savagely. She struck her head with both fists. Gina could see ripped-loose strands of hair between Fromma's fingers. Fromma pounded her head again and screamed in frustration. Gina eased onto the couch next to Fromma. She reached up to hold one wrist and placed the other arm around Fromma's shoulders.

"Oh Lord," Gina prayed. "Please enter into this moment and bring Your peace. Lord, calm us."

As Gina prayed, Fromma stopped beating her head and face and sat with shoulders hunched, eyes and nose dripping onto her nightgown.

"Honey, you're really in a bad way," Gina said.

Fromma nodded. She sniffed and wiped at her nose.

"You're angry at Leo and yourself." Gina rubbed Fromma's back soothingly.

Fromma nodded again.

"Something happened. Something big?" Gina put a note of question in her voice. "Something painful? Something you *need* to talk about?"

"Had a fight," came Fromma's voice, weak.

Better than the wailing, thought Gina. She rubbed Fromma's back some more.

"I hit him in the eye with a dish and it cut his face. He was so angry with me that he slammed his fist through the wall and yelled for me to 'get out of *his* house.' It's not *his* house. We've been married a year and a half. It's mine too now. But I was so mad and he was so mad that I needed to leave so we wouldn't hurt each other again."

Gina touched the red mark on Fromma's cheek. "Did he hit you?"

Fromma touched her own cheek. "No, he only slammed the wall. I just hate myself. I hit myself. I've done it since I was a kid." She screamed in frustration again.

Gina held Fromma's shoulders firmly, and Fromma slumped.

Fromma said, "I snatched up my keys and stormed out of the house. I've been driving around for about fifteen minutes. I ought to go home and confront the—" She swore. "Then I thought I'd better come and talk about it first. I know we're going to get a divorce, but I refuse to let him have the house too. He's so self-centered. He never thinks of anybody but himself." She swore again, several times.

"That's what started the fight. He can't think of anyone but himself. He wanted to enter a 10K race even though we've been planning a trip to Mother's for three weeks. We've been doing so *well* for about three months. Getting along. Happy. Making love more. Everything. Then he has to mess it up."

"You feel like he's spoiled your marriage when it was improving."

"Right. I thought we were getting a handle on marriage. Was I ever wrong."

"And now you feel that you're going to get a divorce."

Fromma blew her nose into the tissue, folded it, and wiped her eyes. "He'll never forgive me for hitting him with the dish. It's hopeless."

"Before the blowup tonight, though, things were going well."

"They were! Now I've blown it. I deserve misery. I'm worthless garbage. I've never been worth anything. I deserve a bully like him. Maybe my fate is to live with him forever and to have to put up with his selfishness."

"I think you should tell me about tonight's argument."

What Are Crises?

Definition

Fromma and Leo are in crisis. Fromma brought her crisis to Gina, which created a crisis for Gina too. A crisis is a temporary period, usually triggered by a traumatic event, in which a person is upset and distressed because the person doesn't know how to act.

Examples

In marriage, possible crises are legion, but some situations lead to crises more than others. Traumatic events, by themselves, don't produce crises. Two people may experience the same trauma. One copes; one doesn't. Some traumatic events are discovering an unexpected pregnancy; making a job decision that has serious implications for the marriage; sudden changes in life or sudden realization of gradual change of life; an event that dramatizes the demands made by a spouse who is depressed, physically diseased, or troubled; out-of-control conflict; a physically or sexually abusive incident; discovery of incest by one partner; a serious disillusionment or violation of expectations; or a discovered or revealed affair.

Types of Crises

Crow said that crises come in three colors: yellow (anxiety), red (anger), and black (depression)—reflecting the emotional mood of the crisis.[1] For example, examine the traumatic events I mentioned earlier. Most have strong elements of fear (yellow) because trauma casts doubt on the future. Conflicts, though, are shaded red because anger dominates. Violations of expectations take on a black shadow as the future is obscured. In each crisis, regardless of the main mood, people are upset, distressed, and uncertain.

Stages of a Developing Crisis

A crisis may occur almost instantaneously or may build slowly over time with a crescendo of seriousness in the final stages. Regardless of the speed at which the crisis develops, though, the crisis passes through the same seven stages prior to some resolution (see graphic on next page).[2]

An event (Stage 1) threatens the person (Stage 2). Some people react to the threat by denial; others by intrusiveness (Stage 3). Denial numbs. The person ignores the threat. Each step closer to disaster is denied until the threat is so imminent that the person must acknowledge it. Intrusiveness consumes. The threat and its catastrophic implications intrude into thought and behavior. The person worries about the impending crisis, thinks about it, engages in ritual attempts to solve the problem, and can't get the problem out of his mind. Neither denial nor intrusiveness solves the problem, and the threat mounts.

Most people try to solve the problem (Stage 4), and they often succeed using approaches they typically employ to deal with similar threats. Crises don't yield to habitual problem-solving tactics. As the person tries and tries again, tension mounts. He or she employs other problem-solving strategies, which also fail (Stage 5). Tension builds further as the person runs out of options.

Emotions rage (Stage 6). Fear permeates every crisis. *What if I can't solve this? What will I do next? Will I have a nervous breakdown? Will I lose control?* Thoughts such as these flood the person's mind. Anger at both the situation and the self bubbles up. Anger whips the person into a problem-solving fury—a last-gasp attempt to solve the problem and remove the threat. Depression mingles into the emotional mire of a crisis as the person is repeatedly defeated in problem-solving efforts and senses helplessness, hopelessness, and powerlessness, which are the core elements of depression. The person develops a negative view of others, the experiences, and the future. One emotion usually dominates, giving the crisis the yellow, red, or black tinge.

As the person tries progressively more solutions and each is proved inadequate to the task, a breaking point is approached (Stage 7). Emotions intensify. Fear becomes panic. Anger becomes violence. Depression becomes helpless apathy. A person may cry out for help dramatically—asking for help emotionally, making suicide gestures, or developing psychological symptoms. If the breaking point is reached, social relationships and psychological and emotional functioning may crumble.

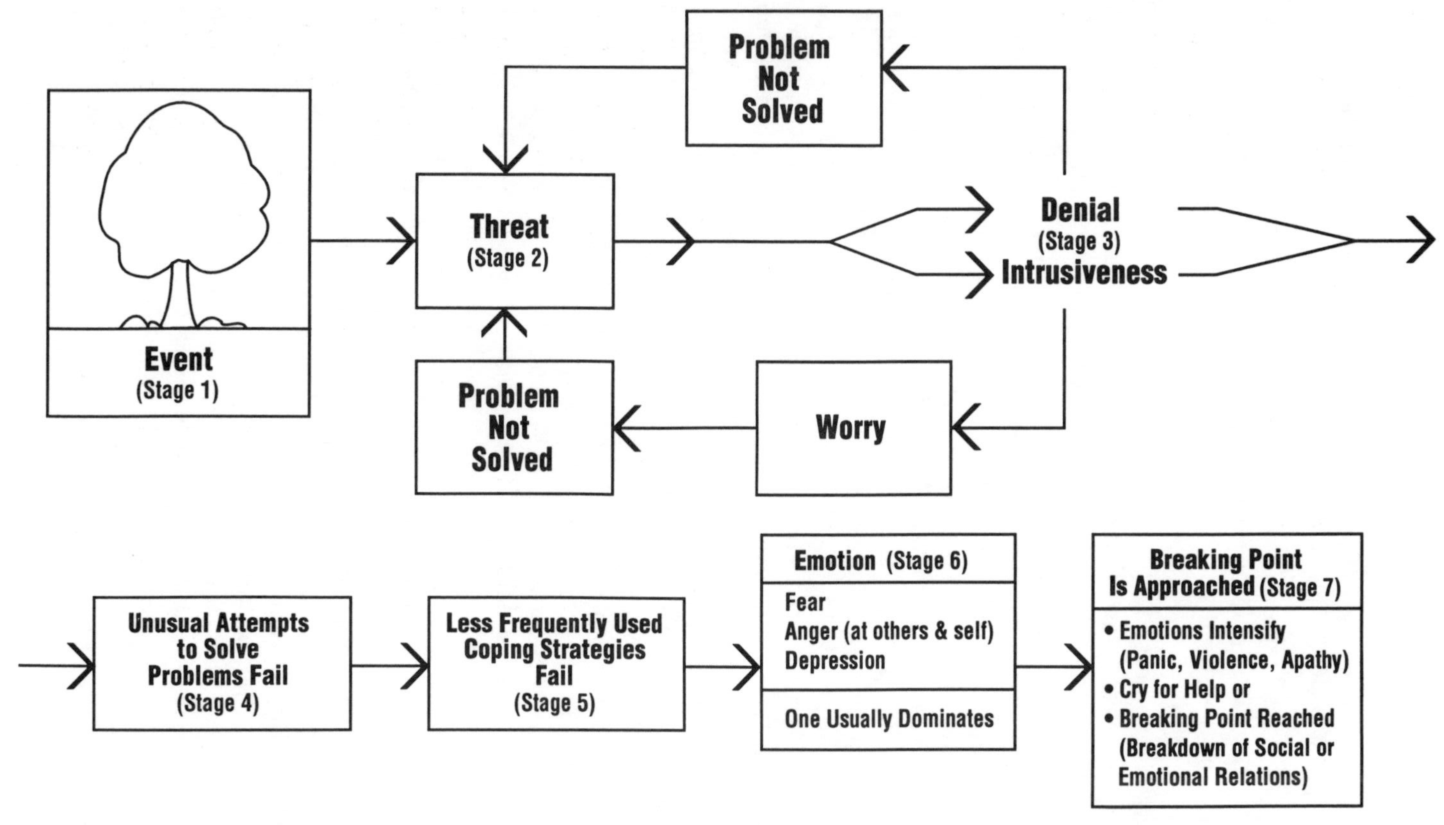

Event
(Stage 1)
Threat
(Stage 2)
Problem
Not
Solved
Denial
(Stage 3)
Intrusiveness
Worry
Problem
Not
Solved
Unusual Attempts
to Solve
Problems Fail
(Stage 4)
Less Frequently Used
Coping Strategies
Fail
(Stage 5)
Emotion (Stage 6)
Fear
Anger (at others & self)
Depression
One Usually Dominates
Breaking Point
Is Approached (Stage 7)
• Emotions Intensify
(Panic, Violence, Apathy)
• Cry for Help or
• Breaking Point Reached
(Breakdown of Social or
Emotional Relations)

Eventually, the crisis will resolve. Either the person will solve the problem, the threat will dissolve due to outside influences, a helper will help solve the problem, or the person will escape the problem by a social or psychological breakdown. After the crisis is resolved, people may experience flashbacks, or vivid (and stressful) memories or dreams of the crisis. Resolution of the crisis depends on the severity of the precipitating event and the person's personal and social resources. The resolution usually involves change. Having gone through the crisis, the person is a different person with powerfully different experiences. Return to normal functioning involves some working through of the crisis—and its meaning for the person—to some psychological completion. Most crises will be resolved to completion in four to six weeks.

Ways of Coping with Crisis

Problem-focused versus emotion-focused coping. Lazarus and Folkman have identified two general styles that people use to cope with stress and crises.[3] Problem-focused coping strategies attempt to change the problem directly by intentionally changing or avoiding the situation. Examples are seeking information that allows accurate expectations and making action plans. Emotion-focused coping strategies, on the other hand, are usually employed when problem-focused coping strategies are not thought to be possible. The person doesn't try to solve the problem directly but tries to control his or her emotions by relaxing, distracting himself or herself from the problem, denying that a problem exists, minimizing the threat, or using wishful thinking.

Which style of coping is better? At first blush, it might seem that problem-focused coping is a better way to handle a crisis. It isn't that simple. First, some people may simply prefer emotion-focused coping and consequently have not practiced problem-focused coping. In crises, problem-focused coping strategies seem foreign and ineffective. Second, the nature of the situation is extremely important. The importance of the situation was dramatized by research of my colleague at Virginia Commonwealth University, Stephen Auerbach, along with Thomas Strentz.[4] They investigated the ways that people coped with a simulated, but realistic crisis: being held hostage.

Thirty-nine airline flight attendants and eighteen pilots participated as hostages in a four-day exercise staged by the FBI to train negotiators and swat team personnel. Six exercises were run in Strentz and Auerbach's 1988 study—two exercises for each of three types of training. Two groups were trained in problem-focused coping. They were shown ways that hostages could help each other during captivity, how to interact with their captors, how to communicate using the prisoner-of-war tap code, how to gather intelligence via smell and sound. Two groups were trained in emotion-focused coping. They were told of the range of emotions they would likely experience and were taught to use deep breathing, relaxation, thought stopping, and distracting imagery to control their fear, anger, and depression. Two groups served as the experimental controls. They were given information about the history of the field exercises and other matters that weren't relevant to how to cope with their captivity.

Five FBI agents dressed as masked terrorists shot (with blanks) and "killed" two other agents and kidnapped the airline personnel. (The killing was so realistic that several airline personnel later said they thought they had really been kidnapped.) Airline personnel were kept prisoner for three days while terrorists negotiated with FBI negotiators. Negotiations eventually broke down and the swat team burst violently into the room firing noisy blanks. Burst blood bags contributed to a gory massacre scene. The rescue was affected.

Who fared the best during the crisis? Most people used some problem-focused and some emotion-focused coping strategies, but people tended to use more of the strategies in which they had been trained. The hostages who were trained in and used emotion-focused coping coped the best with their captivity. The hostages who had been trained in problem-focused coping fared worse on some measures than did controls, who received no training in coping. Generally, when there was no real chance of escape, emotion-focused coping provided the only effective way to cope. People who persisted in thinking of escape upset themselves. Effective coping depended more on training and on the situation than on the hostages' personalities.

Symptoms

Crises breed disorganization, disequilibrium, vulnerability, defensiveness, breakdown in coping, and a loss of sense of self-sufficiency.[5] In crisis, people feel they have lost the ability to cope normally because their coping mechanisms seem inadequate to deal with the threat. People feel panic, emotion, confusion, and inability to decide. Depending on the point of the crisis trajectory where the person asks for your help, you might see more or less extreme emotional reactions.

When a friend asks for help, he or she is generally quite open to influence. Repeated failures of normal coping attempts have eroded self-sufficiency.

Crises can be broken into two periods—the initial stages in which first aid is necessary and the resolution stages in which the person must reestablish normal living and work through the crisis to understand its meaning. The second period resembles normal counseling, so I'll spend most of the remainder of this chapter outlining how to administer crisis first aid.

How to Give Crisis First Aid

First aid is care given first—minutes to hours after the person feels in full-blown crisis. The goal of crisis first aid is to restore the person to non-panicked functioning. This is generally done by giving support, reducing the risk of harm, restoring some equilibrium, helping the person regain some sense of balance and control, giving the person an immediate game plan, focusing the person on the Lord, and linking the person to secondary crisis support people (such as a pastor or counselor).

In crisis first aid, be more active, directive, and goal-oriented than in crisis resolution or long-term helping. Generally, people in crisis want a solution. Fast. But don't be lured into immediate problem-solving without listening to the entire story and assessing your friend's emotions and attempts at coping. Help your friend calm down and make immediate decisions. You may need to help directly—call a spouse, drive your friend somewhere, or provide shelter. Determine what can be put off until more thoughtful decisions can be made. Before you finish first-aid helping, try to mobilize personal coping resources and the person's social resources as well.

Rule #1: Stay Calm, Manage Your Own Crisis

While your friend describes his or her crisis, you'll get pulled into the emotion—seeing yellow, red, or black—and you'll feel a sense of urgency. Don't interrupt to tell your own story or make suggestions about how to handle the problems. Don't ignore either facts or feelings. Don't judge or take sides. Rather, calm your own rising emotion and panic. Employ emotion-focused coping strategies (relaxing, praying for calm, breathing deeply, slowing yourself, telling yourself that you have time to think and not to become swept into the other person's panic).

Rule #2: Calm Your Friend

Once you have yourself in hand, calm your friend. Buy time so that more reasoned decisions can be made. Don't make immediate decisions. Instead of having your friend blurt out his or her story, offer coffee, tea, or soda. Move casually and appear relaxed, even if you don't feel relaxed. (Naturally if someone reports a situation that must be acted on immediately—such as an injury or potentially harmful situation—act speedily, but generally crises don't require split-second action.) Have your friend sit. Speak softly, which will help your friend speak more quietly and less hurriedly. If emotions run high, ask questions that require your friend to think. Give choices, such as "Would you rather talk in here or go outside on the patio?" Whatever causes thought lowers emotion. If you cannot understand your friend because he or she is too disorganized or confused, pause and say, "I want to understand you, but I can't. Start at the beginning and tell me what happened." Prompt your friend with questions if he or she omits crucial events.

Rule #3: Listen Before You Give Advice

When you listen to a person who is in crisis, you are sometimes overwhelmed with the emotion pouring out. Ask yourself, "What's the problem?" If you can't tell what the problem is, you won't be able to help solve it. Early in your conversation, determine whether someone might be harmed—either your friend or some other person (perhaps even yourself). A primary objective of crisis first aid is to ensure people's safety. Therefore, know the facts. Ask open-ended, not yes-no, questions. You'll learn more by letting your friend tell what is going on than by trying to guide him or her. Reassure when concerns are easily addressed, but don't give too much reassurance, which weakens your credibility because you are perceived offering advice when you do not understand the problem.

Rule #4: Think

Your friend's thoughts have been directed down a narrow channel. As he or she tells the story, your thoughts get directed down the same channel. Don't get tunnel vision looking down that channel.

Don't leave issues or obstacles to action unexplored because the person dismisses those alternatives. You might see things that a person who is involved in the issue cannot see. Don't accept a jumble of needs without clarifying them. Get the person to set priorities. Find out what must be done immediately and what can be put off until later.

Rule #5: Explore Alternatives

Don't try to solve every problem *now.* Use your friend's priorities to guide your focus. Suggest possible solutions, but be careful. Actions will have consequences, so explore with the person the likely ramifications of all solutions before the person decides to carry out a solution. Encourage the person not to make long-term decisions (such as whether to divorce or separate) now. Instead, emphasize immediate problems (such as where to stay, what to do about deadlines, whether to go home). Explore the obstacles to actions rather than just talking about actions and their consequences.

Rule #6: Choose a Course of Action

People often begin to describe the crisis with a catastrophic conclusion. Recall that Fromma began by saying, "Leo and I are going to get a divorce." Instead of trying immediately to dissuade the person from the most catastrophic possibility, acknowledge that it is indeed one solution, but don't accept it as the only solution. In crisis, give advice but don't coerce your friend to accept your advice, regardless of how convinced you are that your advice is sound and your friend's planned actions portend disaster. Don't emotionally blackmail your friend. Explore the options and let your friend make his or her own decisions.

Rule #7: Repeat the Plan

Have your friend repeat the plan before leaving. What seems to have been a clear course of action to both of you while he or she was under your calming influence may appear stupid and harmful five minutes after leaving you. Or your friend may feel confused and not recall making a decision. To help your friend remain committed to his or her decision, have him or her repeat the plan. (This will also help you see whether the plan has been understood.)

Rule #8: Follow Up

Don't assume that your friend will follow through on the plan. Crises often debilitate and immobilize well-meaning people. Get your friend to agree to allow you to phone him or her the next morning or the next day to check on how things went. Establish a concrete plan for the person to link up with an after-care helper, such as the pastor or a counselor. Make that part of the plan and have your friend repeat his or her intentions to contact someone specific for longer-term help.

An Example of Crisis First Aid

Let's go back to Fromma's crisis. Fromma had thrown a dish at Leo, cutting his cheek, and Leo had slammed his fist through the wall. Let's see how Gina applied the rules of crisis first aid.

Rule #1: Stay Calm, Manage Your Own Crisis

When Fromma arrived in obvious crisis, Gina stalled. She fixed Fromma tea, which allowed Gina to think about how she might deal with the crisis. Later, Fromma began to lose control of her emotions, striking herself in the head and face. Gina moved closer and prayed for calm for herself and Fromma.

Rule #2: Calm Your Friend

Gina calmed Fromma by giving her tea, having her sit, providing a tissue, sitting beside Fromma, rubbing her back, speaking softly, and praying for calm. People in crisis don't calm down immediately merely because we tell them to. Calming must be continued. As the person tells the story, he or she may again become upset and need to be calmed.

Rule #3: Listen Before You Give Advice

Gina encouraged Fromma to talk, then listened actively as Fromma told her story. She didn't give advice and asked only one closed-ended question ("Did he hit you?").

Rule #4:
Think

While Fromma was telling her story, Gina was listening carefully but also frantically thinking. Instead of trying to think of immediate solutions to Fromma's difficulty, she first satisfied herself that Fromma was not in physical danger. Then Gina estimated how much damage had been done to the marriage by the disagreement. She thought about the practical aspects of the problem. What needed to be decided immediately? Should Fromma go home? Could Fromma spend the night with Gina and Nick? What could be done about clothes tomorrow morning if Fromma spent the night? Should they call Leo and tell him where Fromma was? If so, how much danger was there that he might come to Gina and Nick's house and act violently?

Rule #5:
Explore Alternatives

After thirty minutes of active listening, Gina understood the crisis. She began to ask Fromma questions.

"Fromma," she began, "you've had a bad night. I guess you have some things to decide—practical things."

"Like what?"

"For a starter, we need priorities. What must you decide tonight?"

"I don't know."

Gina let Fromma think about it. "I need to tell Leo I'm not coming home tonight. I'll get a motel room. I should let him know."

"So you've decided that you aren't going home."

"We're going to get a divorce, so it doesn't make sense to go home."

"That's a weighty decision to come to with so little time spent considering it. It might be better to think about whether you really want to divorce and find out what Leo thinks and consider the consequences before jumping to that conclusion."

"I guess you're right, but it seems so hopeless."

"I know it does, but a lot of healing can go on."

"Anyway, I don't think I should go home tonight, and I suppose I should let Leo know."

"You can stay on our hide-a-bed, if you want. I know it'd be OK with Nick."

"Thanks."

The phone rang shrilly. And again.

Fromma and Gina looked at each other. "What if that's him?" said Fromma.

Gina asked, "Do you want me to answer it?"

Fromma nodded as the phone rang a fifth time.

Gina strode to the kitchen. "Hello."

In three minutes, she returned to the living room. Fromma was sitting on the edge of the couch.

"It was Leo. He said he was worried sick about you—that he had called everyone he could think of trying to find you. He said he was sorry and that he wanted to speak to you."

Fromma's eyes widened and her brow knitted. "What'd you say?"

"I told him you were safe here. I said I needed to talk to you and that you'd call him back in a while. He seemed relieved to know you were OK. He said you drove off at ninety miles an hour, and he was worried that something might have happened, especially when you didn't come back."

"Did he sound really concerned about me?" she said.

"He sounded truly relieved to know you were safe."

Rule #6:
Choose a Course of Action

For ten minutes, Gina and Fromma discussed what Fromma would say when she called Leo. Depending on how the conversation went, Fromma might indeed return home. Gina assured her that she was welcome to spend the night if she needed to.

With a deep breath and a shy smile, Fromma headed for the phone. While she and Leo talked, Gina cleaned and straightened the living room. In fifteen minutes, Fromma returned, eyes red. "I'm going home. He seemed genuinely sorry we argued."

Rule #7:
Repeat the Plan

"What are you going to do when you get home? Are you going to discuss it or put it off until tomorrow?" asked Gina.

"I don't know."

"It might be good to decide before you get home."

"Since the Bible says, 'Don't let the sun go down on your anger,' we ought to talk about it tonight, if we can."

"Probably a good decision. How about tomorrow? Are you going to see a counselor or Pastor Hank?"

"We could use some counseling, but I don't know what Leo might think. He might not want to go. Of course, after tonight—" She shrugged. "Who knows? He might."

"So what are you going to do?"

"I suppose I'll talk to Leo tonight or tomorrow about calling Pastor Hank and we'll see whether that will work."

Rule #8: Follow Up

"Do you mind if I give you a call tomorrow and see if you're OK?" asked Gina.

"That'd be great. It'll help me to talk about whatever comes up tonight too."

Secondary Crisis Helping

If you've tried to help the person connect with a counselor or pastor who can aid him or her in working through the meaning of the crisis—as Gina was able to do with Fromma—then you can rest easier about your role in secondary crisis helping. If you can't get the person to seek help of a counselor, though, you may be asked to provide support and help as the person tries to make sense of the meaning of the crisis.

In secondary crisis helping, like long-term helping, you'll listen actively and provide support, but you'll make direct suggestions less often than you did in first aid helping. Your goal is to help your friend return to daily functioning with some understanding of what led to the crisis, what happened during the crisis, what the meaning of the crisis was, and what might be done to avoid a similar crisis in the future.

Crisis counseling is an opportunity for people to seek help for a troubled marriage. Their vulnerability during the crisis usually makes them aware that they cannot repair their marriage alone; so it often opens the door for God to work in the marriage.

CHAPTER THIRTEEN

STICK WITH LONG-TERM PROBLEMS

Most of your helping won't be the whirlwind, emotional cyclone of crisis intervention. It will be steady, if somewhat gusty, long-term helping.

Crises differ in goals from long-term helping. In a crisis, the goal is to resolve the crisis quickly and restore a sense of coping to the friend; whereas in long-term helping, the goal is to stick with the friend and provide support while the person is trying to make lasting structural changes in the marriage. In a crisis, your emphasis is on tactics—here and now decisions about what to do next—while in long-term helping, your emphasis is on strategy—plans for a campaign. In a crisis, decision making is immediate. In long-term helping, decisions may be discussed for days or weeks before action is taken. In a crisis, the raging turmoil of volatile emotions threatens to overwhelm you. In long-term helping, the mood of dissatisfaction, depression, or helplessness seems to gnaw at your bones and de-energize you like a blanket of cold.

In most friendships, you may only rarely mention marriage. A friendship is often structured around a few activities—a Bible study, a sport, a place of work—and though conversation may range widely over many aspects of life, people often do not discuss other relationships with their friends when the other relationships are going well. Only when the other relationships turn sour do friends talk about them.

Your Focus in Long-Term Helping

In long-term helping with a friend, you'll explore marital difficulties. Try to understand marital problems in terms of failures in love; unwillingness to work on the marriage; or weaknesses in faith either in God, in the likelihood of making any change in the marriage, or in the marriage itself. Examine the marriage closely to see where the failures in love, work, or faith show up.

Do they show up in the Christian core of marriage—the Christian beliefs and values of the partners, the core beliefs of marriage, or the willingness of the partners to confess their faults and forgive the transgressions of the other person? Or do problems show up in the four areas that make up marital contentment—closeness, communication, conflict management, or cognition? Are complicating factors involved? Has trouble eroded either partner's commitment? The long-term perspective is aimed at helping identify the causes of the marital difficulties and building faith working through love at each area of the marriage that is affected.

To tackle long-term marriage problems changes the friendship. It opens a doorway into a new type of relationship. Sometimes walking through the doorway is like walking from the living room to the kitchen—no big deal. But sometimes the doorway is more like the one in Dorothy Gale's Kansas house that had been transported to the land of Oz by the cyclone. A different world lurked beyond the door, one populated with unknown creatures: wizards (who may in the end turn out to be humbugs), new (needy) friends, and witches to slay. Like Dorothy, we must decide whether to risk entering the land of Oz and then live the adventures that come our way. Many times we wish for the magic slippers that we can tap together and exit the friendship; but we're stuck in Oz with our friend until the quest is done, effortful and risky though it may be.

But first, we must pass through the doorway.

The Doorways to Long-term Helping

There are three usual doorways into long-term helping relationships: the request for help, your focus on the presenting problem, and good listening.

The Request for Help

The letter. Requests for help from family members often come via letter. Don't over-interpret the person's need when you receive an account of his or her marital difficulties. People usually put off writing until news has accumulated, then they compress the usually negative events into a few pages, often empowered by a crisis. Letters often make the marriage sound worse than it is. Don't panic. Phone and determine what's up.

The phone call. When you receive a phone call requesting help, often the friend is in the midst of a crisis and is seeking crisis first-aid. Sometimes, though, the friend has experienced long-term problems and has finally decided to confide in you and seek your help. Phone calls frustrate some helpers because they cannot see the person's face. For others, though, telephone helping is a godsend, allowing the helper to provide help while doing the dishes or some other task.

The visit. Visits might be drop-in visits from a nearby friend, appointments arranged in advance, or occasionally visits from distant friends who happen to be passing through your city. We have some dear friends who now live in a faraway state. They happened to be within a hundred miles of Richmond visiting relatives, so they called and asked if they could drive by. When we met with them, it quickly became clear that the wife was depressed. In an afternoon, we discussed many decisions the friends had to make, and they left determined to tackle the problems.

The conversation. When Jim called and suggested that we go to lunch together—the first time he had ever made such a suggestion—I suspected that he had something on his mind. Over spicy Chinese food, he looked around, as if checking to see whether the FBI might be listening with some covert spy device. "Helen and I are separated," he said. "I wanted to get your opinion." As it turned out, they reunited the next week but were left with severe marital problems to deal with. The lunch with Jim became the first step in a six-month consultation about how to deal with his deteriorating marriage.

Make It Easy to Request Help

We automatically think of some friends when we need help, but others never enter our minds. Why? Are you perceived as someone who will be warm, supportive, wise, and helpful? You'll probably often be asked for help. But other qualities scare friends away:

- Critical or judgmental of others,
- Always complaining about too much to do,
- Reluctant to discuss your own vulnerabilities,
- Self-absorbed.

To attract friends, be accessible.

Focus on the Presenting Problem

When your friend requests help, he or she is not committed to continue to consult you. Whether he or she asks for more help will depend less on whether you provide some earthshaking insight into the problem than whether you seem interested in your friend and communicate your love. Communicate your interest by focusing on the problem. Ask what happened. Find the facts. Ask about feelings. Explore problems.

Listen Actively

The third doorway into the long-term helping relationship is listening. Listen actively, not passively. Assure your friend that you understand the problem and support him or her in its solution. Most people think good listening is merely paying close attention to the speaker. Not true. A good listener talks almost as much as the talker, clarifying, encouraging the talker to continue, asking questions, reflecting what is said, trying to channel back the feelings that are being expressed, paraphrasing the content of the person's story, and at convenient points, summarizing a chunk of the story into a condensed version.

As your friend describes the marital problems and the events surrounding and leading up to the problems, occasionally—when it fits—put the problems into the context of failures in faith working through love. Ask how problems in separate areas affect each other (e.g., how poor communication affects intimacy, and vice versa). Expand the areas you inquire about until you have asked about the Christian core, the factors affecting contentment, complicating factors, and commitment.

Your Attitude

Battling long-standing marital problems demands the stamina of a marathon runner rather than, as with crises, the quickness of a sprinter. Develop a positive attitude for dealing with long-term problems. Staying renewed to fight the same battles, even when you aren't winning, requires dogged determination and good preparation.

Running the Marathon

To run the marathon, train regularly. Intersperse running with rest to allow sore muscles to heal. Eat lots of carbohydrates the last couple of days before the race to provide energy for the long haul. Develop a race plan. Get a good start, but don't burn out in the first mile. Run at a fast but steady pace.

Before the race is done, each runner meets "the wall." At "the wall," the body's energy stores are depleted, and the runner feels like he can't continue. When you find you want to quit, run through "the wall." When you are defeated, take it in stride. You're mainly racing yourself, not others. Don't get discouraged when another competitor runs away from you. Finally, be aware of pain. Let it speak to you. Marathon runners don't ignore pain. They listen to its message. Does the pain signify fatigue or injury? Learn to discern.

Long-Term Helping

Train, too, for long-term helping. Although you could help a friend without advance preparation, your chances of sticking with the person through the ups and downs of marital problems are better if you have helped others previously and have a tough mental attitude.

The carbohydrates of long-term helping are anticipations of difficult situations. Although you can't predict each crisis, you can predict some. For instance, if you sense that a couple is close to separation, you can bet that you will be called more often. Prepare.

Develop a race plan. Don't fire out of the counseling blocks and burn out in the initial part of a marital problem. Pace yourself. Anticipate "the wall." In long-term helping, progress is never steady. There are ups and downs and there are times when you have no energy left to help. Anticipate these times and prepare to run through "the wall."

Don't let defeats discourage you. Your suggestions will be rebuffed. Your friend will stumble. You're not competing against your friend. Rather, concentrate on doing your best and let the chips fall where they may.

Finally, let pain speak to you. Try to avoid injury. If your spirit is being hurt because you're too invested in the helping or you're trying too hard, then step back, take some pace off, and finish the race without injuring yourself.

Encouraging Your Friend

How can you keep your friend's spirits high during the lengthy ordeal of long-term helping?

The same things motivate and demotivate your friend and you. Help your friend train for the marathon of trying to repair his or her marriage. Suggest periodic rest for recuperation. Help him or her anticipate stressful events and formulate a race plan. Times of discouragement will rise like a wall in your friend's face. He or she must run through the wall. At times, defeat will occur. Attempts to restore the marriage will fall through. Help your friend deal with inevitable discouragements. Finally, the person must be sensitive to the pain that signifies injury rather than the pain that signifies exertion.

Long-term helping is truly a marathon. Through recognizing that, all the participants can make it to the finish line and be tired but fit to race again.

PART FIVE

UNDERSTANDING HOW TO HELP IMPROVE MARRIAGE

CHAPTER FOURTEEN

HELP STRENGTHEN THE CHRISTIAN CORE

We are assailed on all sides by images of marriage. Perhaps the most insistent images are those created in our family-of-origin and in our existing and past relationships. Those target images are saturation-bombed by other images from television, movies, books, magazine articles, sermons, friends' opinions, teachers' pronouncements, and politicians' rhetoric until our coherent picture of marriage looks like a ragtag puzzle with pieces missing.

In the midst of image overload, how can you hope to affect a friend with a troubled marriage? How can you help reshape the image toward a Christian-based image of marriage?

A friend's Christian core consists of three main parts: the friend's (1) Christian values and beliefs, (2) Christian vision of marriage, and (3) willingness to confess and seek forgiveness for sins and to forgive the partner. Early in helping, address the friend's Christian values and beliefs and Christian vision of marriage. Near the end of helping, as the problem nears resolution, discuss confession and forgiveness. In the current chapter, I'll cover the first two parts of the Christian core and, in Chapter 20, I'll address confession and forgiveness.

Understanding the Christian Core

We usually think of living out our Christianity through our:

- profession of faith,
- church activities,
- compassion for the poor and disadvantaged,
- missions or ministry.

Each of these evidences of faith is but part of Jesus' summary of Christianity (Matthew 22:37–40 RSV): "You shall love the Lord your God with all your heart, and with all your soul, and with all your mind. This is the great and first commandment. And a second is like it, You shall love your neighbor as yourself. On these two commandments depend all the law and the prophets." The whole of those two commandments is having faith in (knowing, trusting, obeying) God (through Jesus), loving God and others, and working to show that faith and love practically—faith working through love.

As Christians, then, we accept a right relationship with God through Jesus and seek to help others find a saving relationship with God through Jesus (that is, become Jesus' disciples). Jesus tells us, "Go therefore and make disciples of all nations, baptizing them in the name of the Father and of the Son and of the Holy Spirit, teaching them to observe all that I have commanded you; and lo, I am with you always, to the close of the age" (Matthew 28:19–20 RSV). In Acts 1:8b (RSV), Luke tells us that Jesus said, "You shall be my witnesses in Jerusalem and in all Judea and Samaria and to the end of the earth." We are to make disciples beginning close to home, extending outward to the church, the city, the nation, and the world.

Discipleship begins in the home.

Christian life, disciple training, begins with the most intimate relationships we have: between husband and wife and parent and children. The marriage, seen in biblical context, is the starting place for helping each other become stronger disciples of Jesus Christ. Marriage is the proper arena for practicing faith working through love and helping the spouse grow in faith working through love.

Marriage is working together to help each other mature in Christianity. Each partner contributes his or her strengths toward helping. Each is concerned about the other's growth.

The disciple-making relationship between spouses is not as superior-inferior but as yokefellows (Philippians 4:3), as each other's helpers (Philippians 2:4), as those who rejoice together and weep together (Romans 12:15), as those who stir each other up to love and good works (Hebrews 3:13; 10:24).

When people marry, they become one flesh (Matthew 19:5). They become an integrated body, acting together for their mutual benefit. Paul also uses the body as a metaphor to describe the church (1 Corinthians 12:12–13). In both the marriage and the church, the central function is disciple-making. In both relationships, members of the body help each other practice faith working through love.

Understanding marriage as a key way to practice Christian disciple-making creates a vision of marriage that springs from and unifies Christian values, beliefs, and practices and one's vision of marriage. People with this understanding of marriage will continually ask themselves, *How am I growing in faith and helping my partner grow in faith? How am I showing love and helping my partner grow in his or her ability to show love? How am I doing the work that springs from a loving, trusting relationship with God through Jesus Christ, and how am I helping my partner to joyfully do that same work?* If marriage partners can retain those questions continually on their minds, they will guide their marriage along Christian lines. (When they fail, confession and forgiveness—the third aspect of the Christian core—are needed.)

Promoting an Understanding of Marriage as Discipleship

Helping Christians and Non-Christians

Needy people will seek your help. Not all will be Christians, but even with non-Christians, you can still conceptualize marriage as discipleship to decide how to best help them.

With Christians, you have a common language. Most understand when you speak of faith, sin, confession, repentance, forgiveness, and covenant. Many people who aren't Christians—especially if they were not reared in a Christian home—don't know what such terms mean. If you use Christian language in helping them, they won't understand (at best) or will be turned off (if they are hostile to Christianity).

One challenge of discipleship is to communicate in a language that people understand. Christian apologists since the first century have devised ways of communicating the gospel to those who hadn't heard it or didn't understand it, though each culture differed. Paul, in the first century, communicated differently to Jews than to Greeks. His language, symbolism, metaphors, examples, reference to other sources, and style of persuasion differed with Jews and Greeks.

Even Christians differ in their understanding of Christian concepts. They differ in theological understanding, emphasis, and sometimes even in words they find acceptable. Faithful, loving, working Christians may disagree about how Scripture is interpreted, divorce, remarriage, submission, what the man being the "head of the woman" means, the role of women in ministry (especially in leadership roles), the pastor's authority, the way faith is appropriated, and whether psychology is inherently anti-Christian. Ways that Christians can misunderstand each other are legion.

Like Paul, we must adapt our communication to the people we are helping—Christian or non-Christian.

The task is not as daunting as I have initially made it sound. Both Christian and non-Christian couples want to have happy marriages. Both understand the need to value the partner, to show love, to work to better the marriage, to forgive the partner when the partner hurts them, and to seek forgiveness when they have hurt the partner. Both understand that mutual trust is needed and that commitment results in happier marriages than not being committed. It is the *basis* for valuing, loving, working, forgiving, trusting, and committing that is (crucially) different. As long as you deal with the behaviors and not the Christianity behind the motivations, you'll be understood and your helping will generally be accepted and appreciated. Also, your Christian witness is more likely to be heard when it has been validated and displayed in your life and marriage.

An Example: Helping a Non-Christian

Let's see how this might be discussed. Dan (a Christian) and Jon (not a Christian) service automobiles at a dealership. They have worked together for a year, and their friendship has grown after Dan's initial, gentle confrontation of Jon because of Jon's profanity. Jon reacted positively, swore less, and didn't seem resentful. Dan tried to "witness" to Jon several times after that, but although Jon listened politely, he didn't ask questions and didn't seem interested.

Jon and his wife Rachel developed marital problems. He confided in Dan, who helped.

Jon: We're doing a lot better. When we get mad at each other, we don't stay mad so long anymore. Your idea helped, you know, about apologizing to Rachel when I knew I'd been mean, instead of blaming her for messing up.

Dan: So you've been able to apologize? How'd she handle that?

Jon: She was surprised. It was a switch, me saying I was sorry and asking her to forgive me. She didn't know how to act. She busted out crying the first time I did it.
Dan: And she forgave you?
Jon: Sure did.

Dan had taught Jon about forgiveness, which Jon applied to his marriage. Forgiveness helped restore his marriage. Dan called it "apologizing" at first rather than risk having Jon reject his advice by using the term "forgiving," which is more often associated with Christianity. Jon knew Dan was a Christian, so he might have reacted negatively to the term, not the thought.

As we saw in their conversation, though, Dan spontaneously used the phrase "asking her to forgive me." In my experience counseling non-Christians, I have found that almost all understand the value of forgiveness. They may react to the term, especially when used by someone they know is a Christian, because they believe they are being preached to, but they understand and value a forgiving attitude.

Moving Beyond the Externals

Still, Christians wear Jesus' banner proudly, and we don't want to hide our Christianity. We need to be alert to openings that can allow us to explain the Christian reasons behind our recommendations. Although the openings don't always materialize, or they are closed immediately, we should look for opportunities to present the gospel sensitively. In Dan and Jon's case, Dan offered a mild hint at the Christian foundations to forgiveness, and Jon—instead of rejecting or ignoring the hint—followed up, giving Dan the opportunity to talk with Jon about Jesus.

Dan: I know you probably don't believe it, but you just saw practical Christianity in action.
Jon: Hmmm.
Dan: You know, Christianity is based on forgiveness. It makes you feel good to receive Jesus' forgiveness when you've sinned.
Jon: Yeah, well, I don't know about that, but I know it sure gets a marriage back together.
Dan: It sure does.
Jon: So Christianity is apologizing to God when we mess up, huh? I went to a religious school my kindergarten, first, and second grades. It seemed like a lot of rules, and we got punished, not forgiven, when we messed up.

Dan: It oversimplifies Christianity to think of it as a "bunch of rules" that can be disobeyed and can lead to either punishment or forgiveness.
Jon: How come? That's always seemed like what I understood Christianity to be.
Dan: You learned the K-one-and-two version of Christianity. When kids are young, they need rules, and they don't understand the reasons behind Christianity as adults can.
Jon: So what's the adult version?
Dan: Instead of being just rules, Christianity is about being friends with God. God is completely pure and also completely loving. Does that make sense?
Jon: Yeah.
Dan: God wants to be friends with people, but people don't always want to be friends with Him. When they do, they can't measure up. They're different from God. They're alien. In a way, it's like goldfish trying to be friends with humans.
Jon: I can see that. God's different from humans. That's for sure.
Dan: The main difference is in character. Humans aren't morally perfect, like God, which makes them unfit to live in God's presence. God's too holy. But God loves us. He wants to accept us. Still, it would be against His character to pretend that we were holy, like Him.
Jon: Yeah. Go on.
Dan: The only way people could be holy is if somehow their imperfections—I mean all the nasty parts of their character and behavior—were destroyed. Bad news. That means the death of our character. Compared to God, we deserve only death.
Jon: That's just like I thought. We disobey the rules and we get zapped.
Dan: We deserve punishment. But what if someone volunteered to be punished for us?
Jon: Right. Who'd do that?
Dan: You're right. Even if someone volunteered to be punished, to die for us, it wouldn't do any good because they deserve death and they can only die once. In fact, the only person who could be punished for us, even if the person would do it, is someone who is perfect and doesn't deserve punishment.
Jon: There you have it. Nobody's perfect.
Dan: Except God.
Jon: Right, except God. But that's different. God's not a person.

Dan: But that's exactly what Jesus is. God the Father isn't only holy. Remember, He's also love. He cares about people and doesn't want them to die, as they deserve. So God's Son, Jesus, who Himself is God, also became a human who never sinned. He was God and human at the same time.
Jon: You mean that's what all that stuff about Jesus dying on the cross is about?
Dan: Right. He died for us, taking our sins on Him, so that if we accept that, we can be forgiven and in a right relationship with God.
Jon: Man, all these years, and I never knew what that meant.

Dan asked Jon if he wanted to accept Jesus' salvation, and they prayed together. Dan opened the door to explaining the gospel, and Jon entered. Often, though, the non-Christian simply isn't interested in hearing. Our response, then, instead of pressuring or continuing to persuade, is to grant the person the freedom to choose his or her time to hear the gospel and to continue to act as a disciple of Christ, whose life will minister to the friend.

Resources for Promoting a Christian Vision of Marriage

Direct Teaching

Perhaps the least ambiguous way to promote a Christian vision of marriage is to teach the person directly about it.

Leo stepped into Mac's office and shut the door softly behind him. Mac dropped his feet from the desk to the floor and brushed sandwich crumbs from his chest. He wiped his hand across his mustache, knocking a few other crumbs loose.

"Hey, Leo, what's happening?"

"I was hoping we could talk. You busy?"

Mac gestured to a chair. "Naw. I was relaxing over my, uh, gourmet lunch—a sandwich with meat of undeterminable ethnic origin, bathed in mustard. Yum. What's on your mind?"

"Fromma and I had a fight last week."

"Um, not so good."

"Yeah. She got angry and left, tore out of the driveway like Dale Earnhart on the NASCAR circuit. I was mad at first, but when I calmed down, I got worried. It took me an hour to find her. She went over to Gina's—a friend she's been talking with a lot lately."

"That doesn't sound too good, buddy."

"She came home. It isn't *that* bad."

Mac held up his hand. "Whoa. I wasn't accusing you of anything.

I was merely observing that fights where someone runs off aren't usually the things marital dreams are made of."

"Sorry, I'm upset and defensive. We talked after she came home, but we didn't resolve anything. I'm worried. Fromma believes that we aren't compatible and we shouldn't have married."

Mac whistled. "Sounds serious. What do you think?"

Leo hesitated. "I, uh, don't know. Maybe she's right. We've had several arguments and we haven't been married that long yet. Maybe we should get a divorce like she says."

Mac rubbed his chin.

"She said she wanted a divorce?"

"Not exactly. She questioned whether we should get a divorce. It makes me question it too."

"So you're questioning your marriage vows."

"I'm *questioning*. That doesn't mean I'm ready for divorce."

Mac looked away, as if he were searching for wisdom in the painted corner of his ceiling. "Then you still feel committed to her."

"Of course I do! But, you know, if commitment doesn't work out, you know—" He shrugged.

"No, I don't know. I believe in a different type of commitment, a permanent one. I didn't always believe commitment was permanent. When Cara and I first married, we argued. One day, I was insulted and left the house, the same way it sounds that Fromma did with you. I eventually went to my pastor and he explained the meaning of a covenant to me. Do you know what a covenant is?"

Leo shook his head. "Something I heard a lawyer mention one time. That's all I know. I guess it means agreement."

"It's more than an agreement. It's a pledge for permanent commitment. It used to be a blood-sealed pledge, like Native American blood brothers."

"Oh."

"Anyway, Christian marriage is based on the idea of a covenant between a man and a woman. Each pledges to treat the other better than the self and to remain faithful for life."

Over the next weeks, Mac continued to teach Leo about covenantal commitment. During that time, Leo and Fromma still argued, but Leo adopted a view of marriage as being more permanent than before.

Your Example of Faith Working Through Love

You create an indelible image of a Christian, friend, and marriage partner through your actions. Calling on the Lord as your strength, you are an example of faith. Sticking with the friend during struggles, you are an example of how to work through long-standing difficulties. Valuing the friend, despite the friend's opinions or decisions, you are an example of how the friend can relate to others despite their differences.

Questions

Questions drag the person along your way of thinking. Someone has compared the question mark at the end of the question to a hook that brings the person along with the questioner.

Use questions sparingly. Balance listening, reflecting back your friend's words, and asking questions. When you question too much, your friend feels controlled and may resist you. If you never question, you may miss essential information or allow the conversation to wander aimlessly.

Examine the conversation between Mac and Leo. Leo asked only three direct questions. First, he asked, "What's on your mind?" which started Leo talking about his problems. Second, when Leo said that Fromma was considering divorce, Mac asked, "What do you think?" which helped Mac assess how seriously Leo was considering divorce. Third, Mac asked, "Do you know what a covenant is?" which led into Mac's teaching about covenant.

Resources

Books about Christian marriage can help shape a Christian image of marriage (see the list on pages 74–76). Don't hesitate to recommend good ones that you've read. Books about the Christian faith can build faith. (There are so many good ones that I couldn't begin to list the best. Anyway, you'll have your own preferences.)

Stories about other married couples and individuals who have faithfully acted and worked in love are a rich source of inspiration and instruction. Scripture is the history of the living God's dealings with people, not just a theological text. God knew the importance of people's stories, and we do well to use those stories as examples of Christian faith and to supplement them with the stories of faithful people we know. Naturally, when you tell a friend about your experience with someone else, protect the other person's confidentiality. If the story has any potential to embarrass its subject, either disguise the details so the person is not recognizable, or (better) don't tell it. Maintaining the trust of friends is vitally important to your integrity and relationships with friends. Also, if you talk about other friends, the person you are attempting to help may believe that you will tell others intimate details of his or her story, which may make the friend reluctant to open up to you.

Prayer

Prayer changes things. Even with direct teaching, our own example, questioning, abundant Christian resources, and inspiring stories, we cannot change a person's beliefs or vision of marriage. Transformation comes from the Holy Spirit's internal work in the person's life. If we are wise, we will pray persistently for our friend, that God would change the person's life and that the change would flow into his or her marriage. True wisdom is total reliance on God to work His will in human lives.

Helping Change the Christian Core

Fromma and Gina

While Mac helped Leo adjust to the first year of marriage, Gina helped Fromma. They met for lunch at an ethnic restaurant in a mall near Fromma's office.

"Leo's been different lately," Fromma said as they munched pre-meal bagels. "He seems—" she struggled to find the right word, "—softer, or something. We still argue, but he doesn't seem to want to escape the marriage as much as he did."

"You felt like he was looking for a divorce?"

"Not exactly. He always said he was committed, but he seemed uncertain of his commitment. Sensing his uncertainty, I wasn't fully willing to give myself to him. That, coupled with some crises—a meaningless disagreement over who took out the trash, the big blow-up about his working too much, and the fight over his basketball when I came to your house—made me feel like we were not right for each other."

"And you questioned your decision to marry him," said Gina.

She nodded. "We came from different backgrounds. Both of us were raised in Christian homes but different traditions. He was Methodist, and his mother ruled the roost. He always did the right thing, was the traditional good student and nice guy—the kind I never liked in high school."

They paused as the waitress served the entrees. Then, after Gina offered a blessing, Fromma continued. "I was raised Baptist and grew up with lots of rules. By my teens, I rebelled, started smoking, dated early, and had a lot of sex. In my first year at college, a friend invited me to an InterVarsity retreat at Windy Gap, North Carolina, and I became a Christian. It changed me, but I still resent my early years. Also, I still struggle with some of the bad habits I had before. I swear, especially around work and whenever I get mad. I quit smoking, of course, but sometimes when things don't go well, I'd give anything for a cigarette."

Gina wiped her mouth. "I'm getting ahead of you on the food while you're talking. Let me see if I'm following. You questioned your decision about marrying Leo because you came from different family backgrounds. Yours led to some rebellious years, and you still feel like you have some bad habits from those years."

"Right. My picture of marriage wasn't good. My parents were awfully strict, and I always saw marriage as joyless. I still mostly feel that way, except— Anyway, I guess I'm doomed to having a poor marriage; I had such poor examples of marriage from my parents."

Gina said, "Parents are important in shaping our view of marriage, but you're not 'doomed' to a poor marriage. God frees us from our past and gives us a positive direction for the future. At any rate, you said that you still *mostly* feel that you'll have a poor marriage and then you said 'except—' Except what?"

Fromma scraped the last of her chicken salad onto a crust of toast. She seemed embarrassed. "Except, you and Nick seem happy. It gives me hope, but I guess I don't think, with Leo's and my different backgrounds, a good marriage is possible for us."

Gina laughed. "Nick and I don't come from the same mold either. Nick's all-Italian. He's expressive and so's his family." Gina waved her hands around and shrugged, Italian-like. "Also, his family gets together three or four times a year. I'm from an English-Scottish background, and my parents were both—" she affected a British accent, "—veddy stiff upper lip. Our early years were wild. After we got our Roman Catholic versus Protestant differences resolved in the first year and most of our ethnic differences resolved in our fifth year when we moved to Richmond, we've had a good marriage. I think Jesus gave us the grace to get through those early years and stick with each other because we both saw the value of a permanent marriage commitment."

The waitress offered dessert, and when Gina and Fromma declined, she presented the check and took their money. As Gina and Fromma rose from the table, Fromma said, "I feel more hopeful whenever we talk. I still don't think we're going to make it, but at least it's nice to know that others have faced these difficulties before. It encourages me."

Gina said, "On our own, I don't believe we can rise above the differences most of us encounter. The forces of our background, our culture, and our religious upbringing are too powerful. But we have an Almighty God. Jesus calmed the storm, and He can calm marital storms too. He brings peace when we believe in Him, and He can bring peace into our marriage too. He sets us free from the domination of a sin nature, and He can set us free from the domination of our family background and upbringing—even our lingering bad habits."

As they left the restaurant, Fromma said, "I want to believe it. I really do."

How Did Gina Help?

Over a single meal, Gina made substantial inroads in changing Fromma's Christian core. Fromma believed that her past determined her future, but Gina didn't accept such fatalism. She repeatedly called Fromma's attention to God's ability to free Christians from their pasts.

Fromma listened because she felt accepted. When Fromma described her past and her present struggles, Gina didn't reject Fromma, lecture about stopping swearing, or preach about her sexual past or her continuing desires for cigarettes. Listening and acceptance readied Fromma to hear Gina.

Even before that conversation, though, the groundwork had already been laid. By observation of Gina and Nick's constant witness of love for each other, Fromma was readied to receive Gina's experience at adjusting to premarital differences. Without Gina's good marriage, Fromma might not have been receptive to Gina's message.

Fromma was not changed in such a brief conversation. Her final comment, though, shows her desire to change. Through sincere desire and prayer, she can allow the Holy Spirit to work in her life to transform her, if she wills.

CHAPTER FIFTEEN

HELP BUILD CLOSENESS

Donnie, thirty-seven years old, has been married to Mitch for thirteen years. Sitting at the kitchen table sipping coffee, she complained to you that the intimacy had died from her marriage. She and Mitch seem to be in different worlds. "I'm an unpaid children-chauffeur and block mother," she said. Mitch is a successful real estate salesman who is out with clients frequently at night. He is involved in church as deacon and adult Sunday school teacher, and he spends one night a month at church programs with his daughter and another night with his son.

Chuck and Anita have been married for six years. When you were at their house for dinner, conversation turned to expressing emotions openly. Chuck said that he can show emotions easily and that he requires a lot of emotional support. Anita said that her family-of-origin never showed emotions readily and that she feels uncomfortable with emotions. Their styles clash. Chuck and Anita asked you to help.

Sue is a vivacious, beautiful Christian. She is twenty-seven, brown-haired, smooth-skinned, and pure as spring. She and Rock have been married six months. After church, you and Sue were talking in the church office when she became tearful and confessed that she and Rock were having sexual problems. She has had only two orgasms since their wedding, and both she and Rock are frustrated.

Both were virgins at marriage, and they think they're not doing something right. She asked for advice.

In this chapter, we will discuss three types of couples who might request help from you for marital problems. In each case, the problem is one of closeness.

Needs for Intimacy, Alone Time, and Social Interaction

In the first case, Donnie and Mitch, in their late thirties, experience little intimacy. Their marriage is failing in faith working through love.

Everyone needs intimacy, alone time, and social time.[1] Everyone's optimal balance of intimacy, alone time, and social time is different. We meet those needs by the way we arrange our time schedules. Every activity contributes to one of the three needs. If we read silently or study, that produces alone time. If we listen to a tape and discuss it in a group, we have social time. If we discuss important goals, ambitions, or values with a close friend or spouse, we feel intimate. Every activity affects closeness. People meet their needs by structuring their time. When their time schedules get out of balance, they become dissatisfied with their lives.

Donnie and Mitch's Problem

That's what happened to Donnie and Mitch. Donnie's activities are heavily social. She relates to her children all day but feels that she never gets enough intimacy. Whenever a friend calls, Donnie feels as if she never has time to herself. Sometimes she thinks she must be going crazy because she can't decide whether she wants more or less intimacy. She's not going crazy. She needs more alone time *and* more intimacy. She is overloaded with social activities.

Mitch is also always on the go, but he doesn't complain about his balance of intimacy, alone time, and social interaction. He has little social interaction and almost no alone time, and he likes it that way.

Helping Donnie

To help Donnie, see whether she unrealistically assumes that Mitch must meet all her needs for intimacy. If she believes that, then she and Mitch are in for conflict and disappointment. If Donnie demands more intimate time with Mitch, he'll rebel. If she doesn't get more intimate interaction somewhere, Donnie will continue to be frustrated.

Donnie needs to rearrange her time commitments. She could

- Spend less purely social time with the children. Carpooling may be one answer.
- Make time with her children more intimate—take them on a picnic instead of being block mother, discuss ideas at the dinner table, read and pray before bed.
- Awaken early for intimate time with God.
- Find intimacy in Bible or fellowship groups.
- Send the kids to bed earlier so she and Mitch have more intimate time.
- Cultivate new friends, which can lead to more intimate sharing.

Although the solutions sound simple, they aren't. Spending less time with her children tugs Donnie's guilt strings. She thinks that she must interact with the children continually to be a good mother. Pulling back means she must loosen her control and let the children relate more with the other children.

Donnie might not be able to find a close friend merely because she wants to. Many women her age are as overscheduled as Donnie is. She could invite women home after a midweek Bible study or arrange a weekly prayer time with a friend from church.

Donnie must take a long-term view. Her time schedule can't be revamped overnight. Her commitments will take time to replace, so she must content herself with little steps of progress rather than expect large jumps.

Helping Mitch

Mitch may also need to change, but because he is relatively satisfied with his life, he may not ask for—nor welcome—your help. If he seeks advice for Donnie's sake, suggest that he spend one night a month with Donnie alone. Also suggest that he prayerfully evaluate his church and other commitments in light of Paul's command that husbands love their wives sacrificially as Christ loved the church (Ephesians 5:25). If Mitch won't change, then remind Donnie that she can only change herself and that she should not try to restructure Mitch's life.

The Failure in Faith Working Through Love

Donnie and Mitch have let their time commitments suggest that they value other activities more than they value each other. If you asked them whether this were true, they would emphatically deny it and proclaim the strong love they feel, but Donnie interprets Mitch's actions as indicating that he doesn't care. They think that they should be able to work out their schedules to have their cake and eat it too, but neither is willing to do the necessary work. Thus, they have lost faith that their marriage is special. If Donnie can establish more intimacy elsewhere, she might stop thinking that Mitch doesn't value her. Mitch must clearly show Donnie how much he values her.

Mismatches in Intimacy Needs

Emotional Distancers and Pursuers

In the second case, Chuck is insecure. He became depressed and complained of headaches and physical pains, but the doctor found no evidence of a medical problem except "stress." Anita tried to help but soon felt overwhelmed at Chuck's neediness. The more Chuck sought her help, the more she felt like running away and living in a cave with wild animals. Both complained that this pattern characterized their six years of marriage.

Then Chuck's attitude changed. He stopped asking for as much help. He said, "Where was she when I needed her?" At first, Anita was overjoyed that Chuck demanded less of her, but then she began to worry. She asked for more time together, but he said no and was highly critical of her lack of emotional responsiveness, which angered her. She told him he was weak and demanding. Now, they have no intimate contact. "It's as if there is a four-inch-thick piece of steel that insulates us," says Anita.

This pattern is commonly called the emotional distancer-pursuer pattern.[2] In this example, Chuck is the emotional pursuer and Anita the emotional distancer. Women are usually the emotional pursuers and men emotional distancers, but not always.

Difficulties in Solving the Emotional Distancer-Pursuer Stalemate

The solution to the emotional distancer-pursuer problem seems obvious. Have the distancer provide intimacy that the pursuer needs and have the pursuer stop demanding so much intimacy from the distancer. The solution sounds easier than it usually is.

First, the couple has solidified a *pattern* of behavior, which each has practiced for years—perhaps for a lifetime. So, the pattern may not be easy to change.

Second, if you tell Anita (the emotional distancer) that she should meet more of Chuck's needs for emotional support, she might just leap over the table and grab you by the scruff of the neck, bite you on the nose, and murmur threats in your ear. Your demands for more intimacy are just like Chuck's. It usually isn't easy for the emotional distancer to change.

The emotional pursuer is usually easier to engage than the emotional distancer, who is adept at running away when anyone gets too close. Encourage Chuck to make fewer demands for support. Of course, Chuck may take you at your word and transfer his need for emotional support to *you*. That would take pressure off Anita, but it might not do a lot for *your* home life.

Solving the Emotional Distancer-Pursuer Stalemate

Therapists treat the emotional distancer-pursuer couple by using three rules.

1. Talk mostly to the emotional pursuer;
2. Treat the emotional distancer with great respect; and
3. Never pursue an emotional distancer.

Marriage therapist Carlfred Broderick believes that the emotional distancer has a "dark fantasy," which is a secret fear that he or she will be overwhelmed by the emotional pursuer and will be unable to cope with the pursuer's emotional outpouring.[3] If that is true, one way to help the emotional distancer is to demonstrate that the dark fantasy won't occur. Therapists usually try to get the emotional distancer to initiate some type of intimate activity during the week. Demands to be intimate are reduced by giving the emotional distancer total freedom in choice of task and choice of time. Importantly, though, the emotional pursuer also has a task: to refrain from asking for intimacy and from criticizing the emotional distancer. Although these are two small changes in behavior, they break up the practiced distancer-pursuer pattern. This allows the pursuer to be more positive and the distancer to initiate closeness, which helps change both partners' attitudes.

Anita and Chuck saw their pastor for help. He assigned them tasks. They had a wonderful dinner alone and a walk around the lake one night, and Anita paid Chuck a surprise midweek visit for lunch. Although that did not undo six years of practiced behavior, it showed Chuck and Anita what good times they had been missing, and they re-instituted their long-forgotten monthly ritual of dining and a movie.

The Failure in Faith Working Through Love

In the emotional distancer-pursuer pattern, the failure in the marriage is in how the partners show each other love. Each has specifically decreed the one and only way that he or she will accept love. The distancer says, "Let me alone and I'll know that you love me. Nothing else that you say or do counts as love." The pursuer says, "Be there for me emotionally every time I ask and I'll know that you love me. Nothing else you say or do counts as love." If either spouse doesn't follow the partner's rules, the partner takes it as devaluing rejection, failure to work on the marriage, and loss of faith that the marriage is salvageable or worth saving.

To help emotional distancers and pursuers deal with their problems in closeness, help them (1) accept love from their partner in ways other than those ways governed by their "rule"; (2) break up the old patterns of distancing and pursuing, which both perceive as rejection; and (3) show love in ways that the partner can receive it (even if it means doing what doesn't come naturally). If they can show and accept love, their faith in the marriage can be restored.

Sexual Difficulties

Helping People of the Other Sex

In the third case, Sue was frustrated and sad because she and Rock had sexual problems. They had been inexperienced sexually before marriage, and Sue asked for some advice. You are alone with her.

If you are a male, end the conversation gracefully. Each day, "strong Christians" are tempted into sexual improprieties. This is especially likely in situations that involve honest emotional self-disclosure, vulnerability, tenderness, arousing conversation, and a situation in which a man and woman are alone together. Usually, they are not "overcome by passion." At first, they share exclusiveness and tenderness. Over time, a sexual relationship may develop. Prevent the risk by not talking about sexual intimacies. If you must, invite your friend's spouse, your own spouse, or a third party.

Helping People of the Same Sex

If you are a woman helping Sue, advise her about her sexual relationship. Remember, though, that you are not a sex therapist, so pose suggestions tentatively. For example, say, "This works for some people.

It might work for you, but you and Rock need to do what fits you." There is incredible variety in what people consider "normal" sexual behavior. As a marital therapist, I have heard committed Christians describe unusual sexual behaviors as "normal." If they do not hurt or degrade someone or are not a serious health risk, then I treat those behaviors as "normal" (though I don't rush home to try them out).

Giving Advice About Sexual Matters

Most of us think of ourselves as "normal" sexually, even if we do some "exotic" things to arouse our mates. (What we do is "exotic"; what others do is "weird.") We advise others to do what works for us. Be careful as a Christian helper that what you suggest pleases God and isn't a stumbling block to others.

With sexual difficulties, especially with the inexperience of Sue and Rock, giving Sue ideas for more sexual satisfaction and recommending books such as the Wheats' *Intended for Pleasure* or the LaHayes' *The Act of Marriage*[4] is a good idea. Recommend that Rock talk to a more experienced married man about other ways that Rock might stimulate Sue. Remind Sue that their sexual relationship is an exciting adventure and what a joy it is that they saved such exploration only for each other in marriage.

The Failure in Faith Working Through Love

Sue and Rock love each other deeply, value each other, and have worked on their sexual expression of their love. By now, though, they have lost faith that their sexual relationship can be fulfilling. They are near to stopping to work on their sexual relationship, accepting the unsatisfying love-making as inevitable, and feeling dissatisfaction and failure.

To help Sue and Rock requires restoring their faith. A male helper needs to stick with Rock and a female with Sue to suggest ways that the couple might find more satisfaction sexually. An older couple would be ideal for the task. With some success would come a large boost in restoring their faith. With newly wedded couples, clearing up some basic sexual misunderstandings or providing specific suggestions can give that boost.

Helping with Intimacy

The Intimacy Problem

Even after the crisis passed and the wound healed on Leo's cheek, Fromma remained furious over Leo's involvement in sports. "Leo goes from season to season, one sport to the next, in an unending stream of sweat and neglect," she complained to Gina one day on their three-mile walk around the neighborhood. "He runs road races in the fall and spring, plays league basketball in the winter and enters two-on-two and three-on-three tournaments in the summer, plays summer soccer, and does master's swimming at the YMCA three nights a week."

"I'll bet he's in good shape," said Gina, trying to keep the conversation light. "I wish I was in good enough shape to jog up this hill. I'm puffing."

Fromma snapped, "Yeah, he's in good shape, but our marriage isn't. He uses sports to build up his ego because he feels like a failure as a man."

Gina winced. "You're really hurting."

Fromma glanced at Gina. "I guess that sounded bitter, didn't it? I can't help it, though. I'm frustrated. I ask him to walk with me, and he has a sporting event. I ask him to talk, and he's catching up with work because he took the afternoon off to run a 10K. We hardly have sex anymore—maybe once a week if we're lucky, if he doesn't have something else to do. When we married, we used to make love three or four times a week. It isn't right what he's doing."

Let's Analyze

We can see seeds of all three problems in closeness in Fromma's brief complaint. From Fromma's point of view, Leo has overscheduled his time without allowing enough intimacy with her. The beginnings of an emotional distancer (Leo) and pursuer (Fromma) pattern are also visible and can especially be seen in the couple's sex life.

We must be cautious in our analysis. We have only Fromma's perspective. She is obviously unhappy and may pay selective attention to the negative. She hasn't mentioned how her behavior fits Leo's expectations.

The Helper's Response

"It seems as if he's intentionally irritating you."

"No, I know that he's not happy with our marriage either and that he wants it to improve as much as I do. But he doesn't want to change his life to make the marriage better."

"Have you changed to let him know you want to work on the marriage?"

"I complain." She laughed. "I guess that isn't entirely productive, is it?"

"Now that you mention it—." They both laughed. "You don't feel like Leo's actions communicate love for you."

"That's the truth! If he would skip one tournament or one race, I'd know he loved me. I need reassurance."

"So he enters *every* tournament or race in Richmond?"

"No, it only seems like it. He skips some tournaments, but I feel like he loves sports more than he loves me."

"Have you told him your feelings nonconfrontively?"

"What do you mean?"

"Have you told him that you need reassurance that he loves you without trying to force him to skip a tournament or race?"

"No. I hadn't understood what I wanted until now."

"What do you want?"

"To know that he loves me. I want him to make some sacrifice that tells me I'm important."

"It's hard for him to know what he was supposed to do if you just figured it out. Have you made a big sacrifice for him?"

They puffed silently for half a block. Finally, Fromma sighed. "No, I haven't done much to show him I care. I've pursued my own interests and put Leo off when my interests conflict with our time together. We do the same things. No wonder we're having troubles."

"You've arrived at an important understanding of your part in the trouble. Would it help to talk with him about your insight and tell him how you've decided to change?"

"Yeah, that'd be good, but I don't know what to change."

"You'll probably want to pray about what to change. What are some of the things that you've done to put him off? Maybe changing some of those will show him that you still love and value him."

CHAPTER SIXTEEN

HELP PROMOTE COMMUNICATION

Here's a short course in how *not* to communicate. In troubled couples, we see loads of poor communication strategies. Recall the little devil, Wormwood, in C. S. Lewis's *Screwtape Letters*.[1] In that marvelous book, Lewis wrote tongue-in-cheek from the devil's perspective so we could learn what behaviors to avoid. Pretend that I too am intent on giving advice guaranteed to mess up a marriage.

- Time the communication in the worst possible way. Your spouse has a miserable head cold, twenty jobs to do at home, and children who need to be transported across town. Discuss the future of the relationship.
- "Go for the jugular." It is more important to win an argument than to resolve differences.
- Use power wisely. Play to win. Demand your way. Threaten withdrawal of love, violence, or divorce. Alternatively, if you lose, spoil your spouse's victory.
- Use double binds (no-win situations). For example, Brenda complains, "Dear, you must become more spontaneous." That's beautiful. If Dear *tries* to be more spontaneous, he is deliberate, not spontaneous, but if Dear doesn't try, he's not spontaneous.

- Cut down the spouse by using Don Rickles-like humor.
- Play psychiatrist. Use psychological labels. Don't describe your wife as humble; she has an inferiority complex. Don't say that your husband likes to make love; he's a sex fiend.
- If an argument develops, say, "I don't want to discuss it further." Frustrating.
- Don't get mad, get even. Hurt the spouse. Never apologize. If the spouse apologizes, never accept the apology. Get even indirectly. Never show your anger because you look like the bad guy. Instead, purchase a new winter wardrobe that you can't afford.
- Use absolute statements when you disagree with your spouse. For example, say things like, "You're *never* romantic," or "*Nobody* makes love *that way,*" or "*Everyone* else hangs up their clothes instead of throwing them over the light."

Obviously I'm not recommending these poor communications. But as in *Screwtape Letters,* sometimes the best way to understand what we should do is to see what Satan wants us to do. Satan is the sworn enemy of marriage covenant, and he often communicates such destructive strategies to us, disguised as a neat, attractive uniform of pride, self-aggrandizement, self-protection, or defense of our rights.

Each poor communication strategy that I parodied above is a violation of faith working through love. Most are defective love, devaluing the partner. How far these attitudes and techniques are from the biblical pattern of acting in love.

Helping Couples with Communication Problems

With friends who have marital tensions, communication difficulties may be standard practice. How can we help? There are things we should avoid doing and things we can do.

What to Avoid

Don't criticize. Don't correct someone else's communication unless you are specifically asked. Even then, be tactful. Don't say, "You're destroying Wayne with your put-down humor. You are cruel, even if you don't mean it to be." (That says to the person: "You idiot. Not only are you cruel, you are too ignorant to realize it." It also destroys the person with a put-down and is cruel, even if you don't mean to be—the very thing you are criticizing.) Rather, say, "It seems like Wayne cringes every time you make a joke at his expense. You might use fewer put-down jokes."

Pick your targets carefully. Avoid pointing out all the communication flaws you see. If you point out more than three in a one-hour conversation, the person won't remember any and may feel overwhelmed.

Listen before you act. Don't correct right away. Listen, then build the person's or couple's good points. Decide which communication patterns are most harmful and discuss those.

Unless there's bloodshed, keep focused. If you are not talking to a couple specifically about communication, and one spouse says something hurtful, weigh carefully whether to comment. Usually, your comment will interrupt the flow of conversation. Unless there is tissue damage, don't take the focus away from other topics you're discussing.

Be reluctant to suggest compromises. Don't get so involved in working out a compromise that you forget that you need to help them change their patterns of communication.

What to Do

Increase awareness of the communication. To help the couple change their communication patterns, help them become aware of their poor communication. One way to do this is to point it out continually. Of course, that's obnoxious. Even paid marriage counselors won't often point out problems repeatedly to a couple. Without a flak jacket.

Better, ask partners to "show" you how they communicate. Have them disagree *a little,* so you can see how they communicate. Don't let disagreements become emotional lest the partners lose confidence that you can help them.

Sometimes one partner will object after they have discussed an issue. For instance, the wife might say, "He's not that way when we're alone. He's just nice because you're here." If the husband disagrees with her opinion, then ask the wife to show you how *he* really is. Usually, she will exaggerate. Although sometimes the spouse will get a little angry, usually the exaggeration is funny. If the spouse gets angry, calm the anger by stopping the conversation and saying, "That looked a little more dramatic than I might have expected ol' Harvey to act. What about it? Did you maybe exaggerate a little?"

Help change attitudes. Once a couple is practicing poor communication, it is difficult to communicate differently. God can change the hearts of troubled couples and help them *want* to communicate better. Usually, this begins through prayer and will continue as long as the person continues to pray. Building new patterns of communication is truly a spiritual battle, and our chief weapon is prayer, at times heartfelt and at times dutiful.

When marital partners have communicated poorly for years, they have been hurt often and are wary and suspicious that they'll be hurt again. They think their partner intentionally hurts them. Couples do hurt each other repeatedly, not because one wants to hurt the other but because one spouse wants to improve the marriage but is doing it ineffectively. Most spouses mean well, but they can't or don't carry out their intentions well.

Help break up the habitual poor communication of two partners by stating aloud their positive intentions. If Margaret nags Gary, who responds with vicious sarcasm, instead of pointing out the negatives, say, "Margaret, you seem to *want* the best for your marriage. I can see your concern because you keep reminding Gary to clean the attic. Even though you mean well, it seems to make him mad, which is exactly the opposite of your intention. And Gary, I can see that you too want the best for your marriage. You seem to want to avoid an argument by using sarcasm, but that, too, has the opposite effect of what you intend. Could you think of other ways to communicate that will show how much you value each other?"

Structure better communication. Once God has given at least one partner the desire to change and the partners believe that they need to change, the person erects structures of more positive communication. These include *listening* to the spouse and trying to determine the spouse's feelings as well as what he or she is saying. It also involves *self-disclosure* of one's own thoughts, feelings, desires, and wants. It requires *respect* for the spouse as a valuable person and partner. It demands *care for* and *caring about* the partner. It involves the *commitment* to meeting as many of the spouse's needs as possible. In short, good communication is just practical love in action.

Many programs have been developed by psychologists to "teach" communication. Do they help? Patricia Noller reviewed five studies with similar findings.[2] Troubled couples, who exhibited poor communication with each other, communicated well when paired with an other-sex stranger. Even happily married couples communicated better in some respects with strangers than with each other. Most people know *how* to communicate, but they get into poor habits with their partners. Noller suggested that general training in communication isn't likely to improve marital communication. Only communication training that occurs with both partners together affects marital communication. God can help change those negative communication habits, but the spouses must help by carrying out the hard work of communicating with each other in love.

As for you, point out a few of the couple's destructive habits, pray for them, and help them understand good communication. By doing those things, you can make some difference in their communication.

Help Understand Communication Differently

When communication fails, it fails in three areas. First, *spouses may not understand what each other means.* For example, Ken and Margo were arguing about their finances. Margo said angrily, "Well, I'm going out to the store, and I'll spend as much money as I please." Ken smiled at her and, pointing his finger at her like Dirty Harry aiming a .44 Magnum, he said flatly, "Go ahead, make my day." Margo stormed out, but as she thought about it, she didn't know how serious Ken was about her not overspending. His joke had sent her a mixed message.

The second way communication can break down is by *the way partners communicate.* Some couples have difficulties because they don't know when to stop arguing; others are too afraid ever to argue so they stew in their juices. Some couples always seem angry with each other; others don't sound angry even when they are. Some people interrupt each other so a thought is never finished. Others clam up.

The third way communications go haywire is by *communicating in a way that has a different effect than was intended.* For example, troubled couples often become involved in power struggles. Although they feel they are simply disagreeing over issues such as household responsibilities, whether the husband spends too much time at work, or whether the toilet seat is up or down at night, an outside observer can usually see that partners are dug in and battling each other furiously. If one partner offers a compromise, the mate rejects it because giving in to *any* suggestion made by the spouse is seen as "losing" the struggle. So, even well-meant suggestions may have an opposite effect to that intended.

Techniques for Helping to Change Communication

Focus on any of the three aspects of communication. Most professional counselors emphasize one of the three areas. Time is too limited to consider all three. Choose one aspect and focus your energy.

Problem: Lack of Understanding

Teach active listening. If you characterize communication problems as being a failure to understand what each spouse is communicating, help the couple learn to listen more actively, using the same listening skills that you use as a helper. As the partner is talking, the listener will attend, encourage the spouse to continue to talk, and invite additional talking.[3] Further, while the person is telling his or her story, the listener will try to better understand the story and to check out the accuracy of the understanding by reflecting content and feeling, repeating short, key phrases, paraphrasing longer statements, and summarizing large blocks of information.

Repeat what the partner said before talking. If partners have difficulty listening and they jump headlong into rebuttals without acknowledging the speaker's message, then slow the speakers and listeners down by imposing a structure on the communication.

Set up the rule that each person should make only a short point, then invite the mate to summarize what the person said. If the summary is accurate, the original communicator becomes the listener (for a short point) and summarizes the partner's message. The communication will be slow because every point must be checked for accuracy, but this method disrupts chronic arguments and allows partners to understand each other.

Emphasize that you don't consider this to be normal communication, but exaggerated conversation that allows them to practice listening to each other. It is abnormal communication that allows their normal good communication to heal, much as a cast is unnatural but allows a broken bone to heal.

Problem:
How They Communicate

The pinch model. Another way you might help couples break up habitual patterns of poor communication is based on changing the way that the partners communicate, not checking the accuracy of their communication. Explain to them Sherwood & Glidewell's "pinch model."[4] A pinch is something that hurts a little—a jab, a dig, an offhand put-down, or a humorous insult.

Joe and Ria are eating dinner, and Joe spills his milk. He says, "Well, it's so cluttered on the table with all these sewing projects that I just didn't see my glass." (Zing.) Both Joe and Ria know that Joe has asked Ria countless times to keep her sewing projects off the table, so both partners realize that Joe is "pinching" Ria. Ria can do any of six things in response. First, she can blow up. Second, she can let it pass and punish him later (no sex tonight; embarrass him in front of company; put *him* down). Third, she can let it pass and then retaliate by bringing it up later. Fourth, she can let it pass and forget it. Fifth, she can say "ouch" and let it pass. Sixth, she can talk about it. There is no single correct way to handle pinches, though blowing up, punishing the spouse, and retaliation are certainly unbiblical ways to handle them. Occasional pinches happen in every relationship, and a couple cannot and should not talk about all of them. Handling pinches avoids a build-up of pinches until Ria retaliates, crunching Joe out of proportion to the most recent pinch.

I have the floor. Howard Markman's Prevention and Relationship Enhancement Program uses a technique for changing the way couples communicate. When members of couples interrupt each other, a piece of floor tile is handed to one partner. That partner can talk when he or she "has the floor." The other person must remain silent until the speaker is ready to give up the floor.[5]

Passing the buck. I use a similar method, usually for a different purpose (though it can also be used to slow down arguments). When one spouse is reluctant to talk (especially when the other spouse is very verbal), I fold a dollar bill into a small ball and hand it to one partner, who is allowed to talk. When the talkative partner slows down, I might say, "You probably are interested in what [Marie] thinks about this issue. How about 'passing the buck' so we can find out her thoughts."

Marie talks. If she hasn't expressed herself very fully, I might say,

"Marie, we're interested in hearing more about your ideas on this topic. Don't pass the buck yet."

If I want to end the discussion to make a point with the couple, I can intercept the buck and say, "The buck stops here." After making my observation about how they are communicating, I can pass the buck to one of the partners again.

The marriage conference table.[6] The couple makes four one-hour appointments to discuss an issue. Appointments start and end on time. The first and third appointments begin with the wife talking. She talks (or is silent) for thirty minutes without interruption. Then the husband talks for precisely thirty minutes. No interruptions, debate, or discussion is allowed. This is the opportunity for partners to have their say and be heard without having to justify themselves or debate. Between sessions, topics discussed in the marriage conference are off-limits, which limits arguments about "hot" topics.

Leveling. Leveling is discussing your thoughts and feelings directly rather than holding them in.[7] Teach those you are helping to level selectively. Before choosing to level, a person needs to ask himself or herself these questions:

- Is this a legitimate gripe, or is something else irritating me (such as a bad day at work)?
- Is it important that I level? Am I over-reacting?
- Am I trying to solve a problem or simply griping?
- How will my partner probably react?
- Is this the right time to level?

If leveling still seems appropriate, then the partner needs to level constructively, not destructively. For example, destructive leveling uses character assassination (name calling), insults, storing up complaints, answering a complaint with a complaint (called cross-complaining), and constant complaining. It is aimed at punishing, putting down, or threatening the partner rather than solving a problem. Constructive leveling, on the other hand, involves specific gripes (such as "when you pick your teeth with your toes, it grosses me out") and deals with one issue and sticks with it until the issue is resolved.

Editing. Editing is a decision to communicate politely by deciding among several things you could communicate. Gottman et al. summarize editing in nine rules, which I have paraphrased below.[8]

- Don't say what you can't or don't want to do; say what you can do and want to do.
- Don't complain or nag; express sincere appreciation.
- Don't be selfish: be courteous and considerate.
- Don't hog the conversation; listen to your spouse.
- Don't interrupt; let your partner finish speaking.
- Don't put down your spouse; express what you genuinely like about him or her.
- Don't put yourself down; criticize your ideas, not yourself.
- Don't rehash the past; solve problems that are current.
- Don't think only of yourself; consider your spouse's needs and wants, too.

Most of these rules are examples of faith working through love. They try to value and avoid devaluing the partner.

Problem: Not Achieving the Effects They Intended

The tape recorder. When people become embroiled in power struggles, they communicate habitually. They want to produce harmony and happiness in their marriage, but they produce discord and unhappiness. How can they break those destructive patterns of communication? Addition of a new person can help. Usually, though, a relative or friend of one partner is not the ideal person to break up poor communication, although a relative or friend can be helpful in some cases. It is easy for each partner to perceive the relative or friend as biased, even when there is in fact no bias.

Given a choice, though, most people do not willingly enter into a friend's or relative's active conflict. An objective third party can often help change the marital communication. The only truly objective third party is an audiotape recorder. Sometimes couples can *explicitly agree* to load their recorder with a blank tape and place it in one of the two rooms most likely to house an argument—kitchen or bedroom. When the argument gets underway, the partner nearest the recorder hits "Record." It's amazing how communication changes knowing that one is recording, even if no one will ever hear it.

Intent-impact. If you become involved in a couple's miscommunication and they ask you to arbitrate, use the intent-impact model to help change their communication. If a statement is misunderstood, ask the partner, "What did you intend to happen when you made that statement? If she had reacted as you would have dreamed, how would she have reacted?"

After the person answers, observe that the statement didn't produce the ideal impact. Ask the spouse, "How could he have communicated to get you to respond like he wanted?" After the spouse provides an example, ask the first spouse to communicate in the way that would make the impact he intended.

Stop rehearsing conversations. When people are offended or in chronic conflict with another person, they silently rehearse conversations (or arguments) with the person. Usually these internal conversations sound like, *Who does she think she is? She can't talk to me like that. She's violating my basic rights and not treating me as a person. Next time she says something like that I'm going to say . . .*

Internal arguments that focus on how offended a person is or how he or she has been wronged usually mean the person has disagreed with a spouse in a fundamentally important way. The conversations exercise their sense of righteous (or unrighteous) indignation. They focus their attention on how they have been wronged and how they will *show* him or her next time. Rather than promote valuing love, they usually promote adversarial thinking and a desire to put down the other person—not an example of faith working through love.

When your friend says he or she has negative internal conversations, internal conversations that tear down rather than practicing to build up, say, "Next time, rather than get angry, pray for your partner and for yourself that you may be a 'living sacrifice, holy and acceptable to God' (Romans 12:1) and that you may 'not be conformed to this world but be transformed by the renewal of your mind'" (Romans 12:2 RSV).

Communication

Communication can't be avoided. Through communication, we penetrate the envelope of the other person and see the personality within. Sometimes it's easy not to like what we see, especially if we have the same faults.

Nothing irritates me quite so much in others is their failures in the areas in which I habitually fail. My frustration in my own inadequacies and, yes, my sin, is so much easier to vent on others, especially those I know best, than on myself. Marriage partners inevitably become mirrors to our own souls.

Lord, give me the grace to see my own failings and the mercy to forgive my loved ones for reflecting my own fallen nature back to me. Build in me humility, not judgment, as I communicate with the precious person You have joined to me in spiritual and holy matrimony. And, Lord, build in me a holy zeal for my own repentance and restoration into fellowship with You.

In helping, Lord, let me be gentle in correction. Help me support change and growth in my friends' communication, not through a superior attitude, but through knowledge of my own imperfections, my identification with fellow sinners, and compassion.

CHAPTER SEVENTEEN

HELP RESOLVE CONFLICTS

I went white water canoeing. I was younger then.

Many times, Kirby and I floated down the Russian River in Northern California. White water canoeing on Georgia's Chatahoochee River wasn't the same. I should have realized the difference when Kirby and her sister, Judy, went over a waterfall the day before, and their canoe snapped in half. The next day, my brother-in-law and I were in a different part of the river, different canoe. As we approached a sharp bend, I dug the paddle into the rushing water to turn us. No effect. I heaved. The water didn't care. We skidded sideways, struck something, and suddenly were in the water, a jumble of foam, froth, and frustration. Sputtering, gasping, bouncing from rocks, I struggled to keep my feet in front of me and corral the canoe. My shins were sausage, ground by bashing every rock in the river. White water canoeing would never be quite as much fun for me again.

When a troubled couple is embroiled in a heated argument, a friend who is trying to help usually has about as much effect as I had at white water canoeing. Marital arguments are powerful currents jerking everyone in the boat toward unseen boulders.

I couldn't control the canoe through the rapid-cluttered bend, but the next canoe went straight through. (I hated them.) Similarly, experienced marriage counselors navigate marital conflicts that friends find treacherous.

Assess your capabilities before becoming involved in a couple's arguments. Evaluate candidly whether the couple wants your help and how much you can do without losing a friend or creating more emotion than you eliminate. Only then should you tentatively try to help.

What Causes Marital Conflict?

Different Backgrounds

When partners marry, they bring different backgrounds and different families to the marriage. The families-of-origin behaved in different ways, and the new husband and wife reacted to those families-of-origins—either liking the ways things were done or not liking them. Throughout marriage, at each new phase, partners must confront differences in expectations and decide how *they* will do things. If the differences are not confronted, partners often feel angry and resentful.

Life Cycle Events

At some times, conflict is more common than at other times. For example, when a partner is under stress, little provocations can create annoyance, which further provokes the spouse. Sometimes it seems that marital arguments only occur when partners are too stressed out to deal with the arguments. That is not an accident. Nor is it the evil intentions of the spouse, who waits until the partner is under stress to broach a touchy topic. Rather, stress provokes conflict.

Power

The power rule. The third cause of conflict is by far the most important. It occurs in chronic conflict. Chronic conflict may be repeated arguments about the same topic, or it may involve many arguments about different topics. Couples argue most often about money, sex, in-laws, chores, and child discipline.[1] Usually, chronic conflict is habitual. Partners disagree over the power rule, which specifies *who has the power to make the rules*.[2]

Two former clients illustrate this. Joel and Ann argued for years about eating out. She complained, "He never takes me out to eat. Is he ashamed of me?"

He countered, "Why should we eat out and spend all that money? She's a better cook than any restaurant chef."

One day, they came for counseling in the midst of an argument. "What's the problem?" I asked.

She said, "He wants to take me out to eat and I don't want to go."

I looked at Joel, who shrugged.

The story unfolded this way. As they entered the office building, Joel said, "You want to eat out. Tonight's your night. Choose the place."

Ann replied, "But I've already prepared dinner. How about tomorrow?"

They ended up shouting.

Their problem was fundamental to chronic marital conflict. They didn't argue about whether he would take her out to eat. They argued about *who could say* whether he would take her out.

If arguments are the leaves of conflict and the topics of disagreement are the branches, then the trunk of the tree of marital conflict is disagreement over who can say how things are done. Spouses argue to determine who can say what rules govern their marriage.

Implications. This means several things. First, if the real issue is not a specific difference of opinion, then the friend usually cannot do much long-term good by solving any specific problem through compromise. The basic issue will remain. Rather, to help a couple resolve chronic conflict, help them clearly define their relationship. Who makes which decisions? How can power be shared satisfactorily? Notice I did not say that power should be shared *equally* or *fairly.* Many partners don't want that. Rather, power should be shared so that partners are satisfied with the way it is shared.

Second, compromise solutions are hard to arrive at. Suppose Sidney and Emily are arguing over where to have dinner. Sidney wants to go to a class joint, like the local hamburger palace. Emily wants something nutritious, like pizza. Impasse. Both have given their best arguments, and neither has prevailed. At last, Sidney proposes a compromise. "Why don't we go to the steak house?" Will Emily fall on this solution like Dracula on a victim's neck? Don't bet on it. If she does, she admits that Sidney can decide where they will eat.

Instead, Emily says, "Sidney, honey, I don't feel like steak tonight. How about seafood?"

Sidney says, "Wrong again, lovey-dovey. I break out in hives when I eat seafood."

Sidney and Emily are going to eat PB&J sandwiches tonight. They're disagreeing over who can say what their marriage will be like.

It's not that couples can never decide where to eat. They do every day. Rather, couples in chronic conflict can't often compromise.

A friend might help in the short term. Neither spouse can accept the partner's proposed compromise without admitting that the partner can control the marriage, but if you offer a compromise, Sidney and Emily might eat out tonight, even though they won't have solved the problem.

The Root Cause of Power Struggles

Self at the root. The underlying cause of a power struggle—the root of conflict—is self-will. Each partner says, "I want *my* way. This marriage should mirror *me.*" To help the couple resolve the power struggle, each person must get the focus off *me.* He or she must think of the partner, think of *us,* think of serving rather than being served, think of self-sacrifice rather than self-protection.

A disagreement. Fromma and Leo continued to disagree about his sports commitments, which took him away from her. Finally, Gina convinced Fromma to see Gina's pastor, Hank. After listening to her, Hank suggested that Fromma think more about Leo and less about herself.

"But that's so *unfair,*" said Fromma. "Some people are selfish and take advantage. Some abuse their privilege. Some people do whatever they want even if you're giving and giving."

"That's true," said Hank. "Some do."

"Leo always wants to do his thing. It doesn't matter what I do or say. If I want anything from our marriage, I have to care for myself. He certainly won't. I can't be a doormat, can I?"

"I don't think God wants any of us to be a doormat and have others wipe their feet on us. But let's look at the Scripture and see what it says."

"Sure, what does it say?"

"In Philippians two,[3] Paul wrote that Jesus had the right to heavenly glory but He laid it down to become a human. He didn't insist on His right. He didn't consider His equality with God something to be grasped or held onto. Rather, 'He made himself nothing,' one version says, even going so far as becoming obedient to death on the cross. In that same section,[4] Paul wrote, 'Do nothing out of selfish ambition or vain conceit, but in humility consider others better than yourselves. Each of you should look *not only* to your own interests, but also to the interests of others.'"

"That goes against everything I've always believed. My mother always said, 'Take care of yourself. No one else will.' I can't believe God would want us to be a doormat."

"It's a challenging passage—especially today because we have a cultural tradition of looking out for number one. Paul does say, 'we should look *not only* to our own interests but also to the interests of others.' Still, we usually don't err by looking toward others' interests, do we?"

"Well, that may have been Jesus' calling, but it isn't mine."

"The Scriptures often challenge us with their message. All you can do is prayerfully consider the Scriptures."

"I'll think about it, but I can't see myself believing this part of Scripture."

The crux of the issue. For Fromma, the crux of the issue is her belief that her rights were violated. She parroted her mother's advice that she must take care of herself. When Pastor Hank zeroed in on her self-will, Fromma balked. Mutual submission in love was an alien concept, and she rejected it.

How To Help Change the Power Struggle

Let's examine how to help a couple or an individual renounce the hold of self-will and break out of a power struggle.

Don't Announce It

A friend can often recognize a power struggle in a couple in chronic conflict, even when they can't. However, if you say to the couple, "You are in a power struggle," they may turn on you and assess your IQ, and you won't like their assessment. They will say, "We are simply discussing this issue" (the ". . . you idiot" is in parentheses), then return to their power struggle. So instead of announcing the problem, help them become more aware of the problem, then help break up old patterns of conflict and form new patterns.

Help Them Become Aware of the Problem

To help couples become aware of their disagreements, have them list the topics about which they most frequently disagree. For each topic, each spouse evaluates how he or she thinks decisions are currently made: by the wife only, mostly by the wife, equally, mostly by the husband, or by the husband only. Finally, each rates how decisions should *ideally* be made. (This adapts a strategy proposed by Richard Stuart in 1980 called the "powergram.")[5]

For example, suppose that Ted and Mary Jo agree that they have four major topics of disagreement: child discipline, where they spend the Christmas holidays, how money is spent, and whether the toilet seat should be up or down in the middle of the night. Ted thinks decisions about child rearing are currently made mostly by Mary Jo and ideally he would like them shared equally. Mary Jo thinks she now makes all the decisions about child discipline, and ideally she would like them shared equally. Ted thinks Mary Jo decides where to spend the holidays, and Mary Jo thinks Ted makes that decision. Again both ideally would like to share that decision. Ted thinks he and Mary Jo share decision-making about how money is spent, but he thinks he should have most of the decision-making authority in that area. Mary Jo agrees; she doesn't want to make money decisions. Finally, Ted thinks the toilet seat should be up at night. He thinks Mary Jo controls that decision but that he should control it. Mary Jo believes the toilet seat should be down at night. She believes Ted controls that decision, and she wants that power. Remember, the fundamental issue is not so much where the toilet seat is but *who can say* where the toilet seat is.

Creative Compromise

How could you help Mary Jo and Ted to break up the old patterns of conflict? First, try a creative compromise. (They might not be in a power struggle.) "How about if you take turns? One week the seat is up, the next week down."

Both object. "Too hard to remember."

"Besides," says Mary Jo, "it's a matter of respect for the partner. It's no fun to stumble into the bathroom half asleep and sit in cold water."

"All you have to do," says Ted, "is feel before you sit."

"If the seat is down," argues Mary Jo, "all *you* have to do is feel and lift it."

Somehow you have the feeling they've had this argument before. So you interrupt. "How about if you do something totally different until you can figure out how the seat should be left? This would be something that neither of you want. It will cause you both problems, but at least it causes neither one more problems than the other. It's temporary. How about if you close both seat and lid. Then both of you must lift something."

If you are lucky, they might adopt this temporary measure. You are trying to break up old patterns of arguing until they can form some new patterns. Neither will feel satisfied with this compromise because it creates problems and is hard to remember. Once someone forgets, the seat will be either up or down, which means someone will feel cheated. When old patterns have been disrupted, help the couple solve the problem and build new conflict resolution patterns.

Becoming Aware of Sin at the Root

There is no easy way to confront a person with his or her sin. Whenever you mention sin to someone today, rather than feeling repentance and a desire to be cleansed of sin and to accept freedom from sin's hold, that person feels put down, judged, criticized, and devalued. He or she may feel that you are making yourself superior and might get defensive, angry, hurt, or sad. It's tragic that our culture has largely lost a sense of the cleansing function of repentance, but we have. Therefore, carefully present the idea, lest you drive people away rather than draw them closer to the Lord. The Holy Spirit convicts of sin. You are merely a loving witness for the Lord. As an example of loving witness in action, let's observe Fromma and Gina as they discuss Fromma's visit to Pastor Hank.

"How'd your visit with Hank go?" said Gina as she and Fromma were walking through the neighborhood.

"Mixed, I guess."

"How so?"

"He gave me some good ideas about how Leo and I could argue less, but he has some archaic notions about submission. Those bothered me."

"What do you mean?"

"He said that Jesus had been submissive, even though He was taken advantage of, and he wanted me to be submissive even though Leo was obviously taking advantage of me. I can't see it. I don't interpret Scripture that way."

"You can't understand how being submissive can help?"

"Right. It seems like a ticket to poor self-esteem, like groveling."

"What did Hank want you to do specifically?"

Fromma paused thoughtfully. "I don't know. I freaked as soon as submission came up. I suppose I should allow Leo to play whatever sport he wants without making any demands on him."

"That doesn't sound exactly right to me," said Gina. "Jesus was obedient to death, but His life makes a strong call on us for righteousness. He practically demands that we copy Him."

"It's puzzling. I know that I'm not behaving like Jesus, and deep down I'm not proud of that, but I don't want to roll over and play dead when it comes to Leo's sports either."

"You have a strong pull from within you to have Leo show you that you're important to him—so strong that even if you have to try to coerce his love from him, you are willing to do that."

"I don't want to coerce him to love me. I can't make him love me. I want him to show me his love."

"By giving in on the sports conflict."

"Right. By giving in."

"So you want him to submit to you, and that would show you that he loves you."

Fromma laughed. "When you put it that way, it sounds terrible. I want him to give in to me, and that would show me that he loves me, but I don't want to give in to him. I don't want to show him that I love him. Ouch. That hurts."

"Because you really do love him, and you want him to know, but your conflict over his sports has forced you to do the opposite of what you want to do."

"It has! I'm being selfish. It hurts to admit that because that's what he tells me when we argue. He says I'm being selfish, I tell him he's being selfish, and we get angrier and angrier. Now I discover that I really *am* being selfish. He's been right all along, and that hurts. Of course, he's being selfish, too."

"But you aren't responsible for his behavior, are you?" said Gina.

"No."

They walked in silence. After a while, Gina glanced at Fromma. Tears were rolling down her cheeks.

"It does hurt, doesn't it?" asked Gina.

"It's like a big lump—" her voice caught and she touched her chest, "right here.

"Lord," said Gina, "set Fromma free from selfishness in her marriage. Help her imitate Your willingness to lay down Your life for us. Lord, help me, too, to love Nick and not value my wants and needs above his."

They continued to walk, Fromma and Gina both sniffling. After a block of walking, Gina said, "As I see you struggling with this, I'm convicted, too. There are so many times when I'm insensitive to Nick and think only of myself. It's painful to admit. It's like when I read. I sit on my leg and mash the nerve, so that my leg sometimes goes to sleep. When it wakes up, it's painful. But I don't mind the pain because it means my leg is getting better."

Becoming Aware of Failures in Faith Working Through Love

If you've worked with a friend for very long, the theme of living in faith working through love should have been oft-repeated. Chronic conflict is another instance of failing in the basic pattern of Christian discipleship. In a power struggle, the person loses faith that the Lord cares for him or her and protects the self instead of relying on God. In a nutshell, that is a working definition of un-faith. Losing faith in God's protectiveness, the person stops working to better the marriage and tries to protect himself or herself and his or her rights. Work is channeled into efforts that unintentionally further alienate the spouses and tend, over time, to erode faith even more. Each spouse feels unvalued, devalued, and unloved. Each withdraws love, and the cycle of self-protection and withdrawal of love intensifies.

Motivating the Couple or the Individual

A person won't change merely by knowing that he or she *should* change. This defies common sense, but we see it every day. We know we should floss our teeth daily, but we don't. We know we should eat sensibly, but we slip. Knowledge is a first step to action, but more is needed. To promote action,

- make specific suggestions for action or have the person think of specifically what he or she wants to do,
- make sure the person knows why it will help to take the specific action, and
- have the person say aloud specifically what he or she intends to do differently.[6]

Putting Motivation Into Action

Using a proven method. Use the program by Fisher and Ury for conflict resolution, described in *Getting To Yes: Negotiating Agreement Without Giving In*.[7]

The problem. The book *Getting to Yes* assumes that people deadlock because they stake out incompatible positions on issues and then argue to support their positions. Because people want to win, they refuse to move from their positions. For example, for Mary Jo and Ted, either the seat is up or down. There are no two ways about it. Both parties experience a compromise as losing because it retreats from the position each has held and defended.

Getting to the solution. Fisher and Ury's solution, though, reminds people *why* they take the position they advocate. What are their *interests* in declaring the position? Mary Jo gave an excellent clue to her interests in arguing against taking turns, which was one compromise position. She said, "Besides, it's a matter of respect for the partner." She wants Ted's respect and love. She may have other interests, too.

Ted, when questioned, said that in the middle of the night he has urinated on the seat and then been "fussed at" by Mary Jo. He doesn't want to be scolded and demeaned for making a mistake. He wants to avoid being devalued and feeling unloved.

Christian interests. In most marriages, partners want to grow in love, not in hostility. In Christian marriages, people also want to grow in faith, to reflect Christ in them (the hope of glory), and to work to promote faith and love.

Make people aware of their Christian interests. Although Christians are interested in more than their own self-interests, they still focus on self-interests during conflict, especially chronic conflict of a power struggle. Like a sore finger draws our attention, marital conflict makes us forget what's going well and focus on what isn't.

Help re-balance the interest-equation. Call attention to each person's Christian interests. Point out the desire to love each other, even though love may require self-sacrifice. Have each person talk about his or her Christian interests.

In paying attention to the Christian interests and motivations, you help reestablish the focus your friend wants but has gradually moved away from. Conflict development can be compared to boiling a frog. A frog is cold-blooded, adjusting its body temperature to its surroundings. If you raise the temperature gradually, the frog will stay happily in the pot until it is boiled. When the marital temperature rises gradually, people adapt to conflict until they, too, are boiling. Help them lower the heat by attending to their love, even in the midst of their conflict.

Figure out solutions. Once the underlying interests are discussed, solutions to the problem may become apparent to the couple. Importantly, *they,* not you, identify solutions. Further, the solutions may actually have nothing to do with the toilet seat (or whatever else is at issue), but may require fundamental assurances in a variety of tangible ways about each partner's value to the other partner.

Intervening in a marital conflict can be a mine field for the friend. Make sure that the couple really asks for your help. Tiptoe gingerly through the mine field of conflict. Strive to be a peacemaker and agent of reconciliation rather than a judge or lawyer for the prosecution or defense. Help each person apprehend God's forgiveness for sin rather than dwelling on self-condemnation. If you promote forgiveness, you'll make peace between spouses and between each person and God. As a peacemaker, you'll do more good and keep more friends.

CHAPTER EIGHTEEN

HELP CHANGE NEGATIVE THINKING

Dorothy and Dan married in their teens because Dorothy was pregnant. Despite the strains of both attending college, rearing two boys, and Dan's holding two jobs, their marriage endured. Over time, little discontents built up. They bickered and fussed but through it all, they held together, thinking of their marriage as indestructible.

Dorothy developed breast cancer. The lump was caught early, and the physician removed it. Still, the brief turmoil over the cancer was like a tornado in Dorothy and Dan's marriage, turning their love for each other upside down and strewing the strong parts of their relationship throughout the marital countryside. After Dorothy's operation, they took up different activities and argued more. As their alienation from each other increased, they pulled away from mutual friends. Both were depressed, negative, and withdrawn.

Marie, wife of Dan and Dorothy's pastor, phoned Dorothy to check on her month's absence from Bible study. Marie hadn't wanted to call. She had her own stresses, but it was curious that Dorothy's attendance had become so irregular after the surgery. Burdened by guilt, Marie picked up the phone, which started a series of phone conversations over six months that eventually changed Dorothy's life.

Gottman's Theory of Marriage Stability and Dissolution

John Mordechai Gottman[1] has studied marriages for more than twenty-five years. Gottman invited couples into the lab to discuss pleasant and conflictual topics.[2] He monitored their physiological responses before, during, and after the discussions, which he videotaped. Later, couples viewed the discussions and commented on their thoughts and feelings during the discussions. Based on his research, he proposed a theory of marriage stability and dissolution.

Marital interactions may be positive or negative. Crucial to marital satisfaction and stability is maintaining a minimum "threshold" of positive to negative interactions. Happily married couples may commonly have five or more positive interactions to every negative one. Unhappily married couples may commonly have more negative interactions than positive. Importantly, the threshold differs for different people, and some people with high expectations for their marriage may require many positive interactions to avoid reaching the threshold.

As long as the ratio of positive to negative interactions doesn't dip to a person's threshold level, the relationship is perceived as positive. Negative interactions are explained away. For example, if the wife yells about the husband's messy desk, the husband says to himself, *She's just having a bad day* or *I wonder what irritated her this morning.* He assumes his wife's love, respect, and positive personality.

If the ratio of positive to negative interactions dips to the threshold, though, the marriage is suddenly perceived as threatened and negative. Negative events are explained differently—as due to the partner's negative, enduring personality traits, marital incompatibility, or some other lasting characteristic. Further negative events are seen as confirming the marriage's basic negativity, while positive events are explained away as temporary aberrations from the normal. A wife might think, *He can be nice for a little while, but he's terrible to live with.*

In positive marriages, people calm themselves by relaxing, soothing themselves or each other, or taking a break from the disagreement. In negative marriages, people remain upset by thinking of themselves as hurt, righteously indignant, sad, angry, and contemptuous (and contemplating retaliation); or as hurt, attacked, and innocent (and whining about the injustice of the marriage, poor outcome of marriage, or fear of what will happen). Once upset, people "rewrite" the marital history, recalling mostly the negative times. The negative thoughts and feelings increase.

Helping Change Negative Thinking

An Overview

Negative thinking due to the events in the marriage. When negative thinking about the marriage, the spouse, and the future of the marriage is evident, it may be relatively easy to change or almost impervious to change. For example, negative thinking can arise from a recent disappointment in the marriage, in which case the person has had little time to garner support for his or her negative perception about the entire marriage. Or the marriage may have eroded over time, and substantial evidence for a poor marriage is available whenever anything negative happens.

Negative thinking due to the person. Even worse, negative thinking may be a relatively stable personality characteristic of one or both spouses. The person may have been pessimistic for years, with the pessimism extending into virtually every area of life. The person might be sensitive to negative events and virtually ignore positive events. Or, the person may think negatively because he or she is temporarily depressed. Depression leads to a negative mindset about the self, others, and the future.[3]

Changing negative thinking is almost never easy. When you hear evidence of your friend's negative thinking—criticism of the spouse, negative expectations, attributions of blame, assumptions about the poor character of the marriage or its bleak future, self-downing statements, and the like—it is tempting to think that you can simply correct your friend's thinking and change the marriage. It's not that easy.

People who view their marriage negatively believe they have mounds of evidence that support their belief. Regardless of what you say, your friend can discount it. A woman might think, *How does she know that my husband isn't to blame? She hasn't lived with him for ten years.*

To help your friend change, help (1) change the focus of attention away from the spouse's failures to your friend's own responsibilities, (2) change the evidence supporting the negative beliefs, expectations, and assumptions, (3) pay attention to evidence that is currently being ignored, (4) change the reasoning that led to the negative conclusions, or (5) change patterns of thinking that reinforce the negative conclusions. None of these changes comes easily.

Help Change the Focus of Attention

"You can't change your spouse." Most people in marital turmoil sing the same song: "If My Love'll Just Change, We'll Be All Right." It has a repetitious chorus.

> What can I do to make him change?
> What can I say to turn him around?
> Why can't I simply make him learn?
> For only then can our joy return.

Catchy, huh? But though more people are singing it every year, it probably won't hit *Billboard*'s Top Ten because the thought is a mere fantasy and people—even as they sing it—know it is a fantasy. They know they can never *make* the spouse change. Yet, like the mythical Sisyphus, who was doomed to roll a boulder uphill forever only to have it roll back, they keep trying.

To help a person stop trying to change his or her spouse say, "Regardless of what you do or say, you can never make him [or her] change. You can't control his [or her] behavior, thoughts, or feelings, as you probably well know by now." (Pause for an answer.) "All you can really control is your own behavior. In that area, you can make a difference."

Although saying this one time may make little impact, repetition will often bring about a change because the idea squares so faithfully with people's experience. They have tried to change the spouse and know they can't. They simply need permission to stop trying and the promise of fruitfulness with another direction to focus their attempts at change.

"How can you change yourself?" Get people thinking immediately about *how* to change themselves, not *whether* they can change. Say, "How can you act differently that might bring love and value back into your marriage?" Focus on their own responsibilities. How are they to act? How would Jesus have them respond to being hurt or devalued? How should they change their communication to show love? How can they act in faith that the Lord will change them and their spouse?

Get people to set practical goals for themselves, such as, "When she curls her lip at me in contempt, rather than blow up, I'll ignore it," or, "When she refuses my sexual advances, I'll ask when we *can* make love rather than get hurt and sulk."

Ask people to think of what they want to do differently. For example, Fred and Margaret have had several arguments in the past few weeks. Having traced the pattern from Margaret's point of view, you might say, "Whenever you and Fred have an argument, you withdraw because you don't like conflict. So Fred thinks you are walking out and don't care. How could you handle your feelings besides walking away?"

"I could tell him I don't want to argue."

"How might he take that?"

"He'd probably think I was walking away again."

"So how could you help him understand you better?"

"I could say, 'I don't want to argue; it scares me. I want to work out our differences, but when we get heated, I can't take it.'"

"How might he react if you said that?"

"Probably better."

"How will you remind yourself to say that when the next heated disagreement begins?"

"I don't know," Margaret might say. When you don't jump in with a suggestion right away, she might say, "I could use the feelings of wanting to get away as a reminder."

"Good."

By getting people thinking about *how* to change their behavior, you help them not blame or take responsibility for things they can't change.

"How can you demonstrate faith working through love?" Negative thoughts or expectations are automatic cues for people to build their faith. Help them become more disciplined—more of a disciple of Christ—by asking directly how they intend to demonstrate faith working through love to their spouse. Focus on specific situations rather than general strategies. Generalities are rarely translated into actions, but planning specific actions that would exemplify faith, work, and love will often be used in those situations and will also generalize to other situations.

Margaret complains about Fred's pessimism.

"Fred is so pessimistic. Whatever happens, he thinks the world is coming to an end."

Not content to let Margaret generalize, you ask, "I don't understand. Can you give me an example?"

Margaret says, "Last night, when we argued over whether his sister could stay with us an entire week this fall, I ended the argument by saying it was too upsetting to talk about, and I walked out of the room. He yelled, 'That's the way it always is. We can't resolve anything. Our marriage is never going to get better.' See, he has no confidence that anything positive will ever happen. He doesn't see that by not getting into a worse argument, I'm protecting us from a worse marriage."

"That did sound pessimistic. Remember, though, that you can't affect his attitudes directly. You can only be responsible for your attitudes. I know you want to act in faith in this situation. Can you think of how you might have acted that would have demonstrated faith working through love?"

"I suppose I could have stayed and talked, having faith that the Lord would have protected us instead of taking things into my own hands by leaving."

"Yes, I'm sure that if you approached Fred with an attitude that you wanted to work out your differences without hurting each other, then the Lord would have honored that desire by helping you not to lose your temper and helping Fred stay under control, too."

"I guess, too, that walking out didn't exactly convey my love for Fred. I could at least have told him that I thought his suggestions were good and that I was interested in them before I told him that I was having trouble dealing with our conflict. That would have said that I loved him."

Helping people strive to act as faithful, loving, working disciples of Christ aims their attention where it should be aimed—on Jesus and His faithfulness, love, and work on our behalf.

"*Prayer is necessary.*" Lasting change comes only with the intervention of the King of kings. Prayer is our access to His throne at which we lay our petitions; it is the work of the Christian disciple. Praying with and for your friend is vital, as is coaching your friend to pray for himself or herself.

"*Focus on solutions instead of problems.*" Negative thinking, by its nature, is an over-concern with problems. Help your friend defeat problem-thinking by asking about solutions. Solution-thinking changes problems into possibilities. Once conceived, possibilities can become probabilities, with effort. Encourage your friend to think about solutions, even if none are immediately forthcoming.

People stuck in a rut of negative thinking can sometimes benefit by a creative approach. Jennie was over-committed to her children, work, church, and PTA. She felt intimacy with her husband slipping away. Stymied about finding a solution to her problem, she consulted Teri, a neighborhood friend. Teri knew Jennie loved mystery novels, so she used that idea to help Jennie become more solution-focused than problem-focused.

Jennie: I don't know what to do. Our marriage is skidding into the pit. I can't break out of the skid.
Teri: Jennie, hon, what you have is a good mystery. Why don't you treat it as a mystery? You know how you like to figure out mystery novel plots before the author gives the solution. Think of this in the same way.
Jennie: The Case of the Vanishing Time, huh?
Teri: Yeah, or The Case of the Too-Pooped Supermom.
Jennie: I suppose bumping somebody off is out of the question.
Teri: You probably should think of yourself as the detective.
Jennie: I wish I could kill some of these tasks. I'm worn out being on the PTA board and the building committee at church. They eat up time and don't seem to be doing anything worthwhile to advance God's kingdom.
Teri: Then, be a hit-man, or a hit-person. What are the arguments for killing those activities?
Jennie: Now, I *like* that idea. I suppose if I dropped out of the PTA board . . .

Jennie took a fresh look at her commitments when Teri approached the problem creatively. While being a fantasy hit-person who bumped off unwanted activities might appeal to few people, it was right for Jennie, and Teri recognized that.

Help Change the Evidence Supporting the Negative Beliefs

Negative beliefs, expectations, and assumptions are woven together in a fabric of evidence. Tugging on the conclusions is like trying to rip new rip-stop fabric. Efforts warp and distort but rarely succeed in tearing apart the web of evidence. Attacking the threads of evidence is the most effective way to change negative thinking—though doing so may sometimes be as time-consuming as trying to reweave a fabric.

Help the person change the evidence by changing his or her own behavior, which will provoke different reactions from his or her partner. The spouse will explain away new behaviors at first, but encourage the person to persevere. Remember, people do not generally change their perceptions of the marriage gradually, so don't expect to see increasingly positive reactions by the partner. Changing perceptions is a dramatic event, a sudden epiphany, in which the spouse realizes, usually within a moment (or at most over a few days) that he or she is loved and valued, that faith in the marriage, the partner, and in the Lord can be restored, and that the partner is working on improving the marriage. Explain to your friend how perceptions change and encourage perseverance. Encouraging perseverance in the face of repeated lack of progress will probably be your greatest challenge in helping.

"I try and try to change," said Fromma. "I try not to put Leo down when he's indecisive, but I keep failing. I get so frustrated that I lose my temper and lash out at Leo, blaming him for our problems. Then I get depressed because I've failed again. It's a depressing cycle."

"You're discouraged," said Gina. "I can hear it in your voice. Changing habits is never easy. I have the same problem with my poor eating habits. But, Fromma, remember how your relationship with Leo was before you tried to change."

"Yeah," she said bitterly. "Terrible."

"Right, and now things are better. Sure, you slip up, once or twice a week—"

"More like four or five times a week."

"OK, four or five times a week. But what did it used to be?"

"Four or five times a day."

"Then, you've made progress. Instead of mauling yourself because you're not perfect, look at the progress. The difference in the emotional climate in your marriage must be large when you compare it with a half year ago."

"It is. But Leo's so slow to change. I'll bet he doesn't even notice any difference."

"He may not, but you notice the difference, and if you keep trying to change, some day he will notice."

The central element in almost every marital therapy is helping spouses act differently toward each other so they can (eventually) perceive that their marriage has become different. For instance, Gottman and his colleagues[4] had paraprofessional helpers assist couples in working through the *Couple's Guide to Communication.* He found that, after two years, none of those couples had divorced as opposed to 50 percent of the couples who did not work through the *Guide.* Gottman has recommended a minimal marital therapy involving only three small, but vitally important changes in communication.[5] Partners are trained in:

- non-defensive and non-provocative speaking, especially in response to the other partner's complaints,
- non-defensive listening and validation of the partner,
- editing (not saying hurtful things that come to mind).

When couples can make these three small changes consistently, they soon provide evidence of their valuing love and work on the relationship, which restores faith in the marriage.

Suggest Paying Attention to Evidence that Is Currently Ignored

Look at the flip side of negative emotions. When people are troubled, their emotions are complex. Some are near the surface, and others are buried. Help them see the emotions they are missing by looking beyond the most obvious emotion.

Anger usually is a response to feeling hurt and may shield a person from feeling fear. When you see your friend acting angry, observe, "You sound hurt." Anger is a hard, divisive emotion, but hurt is a softer feeling, more open to healing.

Sadness protects a person from anger, which he or she may find scary. When your friend cries, say, "Maybe there's some anger mixed with those tears." Identifying the anger or sadness can help give clues about how to repair the damage that caused the anger and how to avoid getting more down on himself or herself.

Encourage reminiscence about close times. Helping people recall positive times helps them feel positive rather than negative emotions. It also gives them a vision of what might be accomplished if they work on their marriage. Ask your friend to describe pleasant times. As the story continues, ask questions, elaborate on details, sharpen the image. Steer the conversation away from criticisms and negative thoughts.

Ask about good communication. Ask about times when marital communication was good. Most people can recall better times, even if they feel negative about their marriage. Ask, What made communication good? How did each person act during disagreements? What did they talk about—their dreams, their goals, their ambitions? In almost every area, asking about what used to work when things were going well will stimulate your friend to try some of those strategies again.

Help Change Reasoning that Led to Negative Conclusions

Show your friend how to question himself or herself. "He's so mean. He says such hateful things. I know he's trying to hurt me." Dorothy tearfully recounted her latest argument with Dan. Marie had talked via phone for weeks with Dorothy on improving Dorothy's marriage, and Dorothy had made genuine progress. Nevertheless, marital storms still raged. Marie realized that Dorothy's conclusions about Dan did not spring from nowhere. They were built on the evidence of events that Dorothy had experienced and interpreted and the logic of drawing conclusions.

Marie had concentrated on helping Dorothy create new evidence of love and discover the evidence of love that Dorothy was prone to overlook during pessimistic times. Today, though, Marie thought that Dorothy could look more closely at her reasoning.

"Dorothy, you're making an assumption about Dan's motives. Are you sure he meant to hurt you?"

"Well, it seems that way. What else could he be thinking when he says such hurtful things?"

Marie didn't hesitate. "You said that you say hurtful things, too, when you argue."

"Yeah, but that's different."

"Oh? How?"

"He provokes me into saying the things. Anyway, I always feel sorry afterwards because I don't mean the hurtful things. They just, well, happen."

"So you say hurtful things but don't always mean them. Is he different from you?"

"Um, sometimes yes, and sometimes no."

"Thinking Dan is out to get you or hurt you doesn't help bind wounds. It keeps you apart. Also, your conclusion isn't necessarily true—at least not all the time."

"You're right. If I look at the marriage in a negative frame of mind, these thoughts happen."

"Question yourself when you start to think negatively."

"What do you mean 'question' myself?"

"Ask yourself whether your conclusions are correct. Ask whether they are the product of habit or discouragement."

"How could I question myself? I don't know how."

"For instance, in the argument you and Dan just had, when you catch yourself saying, 'He's mean. He intentionally tried to hurt me. He doesn't care,' then say to yourself, 'Do I want to hurt him, or do I want to make the marriage better? Why should I expect his motives to be different from mine?'"

"But sometimes I do want to hurt him. He makes me so mad I could scream."

"If your motives are sinful, you can confess those motives and pray for strength to repent and for forgiveness from God."

Find and change the equations that govern moods. Sometimes people behave as if their feelings were governed by simple equations. Here are two (of many) examples.

- Having an argument equals depression; having no arguments equals happiness.
- Getting a positive response to my sexual overtures equals "she loves me"; getting a negative response to my sexual overtures equals "she doesn't love me."

If you ask your friend to examine each equation dispassionately, he or she will quickly admit that the equation is over-simplified. Yet, agreement *in the abstract* that the equation is over-simplified will not invalidate the equation. To invalidate the equation, the person must reason about the validity of each side of the equation. Here is an example of how Marie helped Dorothy examine an equation that governed her life.

Dorothy: We can't keep hurting each other like this. It's as if we're poisoning each other daily. If we continue, our marriage will die.
Marie: It sounds as if you believe that people who hurt each other can never be happy together, and that if people don't hurt each other, they'll be happy.
Dorothy: Hmmm. That's right.
Marie: Tell me again about your parents. You said they had a happy marriage.
Dorothy: They were married thirty-three years before my father died.
Marie: And they were happily married?
Dorothy: Very.
Marie: Every day? They never argued?
Dorothy: No, they argued sometimes. I remember one big argument over whether my father would take a promotion that would require him to travel.

Marie: And in that argument, they spoke reasonably with each other throughout?
Dorothy: Of course not. They got very mad, yelled, screamed. Dad called Mom "stubborn and pig-headed."
Marie: That sounds hurtful. They said hurtful things to each other, but they still loved each other.
Dorothy: (thoughtfully) Yeah, they did.
Marie: So you have shown yourself that your equation—that people who hurt each other can never be happy together—isn't correct.
Dorothy: You're right.
Marie: On the other hand, you know couples who seem never to argue or to disagree about *anything*.
Dorothy: But their marriage is definitely not one I'd like to have. It's dead.
Marie: Right. So it sounds as if both sides of your equation are false. Not arguing doesn't necessarily mean that a marriage is happy, and even people with a happy marriage sometimes hurt each other.
Dorothy: Yeah, I haven't been thinking perfectly clearly.

Change the problem-metaphor into a solution-metaphor. Most people think of their problems in terms of metaphors or similes. They imply or describe their problems as similar to or like something else. For instance, Dorothy described her arguments with Dan "as if we're poisoning each other daily. If we continue," she said, "our marriage will die."

Listen for metaphors. They are usually phrased as insoluble problems, leaving no hope. When you hear a metaphor, think how it might be transformed into a solution-metaphor. For instance, Marie could have said to Dorothy, "Even though you're poisoning each other daily, the solution is to take an antidote that can neutralize the poison. The antidote may be a bitter pill to take. It may require an effort to swallow. But it can bring health. I think your antidote is this: when you feel poisoned, instead of feeding poison to Dan, give him the antidote—practice faith working through love."

Help Change Thinking That Reinforces Negative Conclusions

Catch automatic thoughts. Most negative thinking is automatic. "Have you realized that most of your unhappiness in life is due to the fact that you are listening to yourself instead of talking to yourself?" asked Martyn Lloyd-Jones.[6] We carry on a monologue that reinforces our negative beliefs, assumptions, or perceptions.

Psychologists have found that people can change their attitudes if they talk about, think about, or even read aloud the opposite attitudes. If we practice talking negatively to ourselves, we will come to believe ourselves. The other side of the coin is that we can change our thinking and truly affect our perceptions, as has been recommended by Norman Vincent Peale, Robert Schuller, and others for years. Help your friend detect the negative monologue, then plan a more positive monologue.

Interrupt and argue with negative self-talk. Detecting negative self-talk is a time for assertiveness. Help your friend actively interrupt the internal monologue, not wait wimpishly for it to taper off. Then, help the person argue with himself or herself.

Dorothy: I don't blow up at Dan as often, but I still feel as if I'm going to explode sometimes. He still says hurtful things—not as often as before, but often enough. It burns me up. I think how stupid he is and how our marriage isn't going to work out and how I'd like to just shout like I used to. The more I storm around, the hotter I get. It's all I can do to keep from blowing up.

Marie: It sounds like you need to detect that burning early and douse the flame quickly. (Marie turned Dorothy's problem-metaphor into a solution-metaphor.)

Dorothy: I'm not very good at putting out the fire.

Marie: Well, like a fireman, you need to take away either the fuel, the heat, or the oxygen. The fuel is probably Dan's comments. You can't do anything directly about those except provoking him less, which it sounds as if you're doing.

Dorothy: Right. That helps, but it hasn't stopped the problem.

Marie: The heat is the emotion. It's hard not to get emotional when you feel hurt. If you provide the oxygen—your own thoughts—then the heat will inevitably rise. The only thing you can affect directly is your thoughts. You'll keep the heat down if you tackle those thoughts directly with cool logic.

Dorothy: I'm not a computer. I'm going to get emotional if I feel insulted or put down.

Marie: Of course you will. It wouldn't be natural if you didn't feel angry and hurt, but if you dwell on how much you've been hurt or wronged, you'll feel even more emotional. Yet if you dwell on the reasons those thoughts aren't helpful, you'll get less emotional. You decide whether you want to get more or less emotional. You have a choice. You can't create feelings from nowhere, but you can strengthen or weaken feelings and control their expression.

Dorothy: So how do I control my anger?
Marie: Let's take the thoughts you mentioned. You said you'd think that Dan was stupid, that your marriage wasn't going to work, and . . . I forgot the third thought.
Dorothy: That I wanted to scream at him.
Marie: Right. Let's take them one at a time. Suppose I were you. I think, *Dan's stupid for saying those hurtful things to me.* I could argue with myself. I could think, *Of course, I know he isn't really stupid. He's bright. He's unkind. No, that isn't right either. He's usually kind. Uh, he's making a mistake by saying those hurtful things.* See how I'm reasoning with myself. Don't call Dan names, even in your head. He has many good qualities. That's why you married him. He still has those qualities. His *action* isn't helpful, but that's different from there being something wrong with him. Right?
Dorothy: Right.
Marie: Now, your second thought was, "My marriage isn't going to work." How could you argue against that thought?
Dorothy: I could say, "Of course our marriage will work. We've been through absolute hell during the early years. We have a lot going for us. We can handle this crisis."
Marie: Good. And the third thought—that you'd like to shout?
Dorothy: That's easy. I've tried shouting. That doesn't work. What I've been doing lately—trying to meet him in faith and love—has worked better. So I could remind myself to keep with the program that's working.
Marie: Great.

Avoid ineffective strategies. Almost everyone has tried at times to change his or her thoughts. Sometimes we succeed, sometimes we fail. If your friend has difficulty changing his or her negative thoughts, it may be because he or she is using an ineffective method.

Repetition doesn't work. Repeating a phrase or thought over and over loses any power. Instead, have your friend rephrase the thought. Think of new ways of saying the same thought. That keeps the mind involved and keeps your friend from listening to those automatic negative thoughts.

When friends instruct themselves what *not* to think, that doesn't help. In fact, like saying *"Don't* think about oranges," telling themselves *not* to think about the weaknesses in their marriage accomplishes the opposite. They will think about the weaknesses. Instead of saying, *"Don't* think about the marriage's weaknesses," say "Name the specific strengths of the marriage."

Trying to change thinking once or twice and then giving up is also ineffective. Have your friend realize that any new habit seems awkward at first. Your friend will adapt quickly, though, if he or she persists.

Compartmentalize negatives. Negatives, once begun, spread. Soon the entire marriage is viewed as negative, and your friend rewrites the marital history. Coach your friend to avoid over-generalization of negative thoughts into the whole marriage. There have always been positive aspects of the marriage and those aspects still exist. Your friend's task is to identify and expand those positive aspects.

Help put the negatives into a compartment. When your friend says, "He always insults me," ask, "Do you mean *every* statement is an insult?"

"No," your friend might reply, "he insults me when he's under stress." That's a smaller compartment.

Then see if you can help make the compartment even smaller. "So, *every* time he has been under stress he insulted you."

"No, *sometimes* when he is under stress, he insults me, especially when I correct or criticize him."

Not only does such questioning reduce the size of the negative compartment, it also provides practical suggestions that your friend might use to improve the marriage climate.

Focus on God's ability to do anything. Negative thinking is based on the idea that whatever is true now (negative marital interactions and feelings) will inevitably continue and get worse. This negates God's power to make life-transforming changes. God has always radically changed lives. Why should He suddenly go on strike? God has the ability to change hearts, the heart of your friend, the heart of your friend's spouse, and even your own heart. God wants us to be mature disciples of Jesus. If we approach a marital problem searching for how God wants to build us in our character, there are no limits to what He will do.

Together in Christ

Six months after Marie placed her first call to Dorothy, the tornado in Dorothy's and Dan's lives departed as suddenly as it had hit. A church revival turned the couple around. Over the months, a spirit of brokenness and trust permeated Dorothy. She grew in her faith as she listened and tried to practice Marie's wise counsel. Dan was visibly softened by Marie's changed attitudes, and the couple began to attend church again.

When the pastor gave a week of sermons on the family, Dan and Dorothy were primed to listen. The Holy Spirit, working through His servant Marie, other supportive women in the church, Dorothy, and the revival preacher drew Dan and Dorothy together again within the arms of Christ's body.

CHAPTER NINETEEN

HELP COPE WITH COMPLICATING PROBLEMS

Some problems create havoc in marriages, troubled or not. Among the many serious problems, infidelity, alcohol abuse, and physical abuse are especially damaging. Others (serious chronic physical problems, psychological difficulties, childhood sexual abuse) deserve mention, but space limitations prevent me from dealing with them. I'll briefly describe how to help a friend with infidelity, alcohol abuse, and physical abuse and will provide a few resources for you to consult if you encounter those problems (see list on next page).

Infidelity

Definitions

Infidelity is unfaithfulness, sexual or otherwise. If a person wants to know if an act is an infidelity, Frank Pittman,[1] a family therapist who has written about infidelity in *Private Lies,* says the person should ask his or her spouse, who will quickly say whether an infidelity has been committed. Generally, if a person thinks an act should be kept secret from the spouse, it is usually an infidelity.

Some Resources Concerning
Common Complicating Problems

INFIDELITY

Willard F. Harley, Jr., Love *Busters: Overcoming the Habits that Destroy Romantic Love* (Tarrytown, N.Y.: Fleming H. Revell, 1992).

Frank Pittman, *Private Lies: Infidelity and the Betrayal of Intimacy* (New York: Norton, 1989).

Henry A. Virkler, *Broken Promises: Healing and Preventing Affairs in Christian Marriages* (Dallas: Word, 1992).

ALCOHOL ABUSE

David & Elsie MacKenzie, *Still Married, Still Sober* (Downers Grove, Ill.: InterVarsity, 1991).

Robert S. McGee, *Learning More about Chemical Dependency* (Houston: Rapha Publishing, 1991).

Daryl E. Quick, *The Healing Journey for Adult Children of Alcoholics* (Downers Grove, Ill.: InterVarsity, 1990).

Dale and Juanita Ryan, *Recovery from Codependency* (Downers Grove, Ill.: InterVarsity, 1990).

__________. *Recovery from Addictions* (Downers Grove, Ill.: InterVarsity, 1990).

Pat Springle, *Learning More about Codependency* (Houston and Dallas: Rapha Publishing and Word, 1991).

PHYSICAL ABUSE

James and Phyllis Alsdurf, *Battered into Submission: The Tragedy of Wife Abuse in the Christian Home* (Downers Grove, Ill.: InterVarsity, 1989).

Dale and Juanita Ryan, *Recovery from Abuse* (Downers Grove, Ill.: InterVarsity, 1990).

Adultery is the infidelity of having sexual intercourse with someone other than one's spouse. Adulterous affairs happen for many reasons (see next page), but they are always traumatic.

Why Do Affairs Happen?

People may commit adultery
for any of several reasons.

"Oops": A one-time encounter.

"Cupid got me": A romantic love-affair—harder to get over than a one-time encounter.

"Mid-life crisis": This doesn't happen very often.

"Is all we have just us?": Children grow up, leave home, and reveal a dead marriage.

"The devil made me do it": Repeated affairs may indicate a sexual compulsion.

"Can't stand the heat": Too much intimacy makes partners seek distance by initiating an affair.

"The Terminator": An affair is one partner's way to initiate divorce.

Helping the Unfaithful Spouse

In a marriage traumatized by an affair, you might be asked for help either by the unfaithful or faithful spouse. First, I will discuss how to help the *un*faithful spouse.

Step 1: Reveal the affair. Suggest that the unfaithful spouse reveal the affair. Don't reveal it yourself. An affair usually depends on secrecy for its existence. Once revealed, most affairs don't continue. Affairs, with few responsibilities of marriage, are unfair comparisons with troubled marriages. Partners should try to resolve their differences without competing with the affair.

Step 2: Deal with the trauma of the affair. Once revealed, the affair will traumatize the faithful partner. Ask the unfaithful spouse to examine his or her motives for the affair and intentions regarding a future affair. The unfaithful spouse should reflect on lessons learned from the experience, and he or she should consider confession to the partner and to God, repentance before God, and seeking forgiveness for wronging the partner.

Step 3: Deal with the breach of trust. Often, the unfaithful spouse will emerge from the self-examination of motives, confession, and repentance with renewed commitment to the partner and to the Lord. Unfortunately, that does not heal the scar on the bond of marital trust. Trust must be rebuilt as with a building that has been ravaged by a hurricane—brick by brick. Help both partners realize that time is necessary to heal a fractured marriage.

Step 4: Deal with marital problems. Often, the affair dramatizes the marriage's serious troubles. Direct the couple to counseling and continue to support your friend and the marriage.

Step 5: Prevent future problems. The unfaithful partner must plan how he or she will deal with future sexual temptations.

Helping the Faithful Spouse

Dealing with the faithful spouse follows essentially the same progression as dealing with the unfaithful one.

Step 1: Deal with the shock of the revealed affair. Anger is appropriate, but saying hurtful things will compound problems. The person should be angry but not sin (Ephesians 4:26).

Step 2: Rebuild trust. Trust cannot be rebuilt without first forgiving the spouse. As long as unforgiveness, desire for revenge, or bitterness are present, the faithful partner will hold a grudge and will prevent bonds of trust from reforming. The faithful spouse should declare a specific trial period for rebuilding trust, for six months or a year. After that, the faithful spouse should try to let the matter drop. Although the affair will never be forgotten, it should not be mentioned again.

Step 3: Deal with problems in the marriage. An affair communicates that something is wrong with the marriage. Partners should seek counseling together to repair those difficulties.

Step 4: Prevent future problems. If spouses plan together ways to prevent future problems, often the marriage can survive.

Help with Alcohol Abuse

The average annual per capita consumption of alcoholic beverages in the United States is about 39 *gallons*; 95 percent of the consumption is done by one-third of the drinkers (U.S. Department of

Commerce, 1986).[2] Alcohol affects more people in the United States than any other drug. Between 10 and 18 million people are alcoholic. When family members are considered, alcoholism may directly affect between 45 and 75 million people in the United States alone, not considering innocent victims of alcohol-related accidents or violence.

Alcoholism and Codependency

There are three types of alcoholism: heavy daily drinking, heavy drinking only on weekends, or binges of heavy drinking that last for days, weeks, or months (American Psychiatric Association, 1987).[3] Alcohol abuse involves an inability to stop or stay stopped drinking, continued use despite health problems, and troubles at work or with friends or family. Alcohol dependence involves alcohol abuse plus increasing tolerance and withdrawal symptoms if the person tries to stop.

Alcohol abuse and dependence affect marriages and families. Originally a codependent was a member of an abuser's family who initially railed against drinking, but who later protected the abuser from the natural consequences of his or her abuse and enabled him or her to continue to abuse alcohol. In recent years, the meaning of codependent has been broadened to include anyone who attempts to control and rescue someone from any perceived dependency. In codependency, pleasing another person is more important than confronting the problem. Codependency involves trying to rescue a person by controlling and feeling responsible for him or her. Codependents feel hurt and angry over the other person's dependency, guilty for the problem and for not being able to solve it, and rejected, lonely, and unappreciated.

Codependent Christians have additional characteristics, according to Pat Springle[4] of Rapha, a Christian in-patient treatment program. Codependents are driven to perform. Adding biblical oughts and shoulds to society's oughts and shoulds, codependent Christians are plagued by over-responsibility and guilt. Understanding the concept of God's grace, codependent Christians nevertheless can't allow themselves to experience grace, which makes them feel even guiltier. Burdened with commands, they believe they should always feel love, joy, and peace. They can't. More guilt. They despair, and knowing that God should not be blamed, they take all the blame on themselves, in effect trying to save the Savior from blame.

Treatment of Alcohol Dependency

Examine yourself. Many helpers help because they possess tendencies of the codependent. Do you? Before we discuss treatment of alcoholics and their partners, examine yourself objectively. Test your motives for helping. How do you respond to failure? If you react by increasing perfectionistic efforts, self-punishment, and self-blame rather than confessing, repenting, and accepting forgiveness, then self may be playing a large part of your motivation to help.

Get the alcoholic into treatment. Many people recover without hospitalization, indeed without any formal treatment. Most can't. Relapse rate is high regardless of treatment. Still, as a general guideline, direct alcoholics toward treatment. Some treatments are better than others (see next page for an evaluation).[5]

Most modern treatments of alcoholism have used some detoxification, (perhaps) in-patient hospitalization, some modification of AA's 12-Steps, some sort of individual counseling, active involvement of spouses in alcoholics' lives, aftercare, and relapse prevention.[6] Although family members have been included in many treatments, the role of friends is generally the forgotten or slighted piece.

Helping Your Friend

When will you be asked for help? You won't usually be asked for help by the alcoholic, who typically lives in denial of the problem in its early stages and withdrawal from social relationships and paranoia in its latter stages. Even the alcoholic's spouse will seldom seek support and advice. When a spouse asks for help, usually in the early stage of the partner's alcoholism, focus on supporting, understanding, and giving accurate information. Spouses usually do not request help with codependency. They don't recognize they need help. When you recognize codependency, aim your friend at resources to read or at groups that focus on codependency.

Help the alcoholic. Robert McGee, founder and president of Rapha, a Christian hospital program, has described useful dos and don'ts of helping a friend who is involved with alcohol in his book, *Learning More About Chemical Dependency* (Houston: Rapha).

Effectiveness of Treatments for Alcoholism

Detoxification. Detoxification is effective. It can usually be carried out as effectively in outpatient as in inpatient settings.

Antabuse. Antabuse, a drug (disulfiram) that makes people nauseated when alcohol is drunk after its use, has not been effective. The alcoholic doesn't usually take it.

Aversive Therapy. Aversive therapy pairs unpleasant experiences, like high doses of Antabuse or electric shock, with alcohol consumption. Aversive therapy is sometimes effective, but booster sessions are often needed.

Counseling. Individual and group therapy have had moderate success.

Alcoholics Anonymous. Alcoholics Anonymous (AA) depends on participants' working through twelve steps with high peer support. Attendance at the AA meetings is related to abstinence. AA groups have been effective, and the twelve step program of AA has been adapted widely.

Marital and Family Therapy. Marital and family therapy, while not for all alcoholics, has been shown to produce better rates of abstinence and more positive effects on the marriage and family than has individual psychotherapy.

DON'T

1. confront the person when he is drunk or high.
2. yell, overreact, lecture, or preach.
3. let the person blame you for his or her behavior and its consequences. Don't blame yourself either.
4. accept excuses such as, "Everybody's doing it!"
5. give orders or make empty threats. Follow through with what you say you will do.

DO

1. act calmly. Communicate that you care. That's why you are getting involved.
2. be objective. Don't exaggerate or deny the reality of the situation.
3. plan ahead. Know what your options are. Know what you are going to do in a crisis situation so that you can tell the person clearly and firmly about your plans when the situation occurs.
4. get help. Contact someone who specializes in chemical dependency treatment and/or counseling.

(McGee, 1991, pp. 49–50)

Help the alcoholic's spouse. Your responsibilities are limited.

- Provide Information.
- Encourage Responsibility. The spouse, regardless of how "co-dependent," did not make the partner alcoholic. The alcoholic bears that responsibility. The spouse is responsible for living in faith working through love.
- Help Make Wise Decisions. Help the spouse with decisions about treatment, separation, or divorce if you are asked. Help the spouse explore his or her decisions and likely consequences, then let go of the control. Remain a faithful friend regardless of the person's decision about divorce, separation, or remaining in the marriage. Practice faith, work, and love on your friend's behalf, not control, coercion, and judgment.
- Pray. Without God's intervention, helping the alcoholic or his or her spouse is hopeless. The sheer hopelessness should be a stimulus to prayer for us. Armed with prayer, we can bring our friends to the foot of the throne, which is the only place salvation happens.

Help with Physical Abuse

Gilliland and James estimate that a fourth of United States couples experience at least one incidence of wife abuse during their marriage; about one out of six have at least one incidence a year; about one-tenth of husbands abuse their wives regularly. Wife abuse happens across social classes, ages, and races.[7] It happens even within the church, as has been thoroughly documented by James and Phyllis Alsdurf.[8] The rate of wife abuse by the highly religious is lower than in the population at large, but substantial abuse still occurs.[9]

When abuse happens in religious marriages, women are often unwilling to protect themselves or to end the relationship because of theological beliefs. Furthermore, when a woman seeks help from clergy, she is often advised to return to the marriage and submit to her husband—especially in the more theologically conservative Protestant denominations and in the Roman Catholic Church.[10]

Listening and Understanding

Most abused women will seek advice and help only after they have been beaten. As a friend, your main task is listening and understanding. If you are like most people, you may be appalled by the signs of physical damage to your friend. Your righteous anger may be kindled at the abuser, and you may fear for the woman. You may be tempted to judge and condemn the abuser for his cruelty or the woman for having put up with the abuse. She may want to return to the abusive situation. Keep judgmental attitudes in check. They won't help your friend. They will only drive her away from you and possibly back into physical danger.

Help your friend feel OK for having sought help. The abusive relationship is laden with ambivalence. On one hand, the abused woman may be afraid that telling you about her problems could cause her more danger and pain, especially if her husband finds out. On the other, she wants support. Help her feel good about seeking help.

Suppose Carol has sought help from Gerry.

Gerry: I'm glad you came. You did the right thing. I want to help you, and I'll support you, whatever happens.
Carol: I've never been so scared. Even though Hal hit me before, this was different—it really hurt. But I don't know. I'd better go back. He was upset.
Gerry: You sound confused. I know it's hard to talk about this. It's probably embarrassing.
Carol: It is embarrassing. It's like admitting I'm a failure as a wife. I feel like a betrayer.
Gerry: You're not a betrayer if you've been hit so hard your face is swollen. If a stranger hit you, you wouldn't feel like a betrayer if you stopped the violence. If someone hit your daughter, you'd stop it. That isn't betrayal. Tell me what happened.

Be patient; don't rescue. Because your friend talks about her abuse does not mean that she will take action. Don't impatiently push for action. Instead, get her to talk. If she talks and you support her, she'll eventually decide what to do. You're pulled emotionally to take care of your friend, to rescue her, to repair her problems, and to relieve her from danger. She wants her marriage to return to "normal," and she hopes that telling you will miraculously restore her marriage. Don't accept her fantasy. Abuse almost never stops without formal legal or social intervention.

Carol: I know it seems crazy, but I just want it fixed. I want our marriage to be like it was.
Gerry: You know with part of your mind that you can't ever go back, but with another part of your mind, you want things fixed.
Carol: That's it. I want you to make it better. Can't you and Robbie talk with Hal and me? Wouldn't that help?
Gerry: We *could* talk with you, but I don't think that would fix anything. If Hal's hitting you like this, he isn't magically going to stop. You want to go home, and you hope he won't ever hit you again.
Carol: It's a dream, isn't it? But lately it's worse, not better.
Gerry: You want to fix things, but you don't know what to do.
Carol: I don't. I thought maybe you'd know. I can't change things, and I can't escape. I'm powerless.
Gerry: You have some power. You've come here—that's something. Maybe there's no magic wand to wave to return to the past, but you are doing something.
Carol: Maybe if you prayed for us. Maybe that would help.
Gerry: Prayer always helps, but God doesn't promise to fix everything miraculously.
Carol: I know.

Helping Explore Thoughts and Feelings

Gerry: What were you thinking and feeling while Hal was beating you?
Carol: I was afraid. I thought he was going to knock out my teeth. As a teen, I had braces, so I've always protected my teeth. He hit me on the arms, slapped my face, pulled my hair, and when I covered my head, he hit me in the face. I begged him not to hit me, but he kept on. I was afraid he would kill me.
Gerry: It sounds horrid. So much fear.
Carol: It was only afterward, after he left me on the kitchen floor and drove off, that I began to be thankful. I lay there on the floor and

thanked God that he hadn't done anything worse. I deserved what I got. I yelled at Hal and called him names. I made him hit me.
Gerry: So on the floor in your kitchen you blamed yourself and excused him.
Carol: Pretty stupid, huh? He shouldn't have hit me.
Gerry: But you worked up the courage to come here.
Carol: Not courage. Probably fear. What if he came home and hit me again, you know? Maybe some courage, though. At least I didn't lay there and take it this time.
Gerry: You sound angry.
Carol: I am.

Avoid "why" questions. Your friend must deal with her current situation. Anger helps motivate action. Asking "why?" promotes nonaction and often comes across as being judgmental. Even though you are helping your friend feel anger, don't let her dwell on anger. Instead, steer her toward making plans, even small plans. Help examine the options and discuss priorities.

Ensure safety. Physical abuse is dangerous. Determine how serious the danger is, and if you think she is still in danger, encourage her to seek help. If your friend needs sanctuary, invite her to your house (if you feel that is safe) or contact a local agency (probably listed in the phone book). If your friend has already been physically damaged, evaluate whether medical treatment is necessary. If it is, help her get proper care. Evaluate whether she might act violently. She may be primed for violence either against herself (suicide) or her husband.

Follow up. After the immediate crisis is resolved, don't simply forget it, thinking that the problem has been solved. Follow up. Talk with her about the incident. If she considers divorce, help her wrestle with her thoughts and feelings. Direct her to Scripture. Particularly important is Malachi 2:16. Usually, Malachi 2:16a is quoted, but not 2:16b. The whole verse says, "'I hate divorce,' says the Lord God of Israel, 'and I hate a man's covering himself with violence as well as with his garment,' says the Lord Almighty." God hates not only divorce but also violence.

Separation or divorce? Physical abuse is a serious problem and should not be minimized. The woman may be in danger of being killed or seriously injured, of murdering her partner, or of committing suicide. Regardless of one's attitude about the permanence of marriage—and my view of marriage is high indeed—one must at times get the woman out of an abusive marriage, at least until the police or a professional therapist can intervene and help the abuser and perhaps deal with marital tensions.

When it is necessary to protect the woman, I usually recommend separation, but I don't recommend separation lightly. Most people who separate eventually divorce.[11] This is especially likely in abusive marriages. When the woman gets out of the abusive situation, she often decides that she doesn't want to go back because it's too dangerous. Marriage stability is a metaphor for spiritual stability and faithfulness to God, but an abusive marriage is a destructive metaphor for the individuals involved—both husband and wife.

Dealing with physical abuse is a test for your friend and for you in applying the principle of faith working through love. It is not always neatly, cleanly, and unambiguously resolved. At times our wisdom will be muddled. Faith lifts the situation to God. Helping promote the right balance of love and justice is hard work and can only be achieved through prayer and faith.

CHAPTER TWENTY

HELP PARTNERS FORGIVE

Donna and Raphael, both thirty-five years old, had been married for sixteen years and had a fourteen-year-old boy. They were active in their church and in their local community.

Donna spent a lot of time at the swimming pool during the summer and began a teasing, bantering relationship with Randy, a lifeguard whom she thought of as a "hunk." As the summer progressed, they spent more time talking. She was flattered that this twenty-year-old thought her attractive. Then, he dropped by her house, and they had sex, the first of many times.

At the summer's end, Randy returned to college, and Donna became depressed. She confessed her affair to Raphael. Tearfully, she said it would never happen again, and she pleaded for forgiveness. Raphael felt hurt, betrayed, and dishonored. For him, sex with Donna wasn't the same, knowing of her infidelity. Bitterness invaded Raphael's life. He became cynical and withdrawn, suspicious of friends and of old habits. "I've tried Christianity," he said, "and it let me down." After six months, he moved into an apartment.

Two Triangles

Tragedies like Raphael's and Donna's are extreme examples of what occurs frequently in troubled marriages—failures in forgiveness.

Whereas non-Christian partners must forgive each other to repair the inevitable hurts that occur in any marriage, Christians should be even quicker to forgive. Forgiveness is at the center of Christianity and should be a filter through which Christians view life. Sadly, it isn't always.

Lack of forgiveness is a problem that I represent pictorially by two triangles (see graphic). The topmost triangle, with corners labeled BLAME, SIN, and HURT, describes the problem. The lower triangle, CONFESS, REPENT, and FORGIVE, holds the solution. The third part of the figure is a pyramid made from the two triangles. The person dealing with blame, sin, and hurt must place the solution triangle on top of the problem triangle. When that is done, the solution will actually *change* (not just hide) the problem.

The Problem

Blame

In marriage, problems in blame occur when the spouse tries to figure out *why* the partner is not meeting the spouse's needs. The evaluation we give to our spouse's behavior is like a bank balance. When we have money in the bank, we hardly think about the check. But if we know we may be close to overdrawing, even a little check is threatening.

In the same way, if married partners have had many positive experiences, they can tolerate some hurt with little effect on the marriage. But if the couple has about as many (or more) negative experiences as positive, then each hurt rings an alarm. The spouse might think, "She hurt me intentionally," or, "He always is insensitive." One spouse questions the other's love. Motivation to work on the marriage is eroded, and faith in the marriage is lost.

Blame always names the other person as the cause of the problem and impairs work toward a solution. As blame mounts, the spouse feels unvalued, unloved. Blame justifies itself, so attention is continually focused on the partner's failures, weaknesses, and sins. The partner (along with the spouse) soon feels unvalued and unloved. Faith collapses under the weight of negative expectations and self-fulfilling prophesies.

Sin

Of course, sin is at the root of the problem. When we are hurt, we think, *It's not fair. Doesn't he know who I am? How dare he not be sensitive to me!*

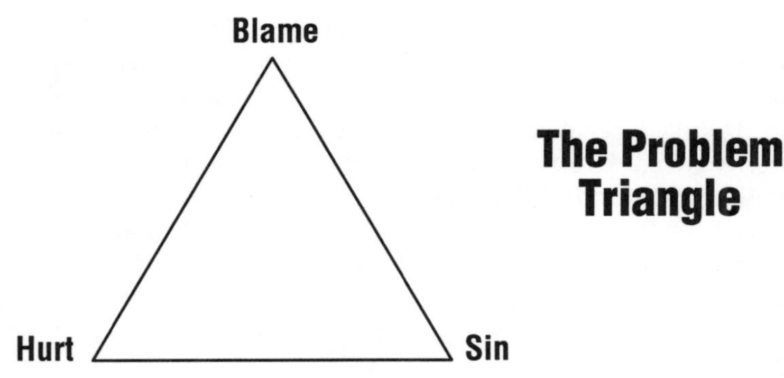
Blame
The Problem Triangle
Hurt
Sin

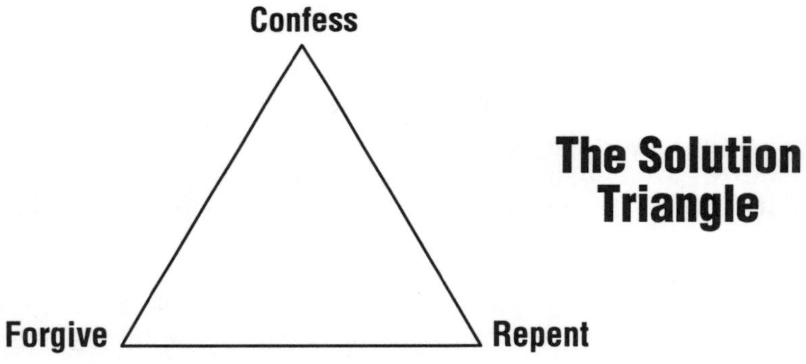
Confess
The Solution Triangle
Forgive
Repent

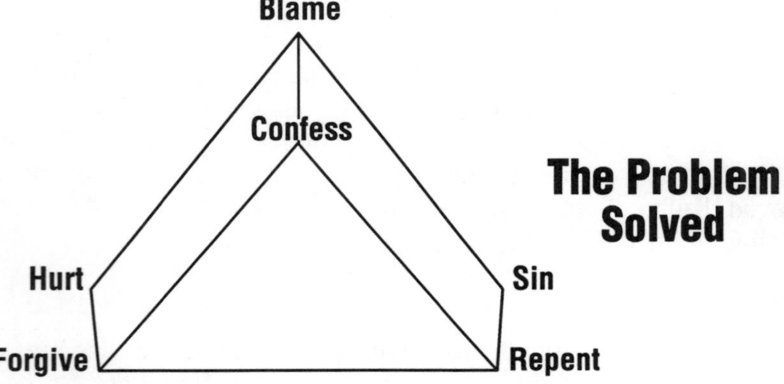
Blame
Confess
The Problem Solved
Hurt
Sin
Forgive
Repent

Sin also begets sin when it is kept in the darkness. Judgment fosters judgment. Anger begets anger. Neglect breeds neglect. Sins feed on each other and, left unattended, they can eat up love, work, and faith within the marriage, like they did with Donna and Raphael.

Donna was unfaithful, but Raphael was unforgiving and bitter. It is a mistake to say that Donna's unfaithfulness was *caused* by Raphael's inattentiveness to her and that Raphael's lack of forgiveness was *caused* by Donna's lack of trustworthiness. Each person was responsible for his or her own sin, not for the other person's sin.

Hurt

Hurt is a stimulus to blame and sin, as well as a response to them. Hurt occurs whenever a marriage partner seems either *unwilling* or *unable* to meet the other's needs. In both cases, there are perceived failures in faith working through love.

When your friend's partner seems unwilling to meet your friend's needs, your friend may feel angry and indignant over the partner's unwillingness to love and failure to work on the marriage. The consequence is your friend's loss of faith in the partner, the marriage, and the future of the marriage.

When your friend's partner seems unable to meet your friend's needs, your friend may feel compassion for the partner but may also feel frustration and resentment. Your friend may feel that the partner *can't* value and love him or her or work on the marriage. Your friend may thus lose faith that the marriage can change. Over time, suspicions may even intrude that the partner isn't trying to change, and feelings of love may be attacked.

Of course, there are times in every marriage when each partner is preoccupied with his or her own needs and can't meet his or her spouse's needs, but those times are usually temporary and balance out over the lifetime. Nonetheless, during times when one spouse is not attending to the other, both partners might still feel hurt and negative toward each other and want to lash back in retaliation.

Blame, Sin, and Hurt

Blame, sin, and hurt are three heads of a monster that devours faith, work, and love. All three heads are joined to the monster's body. If one head is whacked off by the sword of the Spirit, it soon grows back unless all three heads are whacked.

To use another analogy, blame, sin, and hurt are like runners from a shrub I had in my yard in days past—the pyracantha. The runners creep underground, pop up periodically and stab the unwary—and even the wary—with vicious thorns. Underground roots support the shrub, and when the visible part of the shrub is hacked away, the shrub simply pops up in additional places. Such is the nature of sin, blame, and hurt.

The Solution

Confession

Confession turns away from blame. When a relationship has been hurtful, Christian mates' main desire is usually for forgiveness. Of course, usually each thinks *the partner* needs forgiveness.

Forgiveness is not the beginning of healing as many people believe. Rather, forgiveness occurs *after* confession. In any troubled marriage, hurt and sin usually wound both sides. Rather than looking to the partner's hurt and sin, each person must examine himself or herself. Confession should be to God first and perhaps then to the partner. Confession opens the floodgate to forgiveness.

Importantly, confession is not a trick to provoke the spouse into admitting sins. Confession is agreeing with God that we have gone against His will. It is a sincere and truthful admission of our wrongdoing, done because we are told to confess our sins, not as manipulation. We are to confess *our* sins, even if our spouses never do.

Guilt clung to Donna until she confessed her sin of infidelity to Raphael. Sometimes people confess their sins because they know they should, even though they feel little guilt. The important thing is that they agree with God about their sin and that they tell God so and also tell the spouse, when the sin has important consequences for the marriage.

Repentance

Repentance is turning away from sin. Repentance expresses to God one's desire not to sin further. Repentance is both an intention and an effort to follow through with the intention.

Repentance won't change the marriage immediately. When hurt plagues a marriage, both partners are wary that the hurt will continue, so each meets a partner's intent to repent skeptically. Only when effort is observed will defensive walls eventually crumble. One may proclaim trustworthiness but trust may be a while in coming.

Forgiveness

Forgiveness is healing from hurt. Like so much of God's kingdom, the ability to forgive is both a gift of God and an act of the will. Sometimes partners must erect the forms of forgiveness, proclaiming their forgiveness when they don't feel it, and trust that God will pour in the substance of forgiveness later. Sometimes God gives people the grace of forgiveness, and they simply acknowledge that grace when they forgive the spouse verbally.

Don't try to determine whether your friend's forgiveness is "real." When people sincerely bring their efforts at forgiveness under God's care, God will create forgiveness in their hearts.

Forgiveness is not necessarily forgetting. At times, a forgiven debt may be forgotten, but at other times it won't be. In either case, forgiveness removes the sting and poison of bitterness.

Prepare Yourself to Help People Forgive

Pray

The key to promoting confession, repentance, and forgiveness is prayer.

- Pray for the couple to examine their marriage before God. Remember, the Holy Spirit convicts of sin—not you, not the spouse. Motivate the couple to bring the problem to God.
- Pray for your friend. Ask the Lord to convict your friend of his or her role in the marital problems and to prompt repentance.
- If appropriate, pray with your friend for God's Holy Spirit to work in his or her life and for Jesus to minister to your friend.
- Pray for wisdom to know how to be a help, not a hindrance, to your friend's healing and to the future.

Know Your Role

In dealing with blame, sin, and hurt, support the couple through prayer, and act as a signpost that directs them back to Jesus. Promote confession, repentance, and forgiveness. Don't judge your friend's marriage. You, the Christian friend, stand for positive motivations and goals, not guilt and condemnation.

Get Your Attitudes Straight

We each have sinful motivations and actions. Helping a friend deal with confession, repentance, and forgiveness provides a stimulus to examine yourself before God. Why are you helping—for your own glory or peace of mind, or to help another person with his or her spiritual growth? Have you behaved as a good Christian model throughout your relationship with your friend?

Examine, too, your attitude toward your friend. Are you treating him or her as a person whom God has placed in your life to stimulate your growth as much as to receive your help? Regardless of what your friend confesses, do you still regard him or her positively?

Let Your Friend Know That You Support Him or Her

Confessing sin requires vulnerability. People become vulnerable only when they know they can trust their confidant. Let your friend know that you care and will faithfully support him or her.

Promote Confession

Focus on Each Person's Responsibilities

Keep each partner focused on his or her own behavior rather than on what the spouse has done. Don't hesitate to repeat: people cannot change their spouses' behavior; they can only change their own. So, if changes are to occur in the marriage, each partner must change.

Direct Your Friend to Meditate on Scripture

Have your friend meditate on how to love the spouse as Christ loved the church (Ephesians 5:25). I might say, "Do you remember the passage in Paul's epistle to the Ephesians? Jesus loved the church by giving Himself for her. That's always guided me in my marriage. Sometimes when Kirby and I disagree, I want her to change so I won't have to, but when I think about passages like 1 John 4:7–8 and 19–21, I can't comfortably take that stance. Jesus didn't wait for the church to change before He gave Himself for her. Instead, He gave Himself *first.* As a Christian husband, I am admonished to follow Christ's example. Husbands are told that specifically in Ephesians 5. But it's nice to know that Christian wives should also follow Christ's lead."

Describe Empathetic Repentance

Tell couples about Larry Christenson's *empathetic repentance.*[1] Christenson suggests that whenever we see a sin in another person, we should look for the sin (or its close sibling) in ourselves. We often find what we look for. Empathy with our partner can lead to our own repentance.

Christenson observes that we rarely lose our peace over the sin of another. If we are troubled over something our spouse has done, we are probably dealing with our own sin too. For instance, an alcoholic's wife examined herself and found her own lack of self-control in overeating. Through empathetic repentance, the husband of an adulterous woman confided his own failings of fidelity to God.

Describe the Transition Generation

Divorce runs in families.[2] The pain of broken relationships may be passed from adults to children throughout succeeding generations. This brings to mind Scripture verses that sin is visited on the children and children's children up to three or four generations (Exodus 20:5; 34:7; Deuteronomy 5:9–10).

But if divorce and sin can be passed down for several generations, where does it stop? Each person, if he or she seeks God, can be the transition generation that stops the transmission of sin and unforgiveness and begins to pass blessings to succeeding generations. The transition begins with confession of sin, proceeds to repentance from sin, and culminates in forgiveness received (and then given to others in the name of Christ). Describe the transition generation, and invite your friend to break the transmission of sin within his or her family.

Encourage Confession Directly

Talk directly with your friend about sinful behavior and invite confession. Such an invitation depends on an atmosphere of love and acceptance and a sense of trust in you and in what you will do with the confession.

Promote Repentance

Use a Ritual To Promote Repentance

Once the Holy Spirit convicts a husband and wife to change their hurtful ways, they might want to perform some act that symbolizes a new beginning. Sometimes each lists his or her biggest criticisms of the spouse, seals the list in an envelope, and burns the envelope in the other's presence. Others declare in writing their intention to behave more positively and post their intentions on the family bulletin board or in their bedroom. Such symbolic acts are just a start. Good intentions last only a few days unless individuals act differently. Their efforts must be continually undergirded with prayer if they are to succeed.

Set Specific Goals for Repentance

Repentance within marriage usually begins with deciding on exactly *how* the marriage will be different. Recommend that your friend set positive goals. The goals should be simple, written down, and explicit. For example, Jack's goal, "I'm going to be nicer to Marjorie," sounds wonderful, but he won't keep it long because it's too general. Jack will be nicer to Marjorie if she has listed twenty things that Jack could do that she would consider being nice to her and Jack says he'll do three things from the list each week. That is a specific, simple goal. Goals should involve both avoiding the negative and performing the positive.

Promote Forgiveness

Help the Person Forgive Himself or Herself

If emotional healing begins with confession and repentance, it needs to be followed by forgiveness. If you've helped your friend become aware of his or her part in the troubled marriage, help him or her appropriate the forgiveness freely offered in Christ's death. For the committed Christian, your role may be minimal. Proclaim that, "If we confess our sins, he [God] is faithful and just, and will forgive our sins and cleanse us from all unrighteousness" (1 John 1:9 RSV). Assure your friend of the truth of God's Word even if your friend does not feel forgiven.

If your friend is not a Christian, though, explain the basis for forgiveness—Jesus' substitutionary death on the cross. Tell how people receive forgiveness from God, not through their own efforts, not merely through confession and repentance, but through identifying with Christ, who in love already atoned for our sin. Make confession and repentance an act of faith in a loving and merciful God rather than a contractual duty to extract forgiveness from a harsh and unwilling God.

Help the Person Accept What God Has Done

In a study of twenty-nine psychotherapy patients of seven Christian counselors,[3] clients often reported forgiving God during psychotherapy. Although God does not sin (and does not need our forgiveness), people become angry and bitter at God when He acts in unexpected ways. God is greater than humans; He is God of the unexpected. We can anticipate, therefore, that He will often violate people's expectations and incur their anger. Not understanding His ways fully may make people feel that they need to "forgive" God. If they practice the biblical pattern though, they will then examine themselves and confess their own pride at judging God. People's "forgiveness" of God, therefore, generally represents an acknowledgment that God's ways are greater than our own and that we acknowledge our submission to Him.

Help the Person Forgive the Spouse

A partner who is prepared for forgiveness by examining himself or herself, who is aware of his or her complicity in the marital problems, who has confessed those sins he or she has discovered under the conviction of the Holy Spirit, who has repented of further wrongdoing, who has received God's forgiveness and forgiven himself or herself, is ready to forgive the spouse of his or her wrongs. Without the preparatory steps, forgiveness can become condemnation dressed up in Sunday clothes.

To promote forgiveness, help your friend see things from the spouse's point of view. A troubled spouse doesn't want to see his partner's point of view. Wrapped up in his own perspective, he wants you to justify him, not empathize with his spouse. Yet to promote forgiveness, help your friend see the other side. This can only be done if your friend is absolutely sure that you understand him. Thus, showing support, understanding, and caring are necessary to promoting forgiveness.

Raphael couldn't forgive Donna for her affair with Randy, the young lifeguard. Carlos, gray-haired and bristly bearded "patriarch" of the community, talked with Raphael about his inability to forgive.

Raphael: I can't see how she could do a thing like that to me.
Carlos: I know. It's hard. It's an insult to your manhood, a slap in the face.

Raphael: I work hard to provide for her and my son, Miguel. She throws it all away. On a *boy!*
Carlos: Yes, it is a great insult. I can see that it has much affected you.
Raphael: It is of great concern how others look at our marriage.
Carlos: Yes, the men of the church agree that you have done right in not seeking a divorce. It is a very courageous act. And my Linda says that Donna is contrite, much ashamed for her shameful behavior.
Raphael: But I cannot forgive her. I cannot move back home.
Carlos: She has suffered much shame over her disgrace. If I were you, my friend, I too would feel angry and concerned about the thoughts of others. Like you, I am sure, I would want with my whole heart to begin life anew. I would not want my wife to continue in disgrace, and I would not want her to suffer more disgrace by begging me for forgiveness.
Raphael: I, of course, love Donna, and I want a strong marriage—like you say. I should forgive her. I should return home. May God help me.
Carlos: He will, my friend. He will.

Have your friend pray for his or her spouse. Recommend a prayer of thanksgiving, one of petition, and one glorifying God for His work in the marriage. Then recommend a prayer of forgiveness for the spouse. Have your friend recall specific instances in which his partner wronged him and speak forgiveness into each instance. It is important that the friend dwell on seeking the Lord's strength to forgive the partner's sin rather than on the hurtfulness of the sin. If your friend lapses into complaining about the partner's hurtfulness, help him or her get back on track or end the prayer and focus again on confession of the person's own part.

Help with the Healing of Memories

Finally, when hurt has invaded a marriage, wounds are often deep. Jesus heals wounded spirits and marriages. Even the memories can be healed so that, though scars remain, they no longer bring pain. I recommend David Seamands's book, *The Healing of Memories*[4] to couples struggling with hurt. Healing of memories usually is affected when the person re-experiences a hurtful event while meditating on Jesus' forgiving response in that situation. Sometimes counselors ask clients to imagine the event and then imagine Jesus entering the event and ministering forgiveness. Sometimes counselors simply pray that Jesus can change the memory.

Healing of memories is not a counseling technique. It is a work of the Holy Spirit. It can occur without a counselor (or friend) present or under direction of a pastor, counselor, or friend. Generally, if helper and friend are focused on Jesus as the healer and do not have firm expectations about how or even when He will heal, then healing is more likely to occur.

Help Consider Whether Reconciliation Is Appropriate

Reconciliation goes beyond confession of the person's part in the marital troubles and praying for both his or her own and the partner's forgiveness. It involves confessing faults to the spouse, asking for his or her forgiveness, and (perhaps) granting forgiveness to the partner (if asked).

Reconciliation for every sin against a partner is not desirable nor helpful to the marriage. For instance, partners shouldn't confess every critical thought to the partner. Rather, partners should confess those to God. Help your friend decide which sins should be confessed because they promote healing in the marriage, and which, if confessed, would harm the marriage.

Forgiveness is always needed, but many times, reconciliation is not recommended. For example, a partner who chronically physically abuses his spouse should be forgiven, but the abused spouse may not reconcile the marriage. Similarly, spouses of partners caught up in unrepentant alcoholism are called to forgive, but many choose to remain separate from the spouse. Their marriage may never be reconciled as long as the alcohol abuse continues.

Three years after Jane and Edward divorced, Edward moved to Atlanta. He gave up all visitation privileges, saying he wanted to start over. Edward's move relieved Jane, but it triggered other problems. Eddie, then thirteen years old, became bitter toward his father. He began to spend time with a rough gang of boys who skateboarded, dressed in black, and shaved their heads except for a long tuft of hair in front. Many had tattoos referring to death and Satanism. Jane was alarmed about Eddie, but for six months her efforts to influence him seemed to have no effect. Her worries brought back memories of her separation, its helplessness, anger, and bitterness toward Edward. Roberta faithfully befriended Jane in her troubles.

Roberta: Despite all the difficulties with Eddie, I think the underlying problem is that you haven't resolved your feelings about Edward.

Jane: Of course, I haven't. He keeps hurting me. He isn't in Richmond any longer, yet he makes my life miserable by his lingering influence on Eddie. Edward is ruining Eddie, and I have to deal with Eddie continually.

Roberta: Edward is affecting Eddie, even now?

Jane: Look at him!

Roberta: So Eddie lets his memory of Edward dictate his life. It's unfortunate that Eddie allows his memory and his expectations about his father to influence him to act self-destructively, even though Edward is completely out of contact with Eddie.

Jane: You're right. I wish I could get Eddie to see that he doesn't need to let his no-good father cause him to self-destruct.

Roberta: But you can't make him see that.

Jane: No. Eddie's wrapped up in his own world. He won't see what is plain to everyone else.

Roberta: I can see how much this affects you. You want the best for your son, for him to live without being dominated by the past.

Jane: I want it so much.

Roberta: It makes you miserable?

Jane: Wouldn't it make you miserable? Edward has been such a destructive force in Eddie's life.

Roberta: Sounds as if he's been a destructive force in your life, too.

Jane: He has!

Roberta: You care about Eddie, and hope he'll get over Edward's influence, but in the same way, you allow Edward to influence you. (Pauses. After a minute, Jane begins to cry.) You see that, don't you? (Jane nods.) What are you thinking?

Jane: I've become so bitter at Edward, I'm ruining my own life—exactly like Eddie is doing. In fact, my own bitterness may even add to Eddie's problem. I continue to let Edward influence me, even though I'll probably never actually see him again.

Roberta: You're disappointed in yourself.

Jane: Uh-huh. I know I should give up my bitterness. I don't think I could ever forgive Edward, though. He would never admit his selfishness, and I don't want to ever speak with him again.

Roberta: You're confusing forgiveness with reconciliation. You can forgive him for hurting you, Eddie, and the other children without reconciling with him. In ongoing marriages, reconciling is usually important, but in this case, reconciling could be tragic. You need to forgive Edward, though, because your bitterness is imprisoning you.

Jane: I know it is. I want to forgive him. I *need* to forgive him. But how?

Roberta explained that Jesus can heal across time and space, and she led Jane in a prayer for the healing of traumatic memories. For months afterward, Jane felt less venomous toward Edward, which eventually provided a better model for Eddie to deal with his father's memory.

When the relationship remains intact, though, reconciliation is necessary. Your friend should generally offer to forgive his or her partner only after confessing his or her own part to the partner and seeking forgiveness from the partner. If reconciliation is decided upon, help your friend decide on the timing of attempts to reconcile and on how to attempt reconciliation.

Reconciliation is facilitated if each partner thinks the other is sincere. Often reconciliation is helped by physical and psychological contact. Couples in counseling who forgive each other often spontaneously hold hands and look into each other's eyes.

Forgiveness in Action

Fromma and Leo had dinner at Gina and Nick's. After dinner, conversation wound its way to the night of the crisis, months earlier. Despite Fromma and Leo's reconciliation after the crisis, both said they still felt hurt by that night. They hadn't mentioned the night since Fromma had returned home.

Nick suggested that they each hadn't forgiven the other for the trauma of that night, and they agreed. He suggested that Leo tell Fromma how he had contributed to the trauma and that Fromma tell Leo how she had contributed.

Leo tearfully recalled the night and apologized for behaving poorly. Fromma followed suit. Both promised to try to avoid losing their temper in the future. Years later, both Leo and Fromma recalled the conversation with Nick and Gina as the point in their marriage where real healing took place.

Use a Ritual To Celebrate Forgiveness and Reconciliation

Once a relationship has been restored, forgiveness granted and received, the couple may want to celebrate. Like Joshua, who built a memorial to the Lord after crossing (finally) into the promised land, couples may build a memorial to their mutual forgiveness. Any repeatable event can serve effectively as a ritual. One couple went skiing annually to commemorate successful reconciliation. Another designed a scroll attesting to the date of forgiving each other for a multitude of wrongs. Other suggestions include going out to a fancy restaurant, attending a play, taking a trip, having a second wedding ceremony, having a second honeymoon, revisiting the site of the first honeymoon, going camping, and reading aloud Elizabeth Browning's poem, "How Do I Love Thee?"

Reconciliation in Action

Carlos was good for Raphael, engaging him again into the church community from which he had all but withdrawn. Carlos appealed to Raphael's courage at standing up to the insult of the affair, and eventually Raphael returned home to Donna.

They invited Carlos to visit. After dinner, Carlos and Raphael talked at the kitchen table while Donna cleaned dishes.

"I congratulate you, my friend, on the rebirth of your marriage," said Carlos. "Have you made things right between you?"

"Yes, we are one again," said Raphael. "And we owe it to you. You helped me see how little is my capacity to forgive."

Carlos lifted a finger and tilted his head. "Was nothing," he said.

Donna refilled Carlos's coffee mug. "With your permission?" she addressed Carlos.

"Yes," he said.

"I want to thank you for helping us. Raphael told me that you helped him, and he acted with great honor in coming to me. I wanted him to accept my apology, but after he talked with you, he instead asked that I forgive *him.* I do not deserve such a man as he is."

"And I trust he too forgave you?"

"Yes, yes. We have prayed for each other and received the beautiful gift from the God of forgiveness. We praise God for that."

CHAPTER TWENTY-ONE

HELP STRENGTHEN COMMITMENT

Judith and Scott had been married for twenty-six years with no discernible marriage tensions. When they divorced, their friends were surprised. "It came out of the blue," one friend of Judith's remarked. "One day, they were visiting, eating home-made ice cream, laughing, and joking. The next, it seemed, they divorced. What went wrong?"

Judith explained, "We simply realized we didn't want to be married. We never fought, and we communicated OK, but there was no spark. When the kids left home, we realized we didn't want to spend twenty more years together."

Vernon and Ashley divorced because they felt they couldn't communicate. They never talked and felt as if they didn't know each other.

David and Joanie had passion, and they could communicate. Oh, how they communicated. Mostly at the top of their lungs. They fought about everything. Their marriage was made in heaven, but then again, so are thunder and lightning. They ended it after four years. The neighbors were happy.

Brent and Kelley did fine until Kelley got a promotion at work. When she moved into management, her leisure activities changed. She was invited to cocktail parties, concerts, and golf tournaments. Brent was dragged along, but the "hoity-toity" social scene grated on his rural Alabama "good-ole-boy" nerves. "I realized," he said, "that the marriage was turning me into something that I didn't want to become." After that, Brent dug in his heels, and he and Kelley grew further apart.

"One day," said Kelley, "we both started seeing the marriage not as a blessing, but as a burden. After that, we couldn't see anything good with our marriage. I'm not sorry we divorced. We were too different to be compatible."

After fourteen years of marriage, Shari found out that Fredrick had not been a virgin at their marriage. She said she could accept it, but she could not accept Fred's keeping it a secret. Bitterness ate at Shari, and Fred abandoned her after two years filled with mistrust and recriminations.

Marital Satisfaction and Commitment

Each of these marriage commitments was broken for what the people involved thought to be good reasons. In each case, marital satisfaction eroded. For Judith and Scott, their closeness dissolved into a lifeless calendar of passing days. For Vernon and Ashley, communication difficulties spelled a fatal flaw. For David and Joanie, conflict blew their marriage apart. For Brent and Kelley, a negative view of their compatibility drove a wedge between them. For Shari and Fredrick, lack of forgiveness poisoned their togetherness.

Commitment depends on marital satisfaction, which in turn depends on closeness, communication, conflict resolution, cognition, and confession-forgiveness. But commitment is more than marital satisfaction. Many couples remain committed despite being unsatisfied with their marriages, and some couples divorce despite having happy marriages. For instance, Gloria and Clive claimed to have a happy marriage, but Gloria could not abide Clive's continual drinking, and they eventually divorced.

Marital Commitment

A Baker's Dozen Commitments in Marriage

Norm Wright, in his book *So You're Getting Married,*[1] discussed thirteen commitments that partners make when they marry—commitments to:

- Marriage. Marriage commits to your spouse for the remainder of your life.

- Be free from the past. Marriage commits to examine and seek freedom from oppressive patterns that formed in the family-of-origin.
- Love. Marriage commits to philia (friendship-based), eros (need-based), and especially agape (self-giving-based) loves.
- Change. Marriage means commitment through expected and unexpected life changes.
- Understand yourself. Marriage commits to understand your personality, motivations, and limitations throughout life.
- Evaluate expectations and develop goals. Marriage includes unmet realistic and sometimes unrealistic expectations. Partners set goals to achieve the worthy expectations together.
- Make wise decisions. Decisions must be made in love.
- Communicate. Marriages exchange information.
- Listen. Respect each other by listening.
- Resolve conflicts. Marriages should resolve conflicts rather than yield, compromise, win, or withdraw.
- Control anger.
- Build positive in-law relationships. In-laws can be a source of joy or conflict.
- Forgive and pray together. A person cannot be open to God if he or she is closed to the spouse.

If people really understood what they were promising when they took marriage vows, says Wright, there would probably be fewer divorces —and fewer marriages.

Two Aspects of Commitment

Commitment embodies personal dedication and obligation or constraint.[2] Personal dedication is the part of commitment that works for more mutual benefits to the participants. Constraint is the part of commitment providing pressure that makes it hard to change or end a relationship.

Lewis Smedes echoes these two aspects in his book, *Caring and Commitment.*[3] He argues that we have the power to forgive hurts of the past and the power to make commitments or promises for the future. But the promises of the future depend on our adherence to our promises in the past, our faithfulness. Commitments involve consistency (obligations and constraints) and caring (personal dedication).

Consistency keeps the external structure steady. But care breathes lasting love inside the structure. Consistency is the backbone; care is the heart. Consistency is the muscle; care is the warm blood. Consistency is our predictability; care is our personal presence.

The Essential Tension

There is a fundamental tension whenever we discuss commitment. How permanent is commitment? How many exception clauses are permitted, and under what conditions can a commitment be honorably broken?

At the extreme, there are two positions. One suggests that commitment is a tool in service of personal growth or betterment. Any time a "commitment" does not foster as much personal growth or betterment as one would like, the person is considered free to end the "commitment." At the other extreme, a commitment, once made, admits no way out. Marriage commitment is an unbreakable covenant; it is holy wedlock, with the emphasis on the "lock." The perennial wars between individual autonomy and communal responsibility, autonomy and intimacy, psychology and sociology are recapitulated in this conflict over the meaning of commitment, and individuals will arrive at different positions, usually based on their general philosophy about individuality and communality.

Commitment is a balancing act with a foot on each of two cliffs. One cliff is wishy-washy, feeling-dictated agreement to do for others that which we want to do and which furthers our selfish interest. The other cliff is slavish agreement to keep every commitment we ever make, regardless of how small, heedless of the consequences, in spite of God's leading. Sometimes we walk with our weight on one cliff more than the other. On some issues, we hop on one foot along the precipice. Most of the time, though, we bounce back and forth, shifting our weight from foot to foot, maintaining a balanced posture. Most of us lean permanently to one side, conditioned by our personal disposition, family-of-origin, personal experiences, and philosophy.

Whichever way we lean, and however much we change weights, the trick is to balance, even when the sides of the precipice widen as an issue is framed starkly.

Commitment Depends on Three General Factors

Commitment to marriage depends on three general factors. A psychologist named Caryl Rusbult[4] has expressed them in terms of an equation:

Commitment = Satisfaction − Alternatives + Investments

We have already seen how commitment depends partially on satisfaction with marriage. It should seem reasonable that commitment will be weakened if alternatives to the marriage are more satisfying than the marriage itself. The negative sign in the equation means that higher satisfaction with alternatives to marriage erodes commitment.

Alternative satisfactions to marriage include much more than attraction to a rival suitor. Alternatives may include excessive career commitment, over-involvement in church activities, too much time spent with children, or simple accumulation of time and emotional resources spent apart from the spouse.

Investments in marriage are just as varied as alternatives. But investments contribute to increased marital commitment.

- Children. One couple argued frequently. They refused to stop their fighting until they found that it upset their infant son. They soon learned to resolve their conflicts less destructively.
- Length of marriage. Couples are more reluctant to put twenty-five years of marriage aside in divorce than two years of marriage.
- Shared resources, like property held in common or joint banking accounts.
- Opinions of friends and family members that the couple is indeed married for life.
- Perception that the marriage vows are a marriage covenant agreed upon before God.

In recent years, Rusbult has acknowledged an additional component of commitment: salience of the marriage.[5] The more personally important marriage is to a person, the more likely the person is to maintain his or her marital commitment.

Helping Your Friend Strengthen Commitment

Discuss Covenants and Contracts

Talk with your friend about covenantal rather than contractual commitment. Contracts say, "I'm committed as long as you meet my needs." Covenants say, "You are my flesh, and I'm committed regardless of whether you meet my needs."

Here is the picture of God's covenant with Abram (Genesis 15:9–20). Abram killed animals, cut them in half, and laid the halves in parallel rows. God put Abram to sleep, and then God walked between the sacrificed animals and made His covenant with Abram. In Genesis 17, God describes the fidelity that He expected from Abram as his part of the covenant. This was the old covenant. Centuries later, Jesus became the blood sacrifice for the new covenant under which we believers take our new name, the name of Christ, Christians.

Marriage has been long understood as a covenant of man and woman before God. Covenantal faithfulness is expected in marriage. Even in the Christian marriage ceremony, we see the symbolism of the covenant. Bride and groom pass through a divided congregation, blood relations on each side. Bride and groom are married under the sign of the slain Savior, Jesus. The wife even takes a new name to symbolize the permanency of the marriage.

Increase Marital Satisfaction

Marital satisfaction influences commitment. Help your friend establish balanced closeness, good communication, proficiency in dealing with conflict, positive perceptions of the marriage, and the willingness to forgive. Fostering improvement in marital satisfaction will help strengthen marital commitment.

Decrease Competing Alternatives

Alternatives to marriage, such as over-involvement in work, with other friends, with other romantic partners, with hobbies or sports, or with church or other activities, can hamper commitment. To strengthen commitment, help your friend eliminate or weaken involvement in alternatives.

Increase Investments

Investments in a marriage identity can be increased, but increasing investments usually has other consequences, such as affecting marriage satisfaction or increasing competing alternatives. For instance, having a child increases investments, but having a child also frequently decreases marriage satisfaction (Worthington & Buston).[6]

Increase the Importance of Marriage

The marriage can be made more important by pointing out the costs of divorce[7] and benefits of marriage.[8] For example, divorced adults, as compared to married adults, have increased risk of psychopathology, more automobile accidents, more physical illness, higher rates of suicide, more likelihood of being involved in violence or homicide, and higher mortality rates to disease. For women, decrements in health are directly related to divorce; divorced men who are also lonely suffer the most decrements in health.

Divorce also negatively affects children, even into their adulthood (see Gottman for a review).[9] Children of divorce experience more depression, more withdrawal, poorer social competence, more health problems, poorer academic performance, and more conduct-related disturbances. Adults whose parents divorced when they were young experience more stress and report less satisfaction with family and friends, experience greater anxiety, have bad things happen to them more often, have more difficulty coping with life stress, and are more likely to experience divorce themselves than are people whose parents did not divorce.

Helping Your Friend Deal with Threatened Commitment

Many problems in commitment have already been alluded to, but let me examine them in a different light. Problems in commitment may essentially be two-sided or one-sided. Each type poses different problems for you, the helper.

Two-sided Problems in Commitment

In two-sided problems, both spouses' commitment has declined until the marriage's stability is threatened. Usually, this is because of declines in marital satisfaction. Help both partners want to improve their marriage. The best work will be done when both married partners participate together in marriage counseling, usually by the pastor, a professional, or another couple in the church. Encourage counseling.

One-sided Problems in Commitment

In the one-sided problem, only one person is uncertain about his or her commitment to the marriage. Importantly, this does not necessarily mean that the marital problems are *caused* by one person. The marital problems may be due to both spouses' behavior, but only one doubts his or her commitment.

For example, Daniel and Alice experienced years of serious conflict. As the years went on and the relationship did not improve, Daniel threatened divorce. Alice quoted Scripture at him and to all her friends concerning her commitment to the permanence of the relationship, but Daniel continued to threaten divorce. If you were their friend, it would be tempting to assume that Alice was the "good girl" and Daniel was the "bad guy" because Daniel was questioning his marital covenant. In fact, though, both Daniel and Alice probably contributed equally to the poor marriage. True, Daniel is compounding the problem by threatening to divorce, but the sole problem is not whether his divorce threats are right or wrong. If Daniel and Alice talk only about whether Daniel has the right to divorce, their marriage may not survive anyway. The problems responsible for the divorce threats are being ignored.

When a one-sided threat of divorce is encountered, there are two possibilities. You may either be dealing with the one who professes a desire to end the marriage or the one who professes commitment to the marriage.

When your friend wants a divorce. Don't lecture, quote Scripture, or attempt to manipulate with guilt. Most Christians know God's attitude toward divorce, and most non-Christians don't care. If you moralize, your friend will feel judged and will be less open to your help. If a Scriptural perspective on divorce is needed, recommend John Stott's pamphlet, *Marriage and Divorce,*[10] or Stanley Ellisen's book, *Divorce and Remarriage in the Church,*[11] or some other book you believe addresses the issue.

When your friend says he or she intends to divorce, first assess the seriousness of the intention. Some people are determined to divorce and cannot be dissuaded. Others have mixed feelings. If your friend is *determined* to divorce, recommend separation, which most states require prior to divorce anyway, instead of immediate divorce. Never recommend this lightly. Currently, statistics show that about 70 percent of couples who separate divorce rather than reconciling. It is hard for the couple to work out problems when they are separated. Separation can have some positive effects. It will allow partners to see what it might be like to be divorced. For many, separation provides a cooling off period and a time when the marriage concerns can be addressed without the daily frustrations that kept the marriage in an uproar. During the separation, try to get the couple in counseling together. Help the couple improve their marital satisfaction.

For a friend less determined to divorce, don't recommend separation. Recommend marital counseling with a pastor or licensed marital therapist. Support the couple throughout counseling and promote more marital satisfaction and an attitude of faith working through love. Your friend might want a divorce because the alternatives to the marriage have become more attractive than have the satisfactions and investments in the marriage. Recommend reducing the alternatives in order to give the marriage a chance. For example, if Margo is overinvolved in her career advancement, she can work shorter hours so that the marriage will have a chance to revive. If Kip is having an affair, he should end it.

Your friend might want a divorce because the investments in the marriage have suddenly decreased, leaving alternatives to the marriage outweighing marital satisfactions. An example of a sudden decrease in investments might be when the children leave for college, when the last child becomes financially independent of the parents, or when an unemployed spouse achieves employment. When investments in the marriage are rapidly reduced, help the couple compensate by increasing their marital satisfactions, or they will experience a decline in commitment.

When your friend doesn't want a divorce. Your friend may feel self-righteous and can easily blame the other spouse for abandoning the marriage vows. In fact, though, the responsibility for the problems in the relationship are rarely that clear cut. Remind your friend that he or she is not responsible for the partner's decisions, only for his or her own.

The committed spouse should direct his or her efforts at discerning how he or she might improve the marriage, if that is still a possibility. Recommend that the spouse continue to proclaim love for the uncommitted spouse. Steer your friend away from coercing the spouse to continue in the marriage.

Encourage the couple to seek professional counseling, and support your friend. Don't focus all your attention on the spouse's decision to seek divorce. Instead, try to improve the marriage.

When divorce seems certain. If it becomes obvious that the couple will indeed divorce, the committed partner is often quite reluctant to admit that possibility. He or she may have struggled for months or longer than a year to keep the marriage alive, and it is difficult to accept the death of the marriage—even when it is an almost certain conclusion.

This poses a real Christian paradox to those involved. God has the power to heal terminal disease and even to resurrect the dead to new life. But for humans, it is impossible to know exactly when He will do that, for God gives such gifts to those whom *He* wills. So we are caught between encouraging the committed spouse to hold on and pray for a miracle or to take actions that will provide for his or her and the children's futures—actions such as negotiating a fair division of property and equitable terms for child custody, and actions such as preparing oneself psychologically for an impending loss. Tread that line with care, prayer, and discernment. That's no easy task.

In summary, commitment depends on satisfactions, alternatives competing with marriage, and investments in the marriage. In general, recommend counseling for couples struggling with their marital commitment. Even then, you can play an important role. Help rebuild marital commitment, better their marriage, and avoid being sidetracked into theological issues about divorce. Although that *is* an important theological argument, it is usually less important than helping the couple work to save their marriage if they can.

PART SIX

UNDERSTANDING THE NECESSITY FOR HOPE

CHAPTER TWENTY-TWO

HOPE — EVEN FOR THE MOST TROUBLED MARRIAGES

Throughout this book, several themes have been woven together.

1. You can help friends in marital distress. As a Christian, promote hope by sharing your faith, work, and love.

2. Listen and support your distressed friend. Help your friend rethink his or her marriage as an opportunity to make the partner a disciple by practicing Jesus' pattern—faith working through love. Help plan actions that will bring about that understanding. Follow-up on what happens when your friend tries to change.

3. Help your friend build a solid Christian core (Christian beliefs and values, a Christian vision of marriage, and an attitude of confession, repentance, and forgiveness). Help build marital satisfaction through promoting closeness, communication, conflict resolution, and positive thinking. Help deal with complicating problems. Help build covenantal commitment that loves the spouse regardless of what the spouse does or doesn't do.

4. Know your strengths and limitations as a helper.

5. Consult and get supervision if you are not sure of what do to in any instance. Safeguard your friend's trust by maintaining confidentiality about his or her identity and about the details of the problem.

6. Rely on the Lord, not on your own resourcefulness, ability, or skill. Only the Lord can produce lasting change, and you can be His vehicle of change if you seek His will and follow His leading.

Give Yourself a Final Exam

A conversation between Lindsay and Nan opened the book. Reread those few pages to refresh your memory. In Chapter 1, I asked, "How would you have reacted? Would you have been more helpful than was Nan?" You wrote your answer to ten questions (see pages 18–19).

Throughout this book, we have dealt with problems like Lindsay's. You can now demonstrate to yourself what you have learned from the book. *Write* the answer to each of the following ten questions again, and compare your answers with your original answers. Can you see the difference?

For each question, I have provided an answer against which you can test your answers.

My Answers

1. What common mistakes in helping should you avoid?

Don't suggest immediate solutions; resist the urge. Help Lindsay talk more about her situation and her feelings before you suggest solutions. She's looking for answers and demanding them immediately, but you aren't likely to bring peace and tranquillity to her marriage regardless of what you suggest, so plan deliberately. That way, when you do make suggestions, they will be more useful. Don't immediately quote Scripture to her or cut off her expression of feelings by telling her to give her problem to God or to "just pray" about it. Complex problems at root have an answer that's simple to say (but not to carry out), which is to trust the Lord and try to live as a committed disciple of Jesus. However, people don't easily accept that answer in the midst of pain, confusion, and hurt. By saying it as a simple solution, you drive the person away, rather than solving the problem.

2. What is the main root cause of problems in Lindsay's and Patrick's marriage?

The root cause of Patrick and Lindsay's problem is a failure in faith working through love. They devalue each other:

- Patrick's affair devalued Lindsay.
- Both partners yelled at each other, treating each other as objects of rage instead of people whom they love.
- Patrick tortured Lindsay by describing adulterous sex.
- Lindsay reacted violently by throwing a trivet, and Patrick responded violently.
- Lindsay ran away and locked the door, and Patrick reciprocated, leaving early the next morning.
- Patrick tried to kick in the door.

Lindsay showed a failure in faith in the marriage by questioning whether they should get a divorce. Furious and hurt, she seems willing to throw out the marriage without fighting to save it. Faith working through love, the fundamental pattern of Christian discipleship, has crumbled and needs repair.

3. What are the main areas in which the problem is surfacing?

Patrick and Lindsay's marriage needs work in conflict management and communication. The marriage has become so negatively tinged that they can't resolve their conflicts or communicate without hurting each other. The affair communicates that intimacy has been poor, but it may be motivated more by Patrick's desire to hurt Lindsay than by his attempt at closeness with Thelma.

4. How would you help Lindsay deal with her current crisis?

Reestablish contact with Lindsay. Nan should continue to phone, letting the phone ring for several minutes. If Lindsay doesn't answer, Nan should visit Lindsay, especially in view of the reference Lindsay made to "have it be over" and to "end it." The concern about physical danger is real, and Nan should take it seriously.

5. How would you answer her question, "Should I get a divorce?"

A crisis is not the time to make a snap decision about divorce. Neither is it a time for quick assurances that things will work out, or that God is in control, or that divorce isn't the answer (or even that divorce is the answer). Neither is a crisis the time for a theological lesson. To answer Lindsay's question, say, "Divorce is one option, but you'll decide better after you've given it more thought. Right now you need to decide what you want to do when Patrick comes home."

6. Is Lindsay depressed? Is she suicidal?

Lindsay may be suicidal. She shows only a few risk signs—she alluded to suicide, and she has been depressed. We don't know whether she has a suicide plan, how elaborate the plan is, and whether she has the means to carry out her plan. Get additional information before being *alarmed,* but be *concerned.* Ask Lindsay directly about suicide.

7. How concerned are you about each of the complicating factors?

Infidelity. Infidelity is always a threat to the stability of the marriage. In the present case, its hurtful use causes additional concern. If the infidelity is ended, the scars may remain for a long time. Lindsay's forgiveness of Patrick will be a major concern, even if Patrick repents.

Drinking. Drinking is of concern. Apparently Patrick was drunk. We don't know whether this was an isolated incident or a pattern of serious drinking, but drunkenness is one indication of movement toward alcoholism. Get more information to determine how serious the problem is.

Physical abuse. Both partners used physical force, which fed into each other's anger. Neither has hurt the other physically yet, but with this explosive marriage, the risk of physical abuse is substantial.

8. In the longer term, how would you help with:

Intimacy. Lindsay and Patrick evidently have different needs for intimacy, but we aren't told who needs more intimacy and what kinds of intimacy each wants more or less of. Before knowing exactly how to help, we need to know more. Each partner may increase or decrease his or her intimacy through rearranging his or her time commitments. If Patrick is having an affair and drinking, we might assume that he doesn't feel as if his intimacy needs are being met. A group—Bible study, fellowship, or support group—might provide some of his intimacy needs.

Intense conflict seems to impair the couple's capacity for intimacy. As Gottman observed, marital satisfaction is related to the ratio of pleasant to unpleasant interactions.[1] David Myers reports two studies that suggest less frequent arguing and more frequent sex are related to marital satisfaction.[2] In one study, couples wrote down the number of times they argued and had sex each week. Almost every couple who had sex more than they argued reported happy marriages, but no couple who argued more than they had sex reported marital happiness. Decreasing conflict might help Lindsay and Patrick experience more intimacy (and probably enjoy their lovemaking more, too).

Communication. Patrick and Lindsay were unable, and perhaps unwilling, to talk about serious topics, and they often said hurtful things to each other. Modifying those two communication patterns could help reconnect them. Neither partner communicates that he or she values the other. Both partners live in fear of rejection, and they bring about the rejection they fear by staying aloof from each other or by connecting only to hurt each other. Both partners need to edit their negative communication.[3] If they criticize, they need to do so in an atmosphere of love to find solutions rather than to hurt each other.

Conflict management. Reducing arguments and substituting genuine conflict resolution would probably make the biggest impact on Lindsay and Patrick's marriage. It would improve intimacy by making the environment safer and would stimulate more communication. Lindsay and Patrick have proceeded beyond the stage of conflict that can be aided with only the help of friends and family. They need help from a marriage counselor who can allow them to communicate and try to resolve conflict in his or her presence and show them precisely how to talk with each other. As a friend, encourage them to seek counseling and to apply what they learned. Failures would be inevitable. They seem to have practiced an ingrained pattern of communication and conflict, so help them deal with failures by keeping their faith in the progress they will see if they work diligently. Finally, their conflict is serious enough that they may become discouraged. Turn their attention to the redeeming power of God if they bring their marriage before Him.

Negative thinking. Patterns of blame are well established. Further, negative expectations and assumptions about the marriage's future will create a self-fulfilling prophecy unless radical changes occur. Help promote more positive thinking. Encourage their effort and help them see their progress.

9. How would you help strengthen their commitment?

Commitment is a major issue, especially in light of the revelation of Patrick's affair and the hurtfulness with which he flaunted it. Forgiveness will likely take a long time and will be a struggle. Help each partner examine his or her views about the marriage covenant and divorce. Consideration of divorce (by Lindsay) is a serious threat to commitment. If they decide to try to preserve the marriage, clear limits need to be established about ceasing Patrick's affair with Thelma and about his behavior in seeking forgiveness. Restoration of commitment depends on his feeling and showing remorse and demonstrating trustworthiness over an extended period.

10. Do you think Lindsay and Patrick will remain married?

Whether Lindsay and Patrick remain married depends on their willingness to work to rebuild love in their ravaged marriage. Many marriages survive similar threats, and other marriages succumb to lesser threats. The fate of their marriage depends on their ability to practice faith working through love, and on their hope.

Hope

Psychologists have investigated the importance of hope only within the last ten years. Research on optimism and hope have flourished. Technically, optimism and hope are different but are two sides of the same coin.[4] Optimism is a predisposition to react positively when disappointed. Hope is the predisposition to pursue one's dreams. Both optimism and hope are needed to improve a troubled marriage.

We generally think of optimism and hope as qualities that people are born with and that can't be influenced. Not true, say psychological researchers. People can become more optimistic and hopeful. As a friend, you can encourage optimism and hope.

Some Benefits of Optimism and Hope

Martin Seligman, author of *Learned Optimism,* has studied optimism and its benefits.[5] In one study, he tested sales personnel for the Metropolitan Life Insurance Company.[6] He classified the 1,000 newly hired sales people as optimists or pessimists. He also hired 129 "super-optimists" who did not meet the usual qualifications for hiring but showed extremely optimistic outlooks on life and on dealing with failure and rejection. By the second year after hiring, optimists had outsold pessimists by 31 percent. Super-optimists had outsold pessimists by 57 percent.

Optimism and hope not only produce more resiliency to failure and rejection, they also produce better health. George Valliant, of Dartmouth Medical School, tested Harvard graduates between 1939 and 1944. He kept in contact with them and has studied them repeatedly since the 1940s. Seligman classified each graduate as optimistic or pessimistic based on survey responses.[7] By middle age, pessimists had developed more heart disease, high blood pressure, and cancer. Other studies have shown similar results.[8]

Being an Agent of Hope

As Christians, we affirm the sovereignty of God and His grace and power to intervene to change hearts—even in the most troubled marriages. When our friends are hopeless and pessimistic, we have the message of hope, that Jesus died for us and was resurrected. If He can conquer physical death, He can conquer a dying relationship. He can even resurrect a dead marriage.

We have seen evidence throughout this book of helpers being agents of hope. Fromma and Leo were each helped by friends who stuck with them throughout extended troubles and helped them during crises. Carlos, an elder in the community, helped Raphael and Donna recapture their hope after Donna's tragic affair. Roberta was a faithful friend throughout Jane's divorce and the period of recovery afterward. Marie helped Dorothy restore her marriage with Dan by conquering negative thinking. Each helper was God's agent of hope to the couples.

Even if your friend is not a Christian, you still can turn him or her over to the Lord. Bring your friend to the Lord. If he or she comes along, there is healing, life, and hope. If your friend chooses not to drink of the living water, he or she is making a choice.

We have the mandate to bring hope to Christians, not merely to non-Christians. Part of the Great Commission is to make disciples. Disciple-making doesn't just happen in far away places. It happens in our closest friendships. Disciple-making is sharing faith working through love and helping disciples use the principles in the problem areas of their lives.

Optimism and hope—not in themselves but in the proper object of our hope, Jesus—will transform the marriages and lives of our friends and ourselves. As we minister love, the Lord will indeed change us, not just our friends. It is easy to puff ourselves up as we see effects from our helping, but we must remain humble, as agents of hope who are used only by God's grace. Only then can we be true vessels of faith, work, and love.

APPENDIX A

Some Questions to Examine Yourself

CHAPTER 1: "Help, I Have Marriage Problems"

1. Should you feel confident about helping a friend or family member with a marital problem?
2. What is the essential difference between helping with a marital problem and helping with an individual problem like depression or fear?

CHAPTER 2: The Cause of Marital Problems

3. What is the underlying cause of marital problems that is stressed throughout this book? On what Scriptures is it based?
4. How do failures in faith, working, and love show up?

CHAPTER 3: Where Problems Surface

5. What are the three areas of marriage that form the Christian foundation?
6. What are the four areas of marriage primarily responsible for marital satisfaction?

CHAPTER 4: Helping After Marriage

7. What makes newly wedded couples open for help?
8. How well does marriage enrichment work?

CHAPTER 5:
Helping Prevent or Deal with Divorce and Remarriage

9. Give four principles for dealing with disagreements among Christians about the interpretation of Scripture's guidance about divorce and remarriage.
10. How can you help a person deal with the trauma of divorce after he or she has decided to divorce?

CHAPTER 6:
Evaluate Yourself

11. How do experts and novices solve problems differently?
12. List some ways to improve your counseling.

CHAPTER 7:
Mistakes Helpers Make

13. Name five common mistakes in lay helping that are not necessarily concerned with helping people with marital problems.
14. Name four common mistakes in lay helping that are commonly associated with helping for marital problems.

CHAPTER 8:
Become a Better Helper

15. Name four ways to help a friend.
16. In learning better interactional skills, what are the four levels (in the correct order) at which we should practice our skills?

CHAPTER 9:
Bird's Eye-View of Helping

17. Name five ways that effective professional marital therapists differ from ineffective professional marital therapists.
18. Name six stages (in order) that all helping goes through.

CHAPTER 10:
Have a Positive Attitude

19. List two ways that aren't usually helpful at getting people to be more positive about their marriage.
20. List some ways that are more helpful at getting people to be more positive about their marriage.

CHAPTER 11: Use Your Own Marriage as a Positive Model

21. What is the main characteristic of a good model?
22. Name as many ways as possible to use aspects of your own marriage as a good model to copy for the person you are helping. (Try to name at least five.)

CHAPTER 12: Stay Cool in Marital Crises

23. Why is a crisis a good time to help?
24. What is the first rule of crisis first aid?

CHAPTER 13: Stick with Long-term Problems

25. How do you think of long-term marital problems?
26. What are the three doorways into long-term problems?

CHAPTER 14: Help Strengthen the Christian Core

27. The Christian core consists of what three parts?
28. Name six ways to affect your friend's Christian core.

CHAPTER 15: Help Build Closeness

29. Give three rules to use in helping people in the emotional distancer-emotional pursuer pattern?
30. If a person of the other sex asks for help with sexual problems, what should you do?

CHAPTER 16: Help Promote Communication

31. Name five things to avoid doing when helping with communication problems.
32. I listed eleven techniques for improving communication. Name as many as you can.

CHAPTER 17: Help Resolve Conflicts

33. What is the most important cause of chronic conflict and what is at the root of that cause?
34. Explain the basis of Fisher and Ury's method of conflict negotiations.

CHAPTER 18: Help Change Negative Thinking

35. What are five ways to help change negative thinking?
36. Help the person see negative thoughts and expectations as cues to ask themselves: "________________?" (Fill in the blank.)

CHAPTER 19: Help Cope with Complicating Problems

37. How can one partner know if an infidelity has been committed?
38. List some reasons that women stay in marriages where they are being physically abused, even seriously hurt.

CHAPTER 20: Help Partners Forgive

39. What usually is the response when a person says to his or her spouse, "I forgive you," if the spouse hasn't asked for forgiveness?
40. What are confession, repentance, and forgiveness?

CHAPTER 21: Help Strengthen Commitment

41. What are two types of commitment?
42. Commitment is a balancing act between what two extremes?

CHAPTER 22: Hope—Even for the Most Troubled Marriages

43. What are the six main themes of this book?
44. What is the message of hope that we bring to people in troubled marriages?

Answers to Self-Examination

CHAPTER 1: "Help, I Have Marriage Problems"

1. We shouldn't feel confident about helping a friend, but we should realize that lots of people seek help from their friends and benefit from that help. We should feel humble that we are entrusted to help, and we should rely on Jesus' help to steady us when we feel unsure of ourselves and confused. On the other hand, part of Jesus' help can be to direct us to help our friends find a more competent helper within the body of Christ (or in some cases) among professional helpers.

2. The essential difference in trying to help with a marital problem rather than an individual problem is that the married person is covenantally bound to the partner and any changes in the married partner's behavior will intimately affect his or her spouse. The nature of the marital partnership as being two companions who are joined together makes helping difficult because you may have no effect on the spouse and the spouse will likely resist efforts to change that are initiated by the person you are helping. You can usually count on being somewhat frustrated when you begin to help a person in marital difficulties.

CHAPTER 2: The Cause of Marital Problems

3. In this book, I stress failures in "faith working through love" (from Galatians 5:6 and 2 Timothy 1:13) as the fundamental problem in all troubled marriages.

4. Failures in faith are failures to believe God, to believe that marriage can work, and to believe that improvement is possible. Failures in working are seen when partners lose hope that marriage will improve and they stop trying to make the marriage better. Failures in love are instances of unwillingness or inability to value the partner or instances in which partners actively devalue or put down the partner or treat the partner as having little or no worth.

CHAPTER 3: Where Problems Surface

5. These three areas—Christianity, core beliefs, and confession-forgiveness are the heart of the marriage. They are the life blood, pumping vitality into the outer body.

6. Four areas are mostly responsible for a couple's marital satisfaction—closeness, communication, conflict resolution, and cognition (expectations and negative thinking).

CHAPTER 4: Helping After Marriage

7. Generally, newly wedded couples are open for help and advice because they didn't think they would have any adjustment difficulties, but they find that they (a) must resolve more differences than they believed would be the case, (b) face disillusionments because they married an ideal of the spouse instead of an accurate picture of the spouse, and (c) must adapt to new roles and behaviors.

8. Marriage enrichment programs have typically helped the people who already had excellent marriages and not the ones whose marriages were about average. Marriage enrichment programs have been harmful to couples whose marriages were already in trouble.

CHAPTER 5: Helping Prevent or Deal with Divorce and Remarriage

9. When Christians disagree about issues such as divorce and remarriage, I find it helpful to try to adhere to several principles. (You might find that other principles guide your way of dealing with disagreements among informed Christians about how to interpret Scripture.)

- First, I try to understand Scripture, its guidance and its limitations.
- Second, I try to remain humble about my ability to interpret Scripture perfectly.
- Third, I encourage the person considering divorce to try to discern the will of God for him or her through prayer, reasoning, listening and looking for God's guidance, and being willing to follow that guidance.
- Fourth, I must act within my conscience while respecting others' rights to have different opinions.

10. To help a person deal with divorce, you can (1) provide information about divorce and what the stresses and strains will be, (2) help deal with the roller coaster of emotions, (3) provide practical help in times of need, (4) continue to advocate reconciliation and forgiveness, (5) answer questions and respond to ongoing emotional upheaval, (6) counsel against "dating" while still legally married, (7) help the person handle anger, depression, and grief that may occur as the divorce becomes final, (8) (when asked) help deal with continuing conflict between ex-spouses, and (9) provide help in child rearing for the single parent.

CHAPTER 6: Evaluate Yourself

11. Experts have more knowledge about counseling and marriage, better organized knowledge, and more interrelated pathways through which they can make comparisons than do novices. Also experts look at the more important aspects of the problem—such as how people try to resolve conflicts, communicate, or show intimacy—whereas novices look at less important parts of the problem—such as what people are disagreeing about and how to forge a compromise. Experts seek a lot of information before offering solutions, whereas novices try to solve the problem quickly. Experts start with a general plan but may end up at a different destination than they envisioned initially, whereas novices try to work toward a specific destination but have less sense of a plan for getting there.

12. You can improve by:
    - Getting supervision,
    - Getting in a formal training program,
    - Reading about counseling,
    - Keeping a confidential journal, and
    - Watching others counsel (live or videotapes; actual counseling or role-playing).

CHAPTER 7: Mistakes Helpers Make

13. Some common mistakes in lay helping are (1) not finding the balance between being controlled by a formula and having no plan, (2) not recognizing our limitations and thus trying to help someone when we are doing harm instead of helping, (3) violating confidentiality, even if we are doing so with excellent motives, (4) getting trapped in "game playing," (5) giving too much or too little help.
14. Problems common in marital helping are (1) thinking our experience must apply to everyone else, (2) over-identifying with the person we are helping and empowering him or her against the spouse, (3) becoming sexually attracted to someone we are helping, and (4) being too passive.

CHAPTER 8: Become a Better Helper

15. There are several ways that you might help a friend—through providing practical assistance, resources, or information, and through your helping interaction with the person. You might help different friends in different ways. Some friends may require only minimal help; others may require help of each kind.
16. Four levels we should move through as we improve our skills are (1) fundamentals, (2) match-related situations (such as brief role-plays), (3) match conditions (such as realistic role-plays), and (4) the actual match (use of the skills during actual helping interactions).

CHAPTER 9:
Bird's-Eye View of Helping

17. Effective marital therapists have better general helping skills, better help couples not say hurtful things to each other, understand marriage better, use their knowledge better, and motivate people to change more than do ineffective helpers.

18. All helping—professional and non-professional—goes through a beginning phase where the helper understands the problem and communicates that understanding (Stage 1) and helps the person rethink the problem (Stage 2). A second phase involves helping people plan different actions based on the new way of understanding the problem (Stage 3), supporting attempts to carry out the actions (Stage 4), and following up to see how the attempts worked or didn't work (Stage 5). The final part of helping is ending the relationship and restoring the person to normal life (Stage 6). Good lay helpers excel at Stage 1.

CHAPTER 10:
Have a Positive Attitude

19. Two ways that usually don't help people be more positive are (1) tell them directly to be more positive (they agree that they should, but they usually don't change because they already knew that they should be more positive) and (2) coerce them to change by threatening them with Scripture or hell fire.

20. It is usually more effective to (1) ask them to describe the times in their marriage when love grew and see if they can recapture those times or try some of those methods, (2) stress that change will occur because of God's intervention and their initiative, (3) tell them that change takes not only work but time, (4) refocus them on finding solutions rather than describing problems, (5) have them compartmentalize the pain, (6) focus on doing more of what works (once they find some things that work), (7) caution them against expecting the partner (or themselves) to be perfect, (8) help them focus on their own responsibilities rather than their partner's failings, (9) stimulate them to want to make the first change rather than wait for the partner, (10) encourage them to be patient, and (11) orient them toward a merciful

and gracious God who embodies love and reconciliation and wants it for estranged people.

CHAPTER 11:
Use Your Own Marriage as a Positive Model

21. The most important part of being a good model is to be someone the person can identify with. You can be a mastery model (modeling how a behavior should be done) or a coping model (modeling how to deal with difficult situations and how to rise above difficulties).

22. If you self-disclose about your own marriage, your anecdote should be (1) directly about the client's difficulty, (2) clear, (3) short, (4) one central point, (5) presented as one example of how to deal with the client's problem (not as THE ANSWER), (6) phrased to allow the person freedom not to copy your behavior (rather than a demand to follow your example), (7) a positive example rather than a negative one, (8) one of a very few anecdotes about your self (focus on the other person rather than your self), and (9) summarized at the end of the anecdote (or at the beginning) in such a way that the person knows what part of the anecdote you wanted him or her to copy.

CHAPTER 12:
Stay Cool in Marital Crises

23. A crisis can be a good time to help because crises erode a person's self-sufficiency, making them more eager to find a solution and making them more open to God's intervention.

24. The first rule of crisis first-aid is to calm yourself and manage your own feelings of crisis. Then you can calm the other person, listen carefully, think before acting, consider alternatives, help the person choose a course of action, have the person repeat his or her plan, and follow-up to see how things are going the next day.

CHAPTER 13:
Stick with Long-term Problems

25. You should think of marital problems as being caused by failures in faith, in working on the marriage, and in valuing love. Those failures show up throughout the marriage. They show up in the Christian core (Christian beliefs and values,

vision of marriage, and confession and forgiveness). They also show up in four areas leading to contentment with the marriage (closeness, communication, conflict resolution, and negative cognition). The failures also show up in complicating problems. Finally, commitment is eroded.

26. The three doorways into a long-term helping relationship are the request for help (letter, phone call, visit, or conversation), your focus on the problem that bothers the person, and your active listening (which shows your friend that you care).

CHAPTER 14: Help Strengthen the Christian Core

27. A friend's Christian core consists of three parts: the friend's (1) Christian values and beliefs, (2) Christian vision of marriage, and (3) willingness to confess and seek forgiveness for sins and forgive the partner.

28. You can affect your friend's Christian core through:
    - Helping your friend understand marriage as similar to Christian discipleship.
    - Directly presenting the gospel of Jesus Christ's finished work on the cross.
    - Teaching directly about Christianity or Christian marriage.
    - Asking questions that direct the person to Jesus.
    - Referring to Christian resources.
    - Praying for your friend.

CHAPTER 15: Help Build Closeness

29. Three rules for helping people in the emotional distancer-pursuer pattern are (1) Talk mostly to the emotional pursuer; (2) Treat the emotional distancer with great respect; and (3) Never pursue an emotional distancer.

30. If a person of the other sex asks you for help with sexual problems, you can take several courses of action. (1) Don't have the conversation alone. (2) Invite the person's spouse into the conversation. (3) Invite an outside person of the same sex as the help seeker to meet with you. (4) Arrange for the help seeker to counsel with someone of the same sex as himself or herself.

CHAPTER 16: Help Promote Communication

31. In helping change communication, five things to avoid are (1) criticizing, (2) pointing out every communication weakness you see (focus on only a couple), (3) jumping in with immediate corrections (listen well first), (4) getting sidetracked away from the main issue, and (5) suggesting compromises.

32. Ten techniques for helping build better communication are (1) teach active listening when partners often misunderstand each other, (2) have partners repeat the spouse's comment before saying their own comment when the couple often misunderstand each other, (3) teach the "pinch model" when partners say hurtful things to each other, (4) use "I have the floor" and "passing the buck" to slow down interruptions, (5) use the marriage conference table when partners can't make enough time to talk or won't listen to each other when they do talk, (6) teach leveling when one partner holds everything in, (7) teach editing when one or both partners say hurtful things to each other, (8) have the couple tape record arguments when they are in a power struggle, (9) teach intent-impact when the power struggle has become so habitual that the partners automatically misunderstand almost every communication, and (10) have people pray to stop mentally rehearsing their gripes when they are locked in a power struggle.

CHAPTER 17: Help Resolve Conflicts

33. The most important cause of chronic conflict is disagreement over who has the power to make decisions, called a power struggle. At the root of this difficulty is the sin of self-will.

34. Fisher and Ury's method of conflict negotiation has people identify the interests behind the incompatible positions they are taking and then find a solution (or several solutions) that meet both sets of interests. One important common interest for Christian couples is to forge a Christian marriage and to help each other grow in Christian discipleship by practicing faith working through love. You can draw on this common interest to help them decide how to share power in a less

self-centered way than they are when involved in chronic conflict.

CHAPTER 18:
Help Change Negative Thinking

35. To help the person change, you must help the person (1) change the focus of attention away from the spouse's failures to his or her own responsibilities, (2) change the evidence supporting the negative beliefs, expectations, and assumptions, (3) pay attention to evidence that is currently being ignored, (4) change the reasoning that led to the negative conclusions, or (5) change patterns of thinking that reinforce the negative conclusions.

36. Help the person see negative thoughts and expectations as cues to ask themselves: "How can I demonstrate 'faith working through love' in this situation?"

CHAPTER 19:
Help Cope with Complicating Problems

37. To determine whether an infidelity has been committed, a partner can ask his or her spouse. If the partner is thinking about doing something that is questionable, he or she should ask the spouse before doing the action. Hesitancy about asking usually means that the partner should not do the questionable behavior.

38. Women stay in abusive relationships because (a) they fear they will be hurt physically, psychologically, or financially, (b) others advise them to stay, (c) their beliefs or values do not permit them to leave, and (d) they would have to radically alter their lives—affecting their own and their children's well-being.

CHAPTER 20:
Help Partners Forgive

39. If the spouse grants unasked-for forgiveness, the partner usually feels accused and blamed and becomes angry instead of being grateful.

40. Confession is admitting your part in the wrong-doing. Repentance is turning away from the wrong-doing (or at least sincerely trying to turn away from it). Forgiveness is granting (or being granted) pardon for the wrong-doing.

CHAPTER 21: Help Strengthen Commitment

41. Two types of commitment, which both can be factors in any individual's commitment, are personal dedication (wanting to improve the relationship) and obligation or constraint (feeling like one must stay in the relationship). Smedes calls these caring and consistency.

42. Commitment is a balancing act with a foot on each of two cliffs. One cliff is wishy-washy, feeling-dictated agreement to do for others that which I want to do and which furthers my interest. The other cliff is slavish agreement to keep every commitment we ever make, regardless of how small, heedless to the consequences, in spite of God's leading.

CHAPTER 22: Hope—Even for the Most Troubled Marriages

43. The six main themes of this book are these:
    a. You can help friends in marital distress. As a Christian, promote hope by sharing your faith, work, and love.
    b. Listen and support your distressed friend. Help your friend rethink his or her marriage as an opportunity to make the partner a disciple by practicing Jesus' pattern—faith working through love. Help plan actions that will bring about that understanding. Follow-up on what happens when your friend tries to change.
    c. Help your friend build a solid Christian core (Christian beliefs and values, a Christian vision of marriage, and an attitude of confession, repentance, and forgiveness). Help build marital satisfaction through promoting closeness, communication, conflict resolution, and positive thinking. Help deal with complicating problems. Help build covenantal commitment that loves the spouse regardless of what the spouse does or doesn't do.
    d. Know your strengths and limitations as a helper.
    e. Consult and get supervision if you are not sure of what do to in any instance. Safeguard your friend's trust by maintaining confidentiality about his or her identity and about the details of the problem.

f. Rely on the Lord, not on your own resourcefulness, ability, or skill. Only the Lord can produce lasting change, and you can be his vehicle of change if you seek his will and follow his leading.

44. As Christians, we affirm the sovereignty of God and his grace and power to intervene to change hearts—even in the most troubled marriages. When our friends are hopeless and pessimistic, we have the message of hope, that Jesus died for us and was resurrected. If He can conquer physical death, He can conquer a dying relationship. He can even resurrect a dead marriage.

APPENDIX B

An Uncontrolled Study of the Effectiveness of Information About Helping and Personal Problems

In my course at Virginia Commonwealth University on Effective Behavior and Contemporary Psychology, I studied the effectiveness of receiving information about helping and about marital and dating problems.

At the beginning of the course, students rated their perceived ability and comfort at helping a friend with a relationship problem. In one instance, an unmarried friend's steady romantic partner had recently ended their relationship. In the other case, a married friend had marital difficulties. Students were 16 men and 9 women, ranging in age from 19 to 39. Their average age was 27. Only 6 students were majors in psychology. Students were paired. One acted as helper, the other as helpee. The helpee was given the description of the role he or she had to play. The helper counseled as a friend, not a professional counselor. After 8 minutes of helping, pairs were rearranged. Helper in the first scenario was helpee in the second, again for 8 minutes.

After both role-plays were complete, students answered, "How well do you think you counseled this person?" by rating themselves as (1) excellent, (2) good, (3) fair, (4) not too well, or (5) terrible. They then rated their comfort level in the helping as (1) extremely comfortable, (2) comfortable, (3) neither comfortable nor uncomfortable, (4) uncomfortable, or (5) extremely uncomfortable.

After the test, I lectured and showed 7 videotapes of counselors for 12 class hours. I retested students on the same situations (paired with different people, with scenarios taken in reverse order). Then, I lectured for 32 additional hours—6 of those on relationship problems—and on the last day of class, I retested the students on the same scenarios.

Here are the results of the three tests. The percent of people evaluating their performance as either excellent or good (the top two categories) changed from 42 percent at the initial test to 74 percent after learning about counseling to 86 percent after learning about relationships. The percent of people evaluating their comfort level as either extremely comfortable or comfortable (the top two categories) changed from 48 percent at the initial measurement to 74 percent after learning about counseling to 91 percent after learning about relationships.

Obviously, this test is inconclusive. Even though the tests were separated by quite a period of time, students might have experienced a practice effect (making them better helpers) or might have even become bored with the test by the third repetition (making them worse helpers). Nonetheless, if we interpret the results with a large dose of caution, we might still speculate that learning about helping and about relationships each had an effect.

This test suggests that the information in this book—about marriage and how to help—will help you feel more competent and comfortable helping friends.

NOTES

CHAPTER 1: "Help, I Have Marriage Problems"

1. Andrew J. Cherlin, *Marriage, Divorce, Remarriage* (Cambridge, Mass.: Harvard Univ., 1981).
2. G. H. Brody, E. Neubaum, and Rex Forehand, "Serial Marriage: A Heuristic Analysis of an Emerging Family Form," *Psychological Bulletin,* 103 (1988): 211–22.
3. Everett L. Worthington, Jr., "Religious Counseling: A Review of Published Empirical Research," *Journal of Counseling and Development,* 64 (1986): 421–31.
4. Kenneth L. Sell and W. Mack Goldsmith, "Concerns About Professional Counseling: An Exploration of Five Factors and the Role of Christian Orthodoxy," *Journal of Psychology and Christianity,* 7, no. 3 (1988): 5–21.
5. Kenneth C. Haugk, *Christian Caregiving—A Way of Life* (Minneapolis: Augsburg, 1984).
6. Lawrence J. Crabb, Jr., *Effective Biblical Counseling* (Grand Rapids: Zondervan, 1977).
7. Gary R. Collins, *How to Be a People Helper* (Santa Ana, Calif.: Vision House, 1976a); *People Helper Growth Book* (Santa Ana, Calif.: Vision House, 1976b).
8. Jay Adams, *Ready To Restore: The Layman's Guide to Christian Counseling* (Grand Rapids: Baker, 1981).
9. Gary R. Sweeten, *Discipleship Counseling* (Cincinnati: Christian Information Committee, 1983).
10. Horace C. Lukens, Jr., "Training Paraprofessional Christian Counselors: A Model Proposed," *Journal of Psychology and Christianity,* 2, no. 3 (1983): 61–66.
11. William Backus, *Telling the Truth to Troubled People* (Minneapolis: Bethany House, 1985).
12. *Innovations in Learning.* Videotapes on Christian Counseling featuring many well-known Christian counselors. 7018 El Paseo Street, Long Beach, CA 90815.

13. For a good review of research on the effectiveness of lay counseling, especially lay Christian counseling, see Siang-Yang Tan, *Lay Counseling: Equipping Christians for a Helping Ministry* (Grand Rapids: Zondervan, 1991), especially chapter 4, pp. 61–81.

CHAPTER 2: The Cause of Marital Problems

1. Everett L. Worthington, Jr., and Douglas McMurry, *Marriage Conflicts: Resources for Strategic Pastoral Counseling* (Grand Rapids: Baker, 1994); Douglas McMurry and Everett L. Worthington, Jr., *Value Your Mate: How To Strengthen Your Marriage* (Grand Rapids: Baker, 1994).

CHAPTER 3: Where Problems Surface

1. Larry Christenson, *The Renewed Mind* (Minneapolis: Bethany House, 1974).
2. For additional research support that the couple who prays together stays together, see David G. Myers, *The Pursuit of Happiness: Discovering the Pathway to Fulfillment, Well-Being, and Enduring Personal Joy* (New York: Avon, 1992), 173.

CHAPTER 4: Helping After Marriage

1. Everett L. Worthington, Jr., "A Preliminary Study of Guerin's Stages of Marital Conflict," research paper, Virginia Commonwealth University, 1985.
2. S. F. Van Huysteen, "Ministering to Newly Weds," *Journal of Pastoral Practice* 8 (1986): 30–37.
3. William J. Doherty, Mary Ellen Lester, and Geoffrey Leigh, "Marriage Encounter Weekends: Couples Who Win and Couples Who Lose," *Journal of Marital and Family Therapy,* 12 (1986): 49–61; William J. Doherty and B. Walker, "Marriage Encounter Casualties: A Preliminary Investigation," *American Journal of Family Therapy,* 10 (1982): 10–25.
4. Everett L. Worthington, Jr., Beverly G. Buston, and T. Michael Hammonds, "A Component Analysis of Marriage Enrichment: Information and Treatment Modality," *Journal of Counseling and Development* 67 (1989): 555–60.

CHAPTER 5: Helping Prevent or Deal with Divorce and Remarriage

1. A fuller treatment of the different theological positions on divorce and remarriage may be found in H. Wayne House, ed., *Divorce and Remarriage: Four Christian Views* (with contributions from J. Carl Laney, William Heth, Thomas Edgar, and Larry Richards) (Downers Grove, Ill.: InterVarsity, 1990).
2. Several authors have identified "stages of divorce": P. Bohannan, "The Six Stations of Divorce," in P. Bohannan, ed., *Divorce and After* (Garden City, N.Y.: Doubleday, 1970); D. J.

Froiland and T. L. Hozman, "Counseling for Constructive Divorce," *Personnel and Guidance Journal* 55 (1977): 525–29; S. Kessler, *The American Way of Divorce: Prescriptions for Change* (Chicago: Nelson Hall, 1975); S. Kraus, "The Crisis of Divorce: Growth Promoting or Pathogenic," *Journal of Divorce* 2 (1979): 107–19; S. Price-Bonham and J. O. Balswick, "The Noninstitutions: Divorce, Desertion, and Remarriage," *Journal of Marriage and the Family* 42 (1980): 225–38; C. J. Salts, "Divorce Process: Integrating Theory," *Journal of Divorce* 2 (1979): 233–40; R. S. Wiseman, "Crisis Theory and the Process of Divorce," *Social Casework* 56 (1975): 205–12.

3. Judith S. Wallerstein and Sandra Blakeslee, *Second Chances: Men, Women, and Children a Decade After Divorce* (New York: Ticknor & Fields, 1990).
4. Constance Ahrons, "After the Breakup," *Family Therapy Networker* 13, no.6 (1989): 30–41.
5. For theological positions on remarriage, see H. Wayne House (ed.), *Divorce and Remarriage: Four Christian Views* (with contributions from J. Carl Laney, William Heth, Thomas Edgar, & Larry Richards) (Downers Grove, Ill.: InterVarsity, 1990).
6. J. Carl Laney, *The Divorce Myth* (Minneapolis: Bethany House, 1981).
7. John Stott, Marriage and Divorce (Downers Grove, Ill.: InterVarsity, 1985).
8. Stanley Ellisen, *Divorce and Remarriage in the Church* (Grand Rapids: Zondervan, 1980).
9. Emily B. Visher and John S. Visher, *Old Loyalties, New Ties: Therapeutic Strategies with Stepfamilies* (New York: Brunner/Mazel, 1988).

CHAPTER 6:
Evaluate Yourself

1. Larry E. Beutler, M. Crago, and T. G. Arizmendi, "Therapist Variables in Psychotherapy Process and Outcome," in Sol L. Garfield and Allen E. Bergin, eds., *Handbook of Psychotherapy and Behavior Change* (New York: Wiley, 1986), 257–310.
2. R. B. Sloane, F. R. Staples, A. H. Cristol, N. J. Yorkton, and K. Whipple, *Psychotherapy Versus Behavior Therapy* (Cambridge, Mass.: Harvard Univ., 1975).
3. Jean Bedard and Michelene T. H. Chi, "Expertise," *Current Directions in Psychological Science* 1, no. 4 (1992): 135–139.
4. Thomas Schacht, "Can Psychotherapy Education Advance Psychotherapy Integration? A View from the Cognitive Psychology of Expertise," *Journal of Psychotherapy Integration* 1 no. 4 (1991): 305–19.
5. W. Chase and H. A. Simon, "Perception in Chess," *Cognitive Psychology* 4 (1973): 55–81.
6. P. J. Feltovich, P. E. Johnson, J. H. Moller, and D. B. Swanson. "LCS: The Role and Development of Medical Knowledge in Diagnostic Expertise," in W. J. Clancey and E. H. Shortliffe,

eds., *Readings in Medical Artificial Intelligence* (Reading, Mass.: Addison-Wesley, 1984), 406–16.

7. Mary O'Leary Wiley and P. B. Ray, "Counseling Supervision by Developmental Level," *Journal of Counseling Psychology,* 33 (1986): 439–45.
8. E. A. Locke & G. P. Latham. *A Theory of Goal Setting and Task Performance* (Englewood Cliffs, N.J.: Prentice-Hall, 1990).
9. Mike Mason, *The Mystery of Marriage: As Iron Sharpens Iron* (Portland, Oreg.: Multnomah, 1985).
10. Sloane et al., *Psychotherapy Versus Behavior Therapy.*

CHAPTER 7: Mistakes Helpers Make

1. Some of the suggestions in this section are from Everett L. Worthington, Jr., "Issues in Supervision of Lay Christian Counseling," *Journal of Psychology and Christianity* 6, no. 2 (1987): 70–77.
2. James F. Masterson, *Treatment of the Borderline Adolescent: A Developmental Approach* (New York: Wiley, 1972).
3. American Psychiatric Association, *Diagnostic and Statistical Manual of Mental Disorders* 3d ed. rev. (Washington, D.C.: American Psychiatric Association, 1987).
4. S. M. Fulero, *Tarasoff: 10 Years Later. Professional Psychology: Research and Practice* 19, no. 2 (1988): 184–90.
5. Gerald Corey, Marianne Schneider Corey, and Patrick Callanan, *Issues and Ethics in the Helping Professions* (Pacific Grove, Calif.: Brooks/Cole, 1993).
6. Eric Berne, *Games People Play* (New York: Grove, 1964).
7. James T. Berry, *Coping with Sexual Attraction at Work: A Study of Psychotherapists, Ministers, and Personnel Managers.* Unpublished dissertation, Virginia Commonwealth University, 1991.

CHAPTER 8: Become a Better Helper

1. Judith A. Marx, Zsuzsanna K. Gyorky, Georgia M. Royalty, and Tina E. Stern, "Use of Self-Help Books in Psychotherapy," *Professional Psychology: Research and Practice* 23, no. 4 (1992): 300–305.
2. Robert L. Quackenbush, "The Prescription of Self-Help Books by Psychologists: A Bibliography of Selected Bibliotherapy Resources," *Psychotherapy* 28 (1991): 671–77.
3. S. Starker, "Promises and Prescriptions: Self-Help Books in Mental Health and Medicine." *American Journal of Health Promotion* 1 (1986): 19–24, 68.
4. G. Halliday, "Psychological Self-Help Books—How Dangerous Are They?" *Psychotherapy* 28 (1991): 678–80.
5. See for example, Everett L. Worthington, Jr. *When Someone Asks for Help: A Practical Guide for Counseling* (Downers Grove, Ill.: InterVarsity, 1982).

6. Everett L. Worthington, Jr., *How To Help the Hurting: When Friends Face Problems with Self-Esteem, Self-Control, Fear, Depression, Loneliness* (Downers Grove, Ill.: InterVarsity, 1985).
7. Shelley Chapin, *Counselors, Comforters, and Friends: Caregivers in the Church* (Wheaton, Ill.: Victor, 1992).
8. *Ministering Couples: A Like-To-Like Marriage and Family Ministry* (Fargo, N.D.: Catholic Family Services, 1990); see Tan, *Lay Counseling,* for others.
9. Gary R. Collins, *Case Studies in Christian Counseling* (Dallas: Word, 1991).

CHAPTER 9:
Bird's-Eye View of Helping

1. Alan S. Gurman and David P. Kniskern, "Family Therapy Outcome Research: Knowns and Unknowns," in Alan S. Gurman and David P. Kniskern, eds. *Handbook of Family Therapy* (New York: Brunner/Mazel, 1981), 742–75.
2. Ibid.
3. Ibid.
4. Roger Fisher and William Ury, *Getting To Yes: Negotiating Agreement Without Giving In* (New York: Penguin Books, 1981).
5. Worthington, *When Someone Asks for Help;* Worthington, *How to Help the Hurting.*

CHAPTER 11:
Use Your Own Marriage as a Positive Model

1. Norman Garmazy, "The Study of Children at Risk for Severe Psychopathology." In J. F. Anthony & C. Koupernik (eds.), *The Child and His Family at Psychiatric Risk* (New York: Wiley, 1975).

CHAPTER 12:
Stay Cool in Marital Crises

1. G. A. Crow, *Crisis Intervention: A Social Interaction Approach* (New York: Association Press, 1977).
2. This figure is a pictorial representation of the model by Steven R. H. Beach, Evelyn E. Sandeen, and K. Daniel O'Leary, *Depression in Marriage: A Model for Etiology and Treatment* (New York: Guilford, 1990).
3. Richard S. Lazarus and S. Folkman, Stress, *Appraisal and Coping* (New York: Springer, 1984).
4. Thomas Strentz and Stephen M. Auerbach, "Adjustment to the Stress of Simulated Captivity: Effects of Emotion-Focused Versus Problem-Focused Preparation on Hostages Differing in Locus of Control," *Journal of Personality and Social Psychology* 55 (1988): 652–60.
5. Karl A. Slaikeu, *Crisis Intervention: A Handbook for Practice and Research* (Boston: Allyn and Bacon, 1984).

CHAPTER 15:
Help Build Closeness

1. Everett L. Worthington, Jr., "Strategic Matching and Tailoring of Treatment to Couples and Families," *Topics in Family Psychology and Counseling* 1, no. 3 (1992): 21–32.
2. Philip J. Guerin, Jr., Leo F. Fay, Susan L. Burden, and Judith Gilbert Kautto, *The Evaluation and Treatment of Marital Conflict: A Four-Stage Approach* (New York: Basic Books, 1987).
3. Carlfred B. Broderick, *The Therapeutic Triangle: A Sourcebook on Marital Therapy* (Beverly Hills, Calif.: Sage, 1983).
4. Ed Wheat and Gay Wheat, *Intended for Pleasure: New Approaches to Sexual Intimacy in Christian Marriage* (Old Tappan, N.J.: Fleming H. Revell, 1981); Tim LaHaye and Beverly LaHaye, *The Act of Marriage* (Grand Rapids: Zondervan, 1976).

CHAPTER 16:
Help Promote Communication

1. C. S. Lewis, *The Screwtape Letters* (New York: Macmillan, 1961).
2. Patricia Noller, *Nonverbal Communication and Marital Interaction* (Oxford: Pergamon, 1984).
3. Sherod Miller, Daniel Wackman, Elam Nunnally, & Phyllis Miller, *Connecting: With Self and Others* (Littleton, Ohio: Interpersonal Communication Programs, Inc., 1988).
4. John J. Sherwood and John C. Glidewell, "Planned Renegotiation: A Norm-Setting OD Intervention," in Warner Burke (ed.), *Contemporary Organizational Development: Approaches and Interventions,* (Washington, D.C.: NTL Learning Resources Corporation, 1972).
5. Mari Jo Renick, Susan L. Blumberg, and Howard J. Markman, "The Prevention and Relationship Enhancement Program (PREP)," *Family relations* 41 no. 2 (1992): 141–47.
6. Raymond J. Corsini, "The Marriage Conference," in H. Norman Wright, *Marital Counseling: A Biblical, Behavioral, Cognitive Approach* (San Francisco: Harper & Row, 1981), 337–51.
7. John Gottman, Cliff Notarius, Jonni Gonso, and Howard Markman, *A Couple's Guide to Communication* (Champaign, Ill.: Research Press, 1976).
8. These rules are taken from a list on pp. 47–48 of Gottman et al., *A Couple's Guide to Communication.*

CHAPTER 17:
Help Resolve Conflicts

1. Philip J. Guerin, Jr., Leo F. Fay, Susan L. Burden, and Judith Gilbert Kautto, *The Evaluation and Treatment of Marital Conflict: A Four-Stage Approach* (New York: Basic Books, 1987), 50–60.

2. Jay Haley, *Strategies of Psychotherapy* (New York: Grune & Stratton, 1963), 117–50.
3. Philippians 2:8.
4. Philippians 2:3–4.
5. Richard B. Stuart, *Helping Couples Change: A Social Learning Approach to Marital Therapy* (New York: Guilford, 1980), 265–71.
6. Park O. Davidson, "Therapeutic Compliance," *Canadian Psychological Review* 17 (1976): 247–59.
7. Roger Fisher and William Ury, *Getting To Yes: Negotiating Agreement Without Giving In* (New York: Penguin Books, 1981); see also Roger Fisher and Scott Brown, *Getting Together: Building Relationships As We Negotiate* (New York: Penguin Books, 1988).

CHAPTER 18:
Help Change Negative Thinking

1. John Mordechi Gottman, "A Theory of Marital Dissolution and Stability," *Journal of Family Psychology* 7 (1993): 57–75.
2. John Mordechi Gottman, *Marital Interaction: Experimental Investigations* (New York: Academic Press, 1979).
3. Aaron T. Beck, A. John Rush, Brian F. Shaw, and Gary Emery, *Cognitive Therapy of Depression* (New York: Guilford, 1979).
4. Gottman, et al. *A Couple's Guide to Communication.*
5. John Mordechi Gottman, *What Predicts Divorce?* (Hillsdale, N.J.: Erlbaum, 1993).
6. D. Martyn Lloyd-Jones, *Spiritual Depression: Its Causes and Cure* (Grand Rapids: Eerdmans, 1965), 20.

CHAPTER 19:
Help Cope with Complicating Problems

1. Frank Pittman, *Private Lies: Infidelity and the Betrayal of Intimacy* (New York: Norton, 1989).
2. U. S. Department of Commerce. 1986
3. American Psychiatric Association, *Diagnostic and Statistical Manual of Mental Disorders* 3d ed. rev. (Washington, D.C.: American Psychiatric Association, 1987).
4. Pat Springle, *Learning More About Codependency* (Houston/Dallas: Rapha Publishers/Word, 1991).
5. U. S. Department of Health and Human Services, *Sixth Special Report to the U. S. Congress on Alcohol and Health* (Rockville, Md.: Author, 1987).
6. G. A. Marlatt and J. R. Gordon, eds., *Relapse Prevention* (New York: Guilford, 1985).
7. Burl E. Gilliland and Richard K. James, *Crisis Intervention Strategies* (Pacific Grove, Calif.: Brooks/Cole, 1988).
8. James Alsdurf and Phyllis Alsdurf, *Battered Into Submission: The Tragedy of Wife Abuse in the Christian Home* (Downers Grove, Ill.: InterVarsity, 1989).

9. Richard Gelles, *The Violent Home* (Beverly Hills, Calif.: Sage, 1979).
10. Alsdurf and Alsdurf, *Battered Into Submission.*
11. Gottman, "A Theory of Marital Dissolution and Stability."

CHAPTER 20: Help Partners Forgive

1. Larry Christenson, *The Christian Family* (Minneapolis: Bethany House, 1970).
2. H. Pope, and C. W. Mueller. "The Intergenerational Transmission of Marital Instability." *Divorce and Separation: Context, Causes, and Consequences* (New York: Basic Books, 1979), 99–113.
3. Everett L. Worthington, Jr., Philip D. Dupont, James T. Berry, and Loretta A. Duncan, "Christian Therapists' and Clients' Perceptions of Religious Psychotherapy in Private and Agency Settings," *Journal of Psychology and Theology* 16 (1988): 282–93.
4. David Seamands, *The Healing of Memories* (Wheaton, Ill.: Victor, 1985).

CHAPTER 21: Help Strengthen Commitment

1. H. Norman Wright, *So You're Getting Married: Commitment: Basis for a Successful Marriage* (Ventura, Calif.: Regal, 1985).
2. M. P. Johnson, "The Social and Cognitive Features of the Dissolution of Commitment to Relationships," in Steve Duck, ed., *Personal Relationships: Dissolving Personal Relationships* (New York: Academic Press, 1982), 51–73.
3. Lewis B. Smedes, *Caring and Commitment: Learning to Live the Love We Promise* (San Francisco: Harper & Row, 1988).
4. Caryl E. Rusbult, "A Longitudinal Test of the Investment Model: The Development and Deterioration of Satisfaction and Commitment in Heterosexual Involvements," *Journal of Personality and Social Psychology* 45 (1983): 101–17.
5. Caryl E. Rusbult, Julie Verette, Gregory A. Whitney, Linda F. Slovik, and Isaac Lipkus, "Accommodation Processes in Close Relationships: Theory and Preliminary Empirical Evidence," *Journal of Personality and Social Psychology* 60, no. 1 (1991): 53–78.
6. Everett L. Worthington, Jr., and Beverley G. Buston, "The Marriage Relationship During the Transition to Parenthood: A Review and a Model," *Journal of Family Issues* 7 (1986): 443–73.
7. B. Bloom, S. Asher, and S. White, "Marital Disruption as a Stressor: A Review and Analysis," *Psychological Bulletin* 85 (1977): 867–94.
8. Gottman, "A Theory of Marital Dissolution and Stability."
9. Ibid.
10. Stott, *Marriage and Divorce.*
11. Ellisen, *Divorce and Remarriage in the Church.*

CHAPTER 22: Hope—Even for the Most Troubled Marriages

1. Gottman, "A Theory of Marital Dissolution and Stability."
2. David G. Myers, *The Pursuit of Happiness: Discovering the Pathway to Fulfillment, Well-Being, and Enduring Personal Joy* (New York: Avon, 1992), 172.
3. Gottman et al., *A Couple's Guide to Communication.*
4. Daniel Goleman, "What Hope Can Do for You," *Self* (June 1992): 112–13, 180–81.
5. Martin E. P. Seligman, *Learned Optimism: How to Change Your Mind and Your Life* (New York: Random House, 1991).
6. Martin E. P. Seligman and Peter Schulman. "Explanatory Style as a Predictor of Productivity and Quitting among Life Insurance Sales Agents," *Journal of Personality and Social Psychology* 50 (1986): 832–38.
7. Martin E. P. Seligman, *Learned Optimism.*
8. C. S. Carver and J. G. Gaines. "Optimism, Pessimism, and Post-partum Depression," *Cognitive Therapy and Research* 11 (1987): 449–62; M. F. Scheier, and C. S. Carver, "Optimism, Coping, and Health: Assessment and Implications of Generalized Outcome Expectancies," *Health Psychology,* 4 (1985): 219–47.

Moody Press, a ministry of the Moody Bible Institute,
is designed for education, evangelization, and edification.
If we may assist you in knowing more about Christ
and the Christian life, please write us without obligation:
Moody Press, c/o MLM, Chicago, Illinois 60610.